◄ T H E ►
CANADIANS

◄ THE ►
CANADIANS
Biographies of a Nation

Volume III

Patrick Watson
and Hugh Graham

McArthur & Company
Toronto

National Library of Canada Cataloguing in Publication

Watson, Patrick, 1929-
The Canadians : biographies of a nation / Patrick Watson.

Companion volume to the television series,
Canadians : biographies of a nation.
Volume 3 written by Patrick Watson and Hugh Graham.
Includes bibliographical references.
ISBN 1-55278-170-4 (v. 1) —ISBN 1-55278-240-9 (v. 2) —
ISBN 1-55278-318-9 (v. 3)

1. Canada—Biography. 2. Canadians : biographies of a nation
(Television program). I. Title.

FC25.W37 2000   971'.009'9   C00-931507-1
F1005.W37 2000

Composition/Cover & Photo f/x: *Mad Dog Design Inc.*
Printed in Canada by *Friesens*

McArthur & Company,
322 King Street West, Suite 402,
Toronto, ON, M5V 1J2

The publisher would like to acknowledge the financial support of the Government of Canada through the Book Publishing Industry Development Program (BPIDP) and the Canada Council for our publishing activities. The publisher further wishes to acknowledge the financial support of the Ontario Arts Council for our publishing program.

10 9 8 7 6 5 4 3 2 1

Contents

◆ Foreword ◆

THE CANADIANS
BIOGRAPHIES OF A NATION
Volume III

The last fifteen years have seen a rapid growth in the interest that Canadians express in their own history. The success of this series of books *The Canadians: Biographies of a Nation* and of the History Television series on which they are based is a modest witness to this, and we feel, immodestly perhaps, even a small contributing cause, as — we like to think — the popular *Heritage Minutes* may also have been. Both have been financed in part or entirely by the Historica foundation and its predecessor, Charles Bronfman's CRB Foundation. Charles and Andrea Bronfman's generous support of these heritage projects, based on their own passionate conviction about the importance to a nation of its people's stories, is impossible to overestimate.

While geography, climate, agriculture, bridges, buildings, and monuments contain and say much of what any nation is about, it is in the stories of its people that the *meaning* of nationhood is found. Much of this is in the small and subtle ways in which we respond to each other, the idiosyncrasies of language and habit, and the attitudes towards values such as liberty, law, and cultural difference. These are a large part of what our stories are about, but ultimately, like all narrative, they are intended to fascinate the reader with something that fascinated the writers: to lead the reader to care about the people the writers came to care about.

Patrick Watson
October 2002

Part One

MARION DE CHASTELAIN
FAMILY SECRETS

In April 2002, a small group of Canadians gathered around a television set, drinks in hand, in a private salon on the second floor of the Slieve Donard Hotel, Newcastle, County Down, Northern Ireland, to look at the documentary on which this chapter is based. Many of them had contributed to the making of the film, most importantly the Irish-born writer/director Patricia Phillips, who is also executive producer of the series *The Canadians.* But the key person in the room that evening was General John de Chastelain, a Canadian soldier of impeccable integrity and credentials, who for nine long years had been a key negotiator in the international effort to persuade the combatants in Northern Ireland to decommission their weapons as a prerequisite to establishing the peace.

General de Chastelain is the only person ever twice appointed CDS, chief of the defence staff, first by Pierre Trudeau, and later by Brian Mulroney who called de Chastelain back from his then post as Canadian ambassador to Washington, to once more take over as commander-in-chief of the Canadian armed forces. He had come to this screening at our invitation, to give us his assessment of the biography's accuracy and relevance. The film's principal subject — in this case it is not excessive to use the word heroine — was the general's late mother Marion de Chastelain.

General de Chastelain has a reputation for honesty and candour, and yet he was raised in a family that dwelt in the twilight world of spies, where lies are routinely conveyed as truths, where people you think you know turn out to be someone else, and where deeds of valour must often be buried, concealed, forgotten, in order to protect the lives of those who carried them out or those who benefited from them. Much of the biography of Marion de Chastelain is just such a story of buried valour, of dangerous unpredictability, unusual characters and connections, deception and war.

Her story contains a famous secret coding machine and the Canadian who helped crack its secrets, an aristocratic saboteur, a female spy who employs the classical tool of sexual seduction to get secrets from men who should know better, and Marion de Chastelain's two children, one of them a Calgary woman named Jacquie Brewster and the other Canada's best-known soldier.

Marion de Chastelain lived her last years quietly with her daughter Jacquie in the foothills of the Rockies, where she died as the twentieth century ended. While our research has been able to piece together a good deal of the story of her wartime service, almost none of it ever came from her lips. As has been the case with many in the spy trade her secrets were buried with her. Even to her closest relatives she had revealed almost nothing. That evening in Northern Ireland her son the General watched the documentary intently, with a half smile on his face most of the time, once shaking his head and muttering over an error (we had given him a birthday a year later than the real one), and then he joined the production group for dinner. "I learned a lot about my family that I never knew before," he said with a grin. In the documentary he had said,

One thing that always struck me was her reticence about herself. I mean she loved talking about her family and other people, and what they had achieved, but not herself. She was very proud of my father of course, and I think she felt that what she had done was much less than what he had done in terms of the war effort.

The war he referred to was World War II, from 1939–45. But our story begins shortly after the 1918 armistice. The story is composed of a number of at first seemingly unconnected subplots, some set in Germany, some in Romania, and some in Britain and Canada. As we began to assemble the documentary film, to set this intricate life story in motion we first opened a number of those subplots.

William Stephenson, who would become famous as The Man Called Intrepid, had started as an engineer in World War I. He transferred to the Royal Flying Corps in 1917 and shot down twelve enemy aircraft before he was shot down himself in July 1918. After the war, the twenty-three-year-old adventurer came home to Winnipeg, intending to become a millionaire by patenting a can opener he had liberated from a guard while he was a prisoner of war in Germany.

At about the same time a nine-year-old girl, Marion Walsh, daughter of an Irish-born New York accountant, found herself in Romania living in luxury. Germany had controlled Romania's huge and lucrative oil fields, but with defeat she lost that control, and companies from

America, Holland, France, and Britain poured into the country, bringing with them educated young men like Marion's father, Jack Walsh. He was alert to the opportunity in Europe for moving his family socially upwards, and so he put his daughter into the best schools he could find, which were in Switzerland. She became competent in seven languages, including Romanian, French and German. She was small in stature, but athletic and courageous, crazy about winter sports and fearless in her specialty, the Luge, hurtling down those breathtaking iced troughs with striking assurance. She revelled in risk.

So the first pieces of our story are found in a world of success and privilege, full of optimism and prosperity, whose denizens were carelessly insensitive to the dark forces building up in the devastation that was postwar Germany. Demoralized by defeat and then beaten into the ground by the overwhelmingly punitive financial reparations the victors had imposed in the Treaty of Versailles, there were hundreds of thousands of desperate, resentful Germans ripe for the rallying cry of someone who could show them a way out of their penury and humiliation. The one who would do this was the young Adolf Hitler. In 1924, serving time in prison for an attempted coup, Hitler wrote a long boring book, *Mein Kampf (My Struggle)* which, astonishingly, became a kind of blueprint for the New Germany. Hitler smuggled the manuscript out of his cell, got it published, and found eager readers who saw in it not only hope for a renaissance of the Fatherland, perhaps even for the conquest of the world, but also the person who would lead them to that glorious end, *Der Führer*, The Leader.

That same year, William Stephenson, the working-class kid from Winnipeg, former World War I pilot and prisoner of war, by now a successful London-based businessman, had come across a "secret writing machine" that was being offered to commercial companies. Whatever was typed into it was so cryptically scrambled that only if you bought the deciphering key — which meant buying the machine — could you return the meaningless characters to their original sense. Stephenson did not, at the time, catch on to the military potential of the Secret Writing Machine. As a business tool it was amusing but cumbersome to use. Stephenson fiddled with it for a while, and then forgot about it.

In 1930, Marion Walsh turned twenty. She had a degree in international law from the Sorbonne, but when she returned home she was at first somewhat overwhelmed by ambitions that had nothing to do with her own, namely, her dictatorial mother's vision of a daughter's place in high society. Marion's daughter Jacquie said, *My mother was actually married in 1931, I believe, to a Count. It was an arranged marriage by her mother. My grandmother was a schoolteacher. Her name was Mary Mulligan from New Jersey. She reminded me very much of Queen Mary, ramrod straight, very tiny, about 4' 11," but when she was there, you knew she was there. And, I think [even] I might have had problems standing up to her — about anything. (Laughs)*

But if Mrs. Walsh had counted on her daughter's continuing dutiful rise into the upper levels of European snobbery, she was soon to be disappointed. Jacquie said,

She did not want the marriage in the first place but her mother did, so she complied to that point and then did her own thing and had it annulled.

Shortly after this, she met the man who would become the above-mentioned saboteur, Alfred Gardyne de Chastelain. He had a pretty aristocratic-sounding name too, but it was the character not the family crest that brought them together. De Chastelain, known to his friends as Chas, had been born in London, studied industrial engineering, and went straight to those Romanian oilfields as soon as he had a degree. "He rode a horse and looked very romantic," Jacquie said. Marion's close Romanian friend Lady Joan Roderic Gordon, who was the daughter of the then Romanian minister of the national economy, watched from her own romantic perspective as the relationship blossomed. "He was very dashing and very good-looking," she told us, waving a slim, heavily jewelled hand, "and very charming I would say, and she was very beautiful. So it was a natural thing that they should meet and get married."

They were married in 1933. Alfred Gardyne de Chastelain was twenty-seven; Marion was twenty-three. She was now the wife of an oil executive, in an environment where oil was *the* field to be in, and at a time when postwar false optimism put a premium on the pursuit of pleasure. The de Chastelains' pleasures were not quite as sybaritic as some. "My father was a racing car driver," the General said, in the film.

Both rally and racing, and he and my mother took part in a number of those kind of events, which involved them with a structure of society in business, and even the royal family. He got to know Prince Michael at the time. They raced cars together. I think it was a vibrant society and largely because of the international nature of the people that made it up.

Marion was Chas's navigator in the rallies. They rode horses together, belonged to the golf club, and enjoyed the nightlife of "The Paris of the Balkans," the General said.

It was a very cosmopolitan city . . . a city in which the arts flourished. My parents lived a fairly affluent lifestyle in comparison to many people in Romania. . . . It was a period of great excitement, great interest, great intellectual challenge and great enjoyment. Now, for people who were reasonably close to the top of the totem pole, that was nice. For those who were struggling at the bottom it wasn't, but I think by and large life in Romania at the time was enjoyable and that's why so many people stayed there.

But in 1933 the smell of smoke was already beginning to drift across Europe from Germany. Hitler's *Mein Kampf* had become the Bible of German recovery, a recovery nourished by a hatred of everyone and everything not "Aryan," especially Jews. Under Hitler's eloquent leadership the National Socialist Party, Nazi for short, was growing exponentially. The swastika and the straight-arm salute were becoming the symbols for the new optimism and for the restoration of the racially pure glory of the *Heimat*, the German homeland. Fascism, the power-based, violence-enforced rule by self-appointed elites rather than by the rule of law, was the new religion. Hitler, the former prison inmate, became the Chancellor of all Germany. German

Jews were feeling the brutality of the Nazi thugs, and so was the whole brilliant world of German culture. The yeasty mix that had given rise to Bach, Beethoven, Mozart, Hegel, and Goethe was now in danger. At the University of Berlin, young Nazis built a huge bonfire to burn hundreds of copies of the world's greatest books, books incompatible with the new doctrine of racial superiority. Germany was predominantly a devoutly Christian country, the birthplace of Protestantism, but with a large and committed Roman Catholic community as well. While it seems contradictory on the surface, the Bible and the whole Christian vocabulary of God, redemption, and salvation were appropriated by the Nazis (who wooed the Vatican but privately distrusted all the Church authorities). "I was sent by Providence," Hitler told the cheering mobs. "The Nazi Party is Adolf Hitler, and Adolf Hitler is Germany," his deputy führer yelled at them, and they yelled back, "Heil Hitler! Heil Hitler! Heil Hitler!"

And that was when the Secret Writing Machine that William Stephenson had fiddled with years before surfaced again. Stephenson was now a millionaire in London. Part of his fortune was made in currency trading, but much of it came from his having invented the wirephoto while still a student at the University of Manitoba, and then a wireless system for the transmission of text and images. It was this invention that brought him to London, where he cannily marketed it to the newspaper companies and built his reputation both as an innovator and a businessman. One of his companies supplied electronics to the International Telephone and Telegraph Company, which was making armaments for Germany. From IT&T Stephenson learned that Hitler was using the Special Writing Machine to code Nazi party communiqués, and that the Japanese military was also using it. Now he recognized the threat. His wide, high-level connections in London snaked through the political and military elite as well as the commercial and social, and he began to compile his own operating list of people he could count on being anti-Nazi. Many Britons were admirers of Hitler and his fascism, among them some who would deeply regret it later, including the poets W.B. Yeats and T.S. Eliot. One of Stephenson's anti-Nazi friends was a man named Desmond Morton (not the Canadian historian), and Morton was a friend and neighbour of Winston Churchill. Churchill had been warning Britain about both Hitler and Stalin for years, had often been called a warmonger for his stance, and had lost much of his influence in the government. However, in 1935, he discreetly assigned Desmond Morton to gather intelligence about German rearmament, and to start quietly putting together an unofficial and clandestine group of specialists in espionage, sabotage, and assassination. Morton brought Stephenson into that group.

In 1936, the Germans were deporting undesirables and declaring that they were going to purify the Master Race. Marion de Chastelain saw an aspect of it first-hand. Pregnant, on a visit to Berlin she was overcome by nausea in the street and had to vomit in public, holding onto a railing. A matronly middle-aged German woman stopped solicitously, patted her on the back, and said: "It's okay, dear, you're doing it for the führer." The child-to-come was

Jacquie, who was born in Bucharest soon after. Her brother John was born in 1937. The following year Hitler occupied the Rhineland and took over Austria. The de Chastelains should probably have left Romania then — it was an obvious target for German expansion — but they hung on. Both Romania and Czechoslovakia looked to Britain for support but none came. Churchill urged those he trusted in British intelligence to convince Prime Minister Neville Chamberlain to take action. Chamberlain did that. He visited Hitler in Munich for a friendly talk.

In light of what happened next, Chamberlain's search for accommodation with Hitler — his critics called it "appeasement" — seems almost criminally wrong. But Britain was only twenty years away from the hideousness of the First World War, still scarred by the waste of it, its meaninglessness, and the cynicism that had led to it. The British — and the French, and probably even the majority of Germans, although they no longer had a voice in national policy — did not want to go through all that again. When Chamberlain announced that his agreement with Hitler meant "Peace in Our Time," he was cheered. But in October 1938 Hitler's *Wehrmacht* marched into the Sudetenland. Czechoslovakia, Romania, and Poland pleaded with Britain to act. Britain stuck to its guns, or rather its rejection of guns. Churchill said bitterly but with characteristic elegance, "Britain and France had to choose between war and dishonour. They chose dishonour. They will have war."

Not only was Britain not arming itself, just in case, but there was also almost no budget for intelligence. The intelligence service had little more to work with than reports from the military attachés in their embassies. The Bucharest legation reported that there had been a secret meeting of Romanian officials to discuss oil with Hitler's *Reichsmarschall* Hermann Goering. Hitler had more than a business relationship in mind, however; he and Stalin were quietly plotting to occupy both Poland and Romania. In March, Hitler took Prague. Marion and Chas went to Germany ostensibly to buy a car, but Chas was already more than idly curious. They saw tanks in the streets, and thousands of soldiers being trucked down the autobahn. "Both my parents realized that the writing was on the wall," General de Chastelain told us,

> *[They realized] that Romania would in fact become involved and that they both decided we should leave. And [my mother] took my sister and me out of Romania by train and took us to England.*

Chas booked them on the Orient Express, and kissed them goodbye at the station. Marion could navigate a road rally, luge down a polished trough of ice at eighty miles an hour, and speak seven languages, but after a life of servants and luxury, finding herself on a train to Paris without the children's nurse was too much. Jacquie remembers that vividly.

> *She was absolutely, totally . . . just didn't know what to do with us. So, my brother ate his way through a box of chocolates and . . . a lady returning to England who was a nanny realized what was going on and offered to help, and she took over and we were in good hands at that point.*

And Jacquie's son Ian Denton, who would become

very close to Marion in her later years, told us,

My grandmother was not what one would call the maternal type. She never seemed to have that sort of stereotypical motherly or grandmotherly attitude. My grandmother would sit in her chair and have her Scotch and cigarette while other people cooked and prepared.

"We had a cook and maid," Jacquie added, "so she didn't have to cook. . . . She could do it if she had to but she hated it."

The destination of that train trip was London, where William Stephenson had just got a tip from an American source that Germany was now mass-producing the Secret Writing Machine near the Czech-Polish border. Code-named "ENIGMA," and far superior to the original commercial model, it had been developed into a device able to instantly encipher messages that stumped even the most experienced cryptologists. Churchill wanted one of these things, and Stephenson had a plan. Not even the Prime Minister was told about the secret mission, which is said to have involved a bit of sabotage and a suitcase switch in Warsaw. The machine arrived in England in late August 1939, without the key. The British found it baffling. A research unit of crack cipher people took over a vast country estate called Bletchley Park. They called the project "ULTRA." At the height of the Bletchley Park operation there were some 12,000 personnel involved, only a small number of whom actually knew what the ULTRA project was about. There was an ULTRA list of insiders: Stephenson and the other key people. Being on that list was to be a member of the most exclusive club of the war effort.

It was September 1st, 1939, when the German invasion of Poland finally pulled Chamberlain to his feet. Britain and France declared war on September 3rd. Largely isolated from the mainstream of policy and executive decision for most of the decade, Winston Churchill's take on Germany was now vindicated, and Chamberlain asked him to resume his old First World War position: First Lord of the Admiralty.

On September 17, Hitler and Stalin divided Poland up between them. Polish refugees started streaming down the roads towards Romania. "And then they'd arrive in Bucharest," Lady Joan Roderic Gordon says, "and we looked after them, took them into our homes." But Romania's neutrality was precarious now that Poland was no longer a buffer between Russia and Germany. The Romanian Prime Minister was assassinated by pro-Nazis. Romanian trade with Britain was nearly cut off. There had been a secret agreement with Britain to destroy the oil installations if the country were invaded. The British began to prepare for this, contacted Chas through the Bucharest legation, and persuaded him to secretly accept a commission in the British army. With his knowledge of the Romanian geography, language, and especially of the oil fields, he would be a prime candidate to lead a sabotage program to destroy the oil installations so the Germans could not use them.

Late in 1939 ULTRA was making some headway with the ENIGMA codes, and had decoded a German message revealing something about Hitler's plan for a *Blitzkrieg*, a Lightning War, which would be a massive, high speed mechanized attack on Western Europe. Chamberlain had received identical information that official intelligence had gotten out of a downed German pilot but had chosen not to believe it. Churchill considered showing him ULTRA's version, but the ULTRA list people persuaded him that the project should still be kept from the PM.

Despite the danger after Germany attacked Norway and Denmark in April 1940, and not saying what she was up to, Marion de Chastelain left her children with their grandparents and, travelling on a British passport, set out to meet Chas in Bucharest. She was en route through France on May 10 when Hitler began the *Blitzkrieg*. Not long after Marion arrived in Romania, the German war machine would sweep through Belgium, France, and the Netherlands. Chamberlain resigned, asking the sixty-six-year-old Churchill to take over as Prime Minister. Almost immediately, Churchill created an instrument to manage all available intelligence through one agency, the BSC, British Security Coordination. The man he assigned to run BSC was William Stephenson, and Stephenson set up shop in Washington, DC, not as an intelligence official but as a distinguished and wealthy businessman. The United States had not come into the war yet, and an open military intelligence operation on American territory would have been impossible.

Stephenson's covert assignment now was to convince the American government to start collaborating with the BSC. He was able to persuade Canada to send to Washington some of the RCMP's best intelligence people, both men and women. Stephenson believed women to be especially adept at the intelligence game.

Back in England, Churchill had added sabotage to the intelligence machine, setting up the SOE, the Secret Operations Executive. Alfred de Chastelain, Chas, was given the Romanian team. "He knew the oil business," his son told us. "It was his life. He knew what were effective targets." Hitler had reminded Romania that Britain was also occupied on the Western front and wouldn't help in the inevitability of a Russian land grab. "We signed our last treaty with England in 1939," Lady Joan told us.

It was signed in our house between my father among some of the British delegation, some of them. And after that the Germans walked in and they said, "You are no more friends of the British, you must be our friends, you see. We can help you, [but] the British, oh they're finished, they've got nothing."

When Stalin made his pact with Hitler in June 1940, Romania was given twenty-four hours to cede them some oil-rich northern lands. As the Germans had predicted, Britain did not interfere. Romania, still technically neutral, was effectively occupied. By September, Hitler had moved in a whole division of the German army, allegedly to train the Romanian army but really to protect the oil installations and to prepare a push against the Russians. "Anybody with a British or American antecedence had to leave," Lady Joan said. "The Germans, although they didn't bother the Romanians, they said, 'Oh, we're here to defend you from the Russians.' But the people who were in the know, they just left."

Chas was suddenly instructed by SOE headquarters to

get his team out of Bucharest and take them to safety in Istanbul for the time being. Marion went back to England to be with the children. John de Chastelain said that at this point his mother had had enough. "And she was quite clear, I think, once she came back. She had decided with my father that we should go to the States and live with her parents."

She was not, however, allowed to drop out completely. When Marion and the children arrived in New York in the fall, William Stephenson knew she was coming. John de Chastelain again:

> So after we'd been in New York for some time — we were living in Forest Hills with my grandparents — she got a call from somebody from the British embassy saying, "Would you like to do something for your king and country?" and she said, "Yes." Because of my father's background, my mother's circumstance was known to the intelligence people in London and therefore to the intelligence people working for Sir William Stephenson in Washington. And it was known that she was a linguist.

Stephenson needed a French speaker who could be trusted. Marion fit the bill. The assignment was top secret. She was going to run a spy in Washington, Betty Thorpe Pack, who was an adventurous and gorgeous woman code-named "Cynthia." Originally from Minneapolis, Cynthia was the daughter of diplomats, had married a British diplomat twenty years her senior, had been initiated into the undercover game in Poland and loved it, and now was about to graduate into that classic combination of espionage and the oldest profession.

Cynthia spoke fluent French. France, nominally a separate nation but in fact run by the Nazi-directed Vichy Government, still had an embassy in Washington. In May 1941, Cynthia was assigned to penetrate the Vichy French embassy, and Stephenson had decided to put Marion de Chastelain in charge of the operation. She had the language, she was a woman, she could get along with Cynthia, and she had a much broader experience of the world than anybody of similar skills in Stephenson's BSC.

It may begin to sound a bit comic book or television sitcom about now. Cynthia, in her Washington home, seduces a Vichy French attaché, Charles Brousse, and somehow — blackmail? a romantic appeal to old loyalties? — somehow persuades him to give her copies of secret documents. Her personal risk was huge. Since the US was not in the war, should her life be threatened, for example, there was no way she could turn to the American police for protection. What she was doing was completely illegal and official America would have been furious. And this was a highly emotional adventurer. She swung from extreme highs to desperate lows. She would come back from one of her assignations and report to Marion in moral tatters, and at other times be sailing high, giddy with risk and success. Marion was the straight one, the stabilizer, a functional link between the romantic adventurer and the serious work.

Marion often travelled six times a week between New York and Washington, rarely getting home to see John and Jacquie or to get some sleep. But December 7, 1941, was different. She had been working sixteen-hour days for some time, and that weekend she told the BSC people not to bother her. But in the middle of the night the phone began to ring and did not stop. She finally got up in a very bad humour, and a voice said, "Marion. Get in here right away. Pearl Harbor's been bombed."

So America was at last in the war, and by that time William Stephenson had so effectively developed his covert co-operative relationships between the American and British intelligence agencies that they were ready to swing into full-scale action together. Stephenson had accomplished his mission, and Marion de Chastelain was one of the key people who had helped him do it.

Stephenson's next assignment brought him home to Canada for a while. The decision had been made to establish a secret Canadian training base for saboteurs and spies, Camp X, on the north shore of Lake Ontario near the small city of Oshawa. They set up a state-of-the art communications centre, with a soaring radio tower, the HYDRA Wireless Station that linked Washington, London, and Ottawa and relayed some of the most sensitive information of the war. Of course, they needed a powerful encryption system. A Canadian electronic genius named Benjamin de Forest Bayley designed an encoding machine called Rock X, a central component of the whole HYDRA operation, and as far as we know, the enemy cipher specialists never broke it.

Marion de Chastelain was still running Cynthia in Washington, and was soon reporting back to Stephenson through HYDRA, sending him, among other documents, Vichy naval materials coded by ENIGMA. In May 1942

Cynthia had moved into the Wardman Park Hotel where Brousse lived in Washington. While it was more convenient to slip into her apartment for a passionate embrace, it was also more dangerous. His wife lived at the hotel too, and it was a favourite residence for other foreign operatives. Marion would take an early morning flight over from New York, and meet with Cynthia at the Wardman Park, using different entrances and exits in case she was followed.

An allied operation along the coast of French North Africa was being developed as a stepping-stone into Europe. The code name for the plan was TORCH. The planners needed to know the movement of the German-controlled Vichy French fleet in the Mediterranean, and so Marion was assigned to get Cynthia to try for the Vichy ciphers and codebooks. Her chance came in June. She arranged to meet Brousse in the embassy at night to pick up the documents. At a crucial moment they heard a guard coming. Cynthia told Marion that at this point she just whipped off all her clothes and when the guard came upon a steamy love scene in the corridor he discreetly turned away and left them alone. "Boy, what a night I had," Cynthia told Marion, and Marion laughed, and headed back to New York and the HYDRA transmission station. The ciphers and other materials made their way, via Camp X and HYDRA, to Bletchley Park in time to be incorporated into TORCH.

Now Chas got involved in Camp X. He had been assigned to enlist a team of Romanians to be parachuted into Europe. They would be trained at Camp X. The SOE said, "Well, you speak Romanian, you'd better go with them." And so when he came to visit Marion in New York, it was to tell her that he was about to do a little drop into their former European home country. "The mission was in fact to try and make a separate peace with Romania before the end of the war," Lady Joan told us. Chas's assignment was at the request of King Michael himself, Chas's old friend. Marion was frightened, but she agreed: he had to go.

By late 1943, the Wardman Park Hotel Caper was finished. Now BSC gave Marion an assignment in England, dealing with the Balkans. We don't know what this one entailed, and characteristically Marion never discussed it. Once again, the children were uprooted, this time travelling across the Atlantic and into the heart of the war. At least she would be with Chas, who was back in London preparing his team of Romanians for the parachute jump. Marion and the children sailed from New York in a convoy of artillery freighters. Jacquie was seven and John only six, but he says he remembers the trip very clearly.

She felt that my sister and me were being spoilt rotten by our grandparents, which may have been the case. Anyway, she felt that we should be back in Britain, over the objections of her parents, who thought this was absolutely crazy. This was not the time to be going to Britain, you know there were still U-boats in the Atlantic. . . . It was an important convoy and it was a big convoy and there was a great deal of concern I found amongst the crew about their own safety. I mean they had been doing this a number of times, but I think the impatience with me making a nuisance of myself was partly the fact that this was deadly serious, and a torpedo at any moment could make life very difficult.

Jacquie said, "My brother loved it and drove everyone crazy blowing the little whistle on his life vest. But I was sick as a dog and I hated it." Arriving in Liverpool just after an air raid they took the train to London. The worst of the Battle of Britain was over, but some bombs were still falling, and from time to time Marion had to take kids into a tube station to sleep. She wanted to get them out of that kind of danger, and sent them off to a boarding school in the north of England. "I remember twice she came up," Jacquie said, laughing. "And I was really embarrassed because she had long, red nails and none of the other moms up in northern England had long, red nails. And, I just wished she would sit on her hands."

On December 21, 1943, Chas and his team parachuted into Romania. They were to radio Istanbul on their arrival at the safe house, but the signal never came. A few days later Marion got a telegram from a Romanian friend. Chas was a prisoner. She assumed the Germans had him. She had shared with him what she knew about UTLRA — which was quite a bit — and was sick with terror thinking that he would be tortured, that he would give something away, that all that work would be destroyed and so would her beloved husband. But then the good news arrived; it was not the Germans who had Chas, it was the Romanians. The Germans wanted him, but the Romanians would not give him up. Lady Joan said,

Chas was very cunning in that way. He pretended he was just a playboy and he didn't know why they parachuted

him and he, oh, he liked to drink and smoke and all this
sort of thing. He told the soldiers, who looked after them,
"Come on and let's have a drink, bring some cigarettes
and bring this," and nobody thought of tormenting him.

The pro-Nazi government had allowed King Michael to
live on at the palace, and he secretly began to organize a
coup. With Germany preoccupied in France after the invasion of June 1944, the young king successfully overthrew
the puppet government, and one of his first triumphant
acts was to release the political prisoners, including his
friend Alfred de Chastelain. His son told us,

The operation my father [had led in Romania], Operation
Autonomous, was bitterly criticized by Stalin and as a
result, after my father was released and King Michael had
taken over the government, he sent him to Istanbul to
reopen communications with the allies. My father had
given a commitment to Michael that he would come back
[to Romania], but he wasn't allowed to, and he was
brought back to Britain, and I think that really ended his
SOE operation as far as action in the Balkans.

When Chas and Marion and the children got back together, the experience of walking down a London street together may have changed John's life. He said,

He was wearing a uniform, he was a Lieutenant Colonel,
and everywhere we walked around Richmond he was get-
ting saluted because there were troops all over the place.
And finally, in disgust, he took his uniform off so he did-
n't have to be saluting all the time. So I knew he was quite
important.

But that was classy stuff, all the same, and the rank,

and the salutes, and the stories that came with them stayed in the boy's mind.

And then came May 1945, and the war in Europe was over. Chas and Marion would have loved to go back to Bucharest; in most ways it was still Their City. They had a house full of furniture there. But the Communists had taken over by then, King Michael had been forced to abdicate, the de Chastelains were able to recover a small shipment of photographs and other personal stuff, but everything else was lost.

Spying is often said to be a kind of aphrodisiac. Once you've entered the secret world of intelligence, once you've had access to secrets, once you've handled intelligence, it's a world that is difficult to leave behind. Chas found it so. He had loved the excitement of a saboteur's life. Marion set about creating the impression that the world of secrets was past, and that getting the family together was the future. But she may have been complicit, with her husband, in continuing the game. Jacquie told us,

When my mother finally found a house for us, it was in Kensington, sort of backing onto the Russian embassy. It never really seemed odd to me until later on, and it just struck me one day, I wonder if that was by design that we backed onto the embassy, or if it was just pure chance.

Pure chance or not, it will never be known. They acted like any other family trying to recover from the war, and if there was something else going on, Marion never talked about it. John de Chastelain said,

My father started a business, a multifaceted business dealing with imports and exports and a particular chemical

process dealing with film. He became a city man, pinstripe
trousers, umbrella, briefcase. Eventually, of course, the
business didn't work out and he went back into the oil
business, which brought him to Canada.

In 1954, the family began a new life in Calgary, but
without John. Perhaps it was the memory of his father in
uniform that made him choose to study for a military
career in Edinburgh. But his father wanted the family
together.

My father suggested that I join him in Canada, and men-
tioned that there was a place called the Royal Military
College that would allow me to do my military service and
get my degree at the same time. So I came to Canada and
went to RMC and joined the army.

Chas and Marion became part of Calgary society. They
joined the golf club and the Ranchmen's Club. Calgary
seemed an unlikely place to run into fellow spies. Lady
Joan said,

I was in Calgary already, having lunch with my husband
and suddenly I feel somebody coming from behind me and
putting his hands over my eyes. He said, "Guess who?"
And I thought that it was a pretty silly joke . . . my hus-
band didn't like those kind of jokes. I turned around and it
was Chas, and of course we hugged and embraced, because
you know you get very fond of the people who lay their life
down.

Twenty years later, John de Chastelain was well on his
way to becoming a Canadian general. His father died
proud in the knowledge that his son was commanding a
battalion in Winnipeg and his daughter had her dream, a

family. On his death, friends remembered all he had done. Romania's King Michael sent a bouquet and a letter of condolence. The Man Called Intrepid came to the funeral, and said obliquely to young John that his father's work had "had an impact," but he never explained what that impact had been, the commitment to secrecy surviving the man in the coffin.

Marion took a job with a Calgary company and kept it until well into her seventies. Every day she lunched at Oliver's. Today the restaurant is called Quincy's, but nothing else has changed, not even the tables. Marion had her own, and it is still there. Few dining at Oliver's would have had the faintest idea what she carried in that secret head. She was just a nice lady who worked across the street, and apparently that's the way she wanted it. The secrets stayed secret.

Her grandson Ian got to know her over those lunches, and found some common ground.

With her sort of car fascination — and I really loved cars — we kind of connected, on sort of a guy level. . . . And, as I said, my grandfather and her used to do rallies through Europe and they collected all these little badges. We talked about that kind of thing a lot and we decided that, why not get together and go on a road trip. So we went to Freehold, New Jersey, where she was born, and we spent a day there and we saw the house where she was born, and were just sort of reminiscing about it and just wanted to see how her life started, basically.

But neither the grandson, nor the son, nor the daughter, ever got her to talk much about exactly what she had done in the war. William Stephenson, now Sir William, had retired to Bermuda, and once a year Marion went to visit him there. "I sure would have liked to be a fly on the wall when those two got together," Jacquie said.

But if there were any flies on those walls, they're not talking.

◆　◆　◆

The History Television documentary was written and directed by Patricia Phillips.

◆ Part Two ◆

ROBERT MARKLE
AN INVESTIGATION

Unlike the other chapters in this Volume III of The Canadians:
Biographies of a Nation, *in which the collaborating authors
Patrick Watson and Hugh Graham would be at a loss to say
exactly which sentences were written by which of them, the fol-
lowing chapter is entirely a first-person narrative from Patrick
Watson, for reasons that will be almost immediately clear.*

In May 1965, my colleagues and I in the CBC production
offices of the current affairs television magazine program
This Hour Has Seven Days were surprised to learn that the
Toronto police had raided a small local art gallery and confiscated a few pieces, charging the gallery owner with having exhibited obscene objects. The show in which these
works had been hung was a major event for the small but
popular Dorothy Cameron gallery. It was called *EROS 65*.
The opening was very much a gala affair, and many
Toronto celebrities had been invited. Pierre Berton con-
ducted the "official" opening, and all of the works hung,
by Harold Town, Dennis Burton, and Robert Markle, were
in one way or another celebrations of sexuality.

The five Markles that had been impounded —
Marlene Markle likes to say that they were put in jail —
were highly stylized nudes, two women in each, and the
women appeared to be making love to each other. It would
later be whispered around town that the person who laid

the absurd charge had been rebuffed as a lover by the gallery owner, Dorothy Cameron, and was exacting some kind of eccentric vengeance. The only reason to give that rumour any kind of credence is that the works, while lyrically erotic and intriguing, seem so innocent today that it is not credible that they could have seriously offended anyone, even in the Toronto of four decades ago.

The *Seven Days* editorial group was unanimous in thinking that there was a story here for us, and I was assigned to interview the twenty-eight-year-old artist, Robert Markle, whom I had not heard of before. The interview went well, but it was not long enough to satisfy me, and I invited him across the street to the Celebrity Club for a beer. One beer led to quite a few more, but more importantly the conversation that began that May afternoon was picked up again over a few more beers a few days later, and became an extended exploration of ideas and experiences between Robert and me that grew into a close and profoundly affectionate relationship. You could say that the conversation begun in that basement bar that May afternoon never really ended until Robert's life ended, and long before that he had become my closest male friend.

So it was with some hesitation that I proposed his biography to History Television for this series, and I sought verification of the idea from producer/director Daniel Zuckerbrot — who knew Robert only as a friend of mine and through the half-dozen canvasses in my house. Zuckerbrot soon came back to say that he was intrigued, that I should not worry about my closeness with the subject, and that the story was eminently worth an hour of prime-time television.

It began in Hamilton, Ontario, where Robert was born in 1936, the son of steelworker Bruce Maracle and his wife Kathleen. Maracle is a common name in the Mohawk reserves at Deseronto and at Tyendinaga where Bruce was born. Kathleen used the spelling Markle — we don't know why — and although he was listed in the Ontario Births Registry as Robert Maracle, Robert always used his mother's version. He had the characteristic features of an Ontario Mohawk, but his personality and intellect were so compelling that it had never occurred to me to wonder about or inquire into his origins. In those first months of our rapidly burgeoning and turbulent friendship, he never brought it up, and when he made some offhand remark about "us Indians," he was surprised that I was surprised.

It was not that he wanted to conceal or suppress his Native origins; in a sense his mother had preferred to be quiet about their Iroquois beginnings, finding that in Hamilton, Ontario, in the 1940s life was a little easier if you were not identified as an Indian. Not until his mid-forties did Robert's curiosity about his origins begin to stir, hesitantly at first, but later strongly enough to take him to the Tyendinaga reserve near Deseronto, which he had never seen, a reserve dotted with mailboxes with Maracle painted on them. It was an experience that transformed both the man and his art.

But that was much later. In 1954 he enrolled in OCA, the Ontario College of Art in downtown Toronto, and there met Paul Young, another artist who became a close friend, and who now teaches at OCA. Young says that the college was very conservative in the '50s and '60s, and that guys like him and Robert had come there to learn the now-established traditions of landscape painting in Canada. Professor Young told us,

Most of the faculty were either realistic painters of the old school or sort of semi-abstract painters of a slightly lower grade. So we weren't terribly impressed with their relevance to modern society as it was in 1955. But as students, of course, we weren't all that hip ourselves. When Robert and I used to go out painting, I mean we were trying to do Tom Thomson and Arthur Lismer, and so on. So we didn't really know what was going on. That passion for landscape eventually left him and I think be began to realize that in a sense it was history and there was no sense repeating history.

But even in those early days, when landscape painting was still the prime focus, Robert Markle, Young says, had a streak of difference, originality, and universally vectored curiosity about him that was noticeable from the start.

The first time we ever went painting together, we were actually drawing. We had brushes and we had ink and everything, and we were down in the Humber Valley. And I got bored with my picture and I went over to see what he was doing. And do you know what he was painting with? He was painting with dirt, and it was the black sludgy muddy stuff and there was another kind of dirt and some other kind of dirt. He had them all sorted out in front of him like a palette and he had his brush and he was painting with dirt. And his picture was better than mine!

From later in his life there is quite a lot of video and film footage of Robert at work and at play that has survived. In some of those moving pictures you can see the tactile, sensual, skin-sensitive curiosity of the mud-painter. The artist bends down, bringing his thick glasses so close to the work that you fear they'll be spattered, and he spreads a thick crescent of wet black ink on the thick toothy paper. He follows up instantly with a piece of wadded facial tissue that he pushes thoughtfully into the wet black, and moves it about almost as if it too were mud that he was shaping as well as painting.

That inked crescent in the old black-and-white film is shadow on the thigh of a naked woman. Nudes in ink, paint, plywood, pencil — who knows, perhaps even in mud — are by far the dominant image in the large legacy of his surviving work (much of it now being collected by the Art Gallery of Ontario, and some as far abroad as the British Museum). Paul Young said,

He loved the strippers. He used to go to strip joints all the time, especially burlesque. It wasn't so much the girls in the bars. It was burlesque that he was really crazy about because the girls were so exotic and so bizarre. They all had enormous breasts and strange acts with snakes and balloons and everything, and he loved all that. He loved the showbiz part.

And while many of his nudes are decorated with the pasties and G-strings of the striptease performer's repertory, the vast majority of these naked bodies are really one body, that of Marlene Shuster. Robert met her when she was in first year at OCA and he in second, and he almost instantly fell in love with her. He persuaded her to pose for him while they were still students. She had never posed in the nude before. She says,

I was going off to art school. Here's a nice little Jewish girl going off to art school. Wasn't supposed to do that in those days. He was the first person and I did it without even thinking. I mean he just drew that out of me. I became, I just became enamoured of him.

Their studies at OCA stopped abruptly when Robert lost his temper over something so trivial he later could never remember what it had been. His reaction was not trivial; it was dangerously furious. Paul Young couldn't remember what caused it either, but the event is still vivid in his memory.

He got into some kind of a hissy fit. I don't know what it was about. But he picked up a bottle and threw it against a wall in a rage. And it turned out that it was a bottle of acid for etching plates. And whatever damage it did to the wall, which I'm sure was considerable, and it probably splattered on other people's work or perhaps somewhere else, I don't know. But the man who ran the print shop would not put up with that kind of stuff. So he was just summarily dismissed from the college and that was it. I don't think he put up much of a fight.

The painter Gordon Rayner, who was not at the college with Robert, says that

Marlene apparently went down to the boss man and said, "You kick him out and I'm leaving too." So they both did. Robert left. The school wouldn't give in. And so Marlene went with him. It was really a great happy ending because

it's how Robert and Marlene got together and stayed together all those years.

They soon got married — November of 1958 — and then both had to look for work. The man who would make his reputation as a provocative painter of the nude female body could then be found lettering cardboard signs for Goodbaum's grocery store on College Street, including elegantly correct Hebrew script for the High Holidays. But that almost instant fascination with the contours and light and shadow on Marlene's body kept its hold on him. He photographed her with a simple stills camera, and then borrowed a 16mm motion picture camera and shot a few exquisitely framed sequences of Marlene posing nude by a rushing stream, supine in the long grass, slipping mysteriously through the shaded trunks of the forest. The film itself is visually gripping — Marlene generously made it available for the History Television documentary on Robert's life — but his primary purpose in filming these scenes was to have her available for his easel and his brush while the real person was out earning their living.

He did so much in the early years that he could draw a line without my being there and it would be the line of my body. He knew my body so intimately that he was able to put a line on the paper of a rib cage or a breast resting on the rib cage or the calf being extended. He always said, "It's yours, because that's how I learned and that's what I draw." . . . Sometimes he'd say to me (chuckles), "I wish I could do something else, you know. But I can't."

She knows, and he knew, that this was a joke: Robert Markle could paint anything he set out to paint. But it was a meaningful joke, for Robert never lost his almost obsessive fascination with Marlene, her body, her conversation, her spirit. She is there in the thick impasto images of him with a saxophone and a glass of beer and she with high heels and pointed nipples at a table in some imagined bar; or in the bed in their farmhouse at Holstein, he watching television (he was a television nut, I thought) and she gazing at the ceiling; or in the next panel of that same brilliant, funny, profoundly affectionate little triptych, she in the bath (there are hundreds of bathtub paintings) and he on the toilet; and in the third panel they are both in the kitchen, at the table, eating and once again watching television.

He called her "The Muse." There is a canvas on the only wall in our house big enough to take it — it is about 200 centimetres by 150 centimetres — of the two of them in the water, a lake presumably, she standing, he apparently sitting for only his ponytailed plump head is out of the water. It is entitled *The Muse Home for the Holidays*.

Robert Markle had an immense sense of humour and an infectious lilting laugh that lit up a room. He was also an arresting writer: essays, narrative journalism of an intense poetic and gossipy character — brief flashes of imagery. Here is a short piece he titled *Statement: The Painter and His Model*.

Into the topless taverns and the gritty bars where the regulars have puke on their shoes and the cleaning lady is a fire hose, the artist goes, searching for his model. The model is his Muse, and he finds her modeling in the raw night of these places, explaining her body the way the artist might explain his art. She writhes under the watch-

ful eye of the artist. She dances to rock and roll, silently mouthing the words as though they had the power to jus- tify. She moves with an amazing and splendid fury, fight- ing, in that bleak interior, not to win a point but to pre- serve her very existence. The artist understands the event, he makes it his own by entering into her celebration, by leaving his.

"The real only exist in the mind of the artist strong enough to contain them and give them form." Lawrence Durrell had one of his Alexandrian Quartet *characters say that.*

Art is not art unless it threatens your very existence.

He was still painting his Muse the year he died.

The strippers he painted were not always Marlene, but Marlene often went with him to the Victory Burlesque on Spadina Avenue just north of Dundas, to legitimize his request as an artist to come backstage and meet and talk with the performers. She would study the G-strings and the pasties and come home and make copies of them and get herself up in the makeup and the tiny slips of fabric and the high heels . . . and he would paint her.

He wanted some of this stuff duplicated at home so that he could work more closely from it. So I'd be sewing costumes and that's how I learned how to make G-strings and stuff, was watching these women and how to move. Robert was kind enough to go out and buy me a record about how to do burlesque and little books, you know. How to do [it] books, how to do the moves and all that. Oh yes, we stud- ied. We studied.

He experimented from time to time with lithographs. There is a 1987 documentary film, *Priceville Prints*, that shows him at work on the stones. His earlier (1975) five-part series of black-and-white lithos, *The Victory Burlesque Series*, changes hands these days at substantial prices — in the rare cases when its owners will part with one of the only fifteen sets that exist. Anna Hudson, the assistant curator of Canadian art at the Art Gallery of Ontario said,

The nude in Robert's early works from the sixties, his burlesque dancers and even his movie star series — when you place these images together, the woman sort of begins to dance. She turns and moves. It's rhythmic. It's hard to take one of these paintings all by themselves and see it in isolation because it's part of a woman dancing or a performance. So each of these images captures just seconds or just a moment. So it's like there's constantly a cinema in Robert Markle's head.

In the spring of 1960 Marlene went to work in the Isaacs Gallery. Avrom Isaacs had started buying and selling paintings when he was scarcely out of college. He was not that knowledgeable, he says, but he sensed a new energy radiating from the canvasses of this group of young Toronto painters, Markle and Rayner, Graham Coughtry, Nobuo Kubota, Dennis Burton, Michael Snow, and Snow's wife Joyce Wieland, and he began to round them up for his gallery. Marlene was working there before Isaacs took Robert on as one of "his" painters. He says that Robert hung around a lot because of Marlene. Robert would try to persuade her to leave work and come over to the Pilot Tavern. Sometimes he'd have a folio under his arm, and when Av eventually asked to look at some pieces, he found them pretty interesting.

Years later, after Robert was gone and Avrom retired, it was through the large Isaacs collection of Markles that a couple of pieces found their way into the British Museum.

In addition to painting, music, talk, beer, and his Muse, he loved his 250 cc Honda motorcycle, and pined for a bigger one. When that Dorothy Cameron scandal broke in the papers in 1965, he and Marlene had jumped on the little bike and driven off to New York together, motoring back just in time to discover that he was famous.

On July 9, 1969, now riding a 650 cc candy-apple red Triumph, Robert was hit by a car and terribly smashed up, most especially, and seriously for an artist, his arms. He was in intensive care for a week. During the months of recovery, his muse became his nurse. She told us,

When he was able to start to work again, get the use of his hands again, it was still in black and white but it was a different kind of imagery because he had to use a big shaving brush. . . . He couldn't close his hand around anything finer. So the image became really bold and broad stroked, not the finesse that he had. But still, very rhythmic — big broad lines covering the page.

As they talk about Markle now — often as if he were just out of the room for a few moments — his friends and colleagues and former students are as eager to tell you about Robert the talker, Robert the jazz enthusiast, and Robert the philosopher and teacher, as they are about Robert the artist. Not just teacher of art, either: he had a natural gift, almost a compulsion to teach, and a gift for philosophic inquiry and clarity that would have propelled him to academic stardom had he ever chosen to study in those often dismally obscure environs. Instead he taught in bars and taverns, or at the little dining table in the kitchen at the Holstein place (where this writer spent many enchanted hours being guided through the elusive craft of painting in watercolours). Not long after settling down in Egremont Township he joined a hockey team, most of whose members spent much of the winter living on their Unemployment Insurance Commission cheques. The team was called the UIC Flyers. Robert designed the logo and cap and sweater badges. You can see some of the boys — most of them getting on a bit now — wearing the badges in their caps, in the documentary, as they talk over a few beers about how life has not been the same since he left them. This was in the Mount Royal Hotel in Mount Forest, where they'd go for a few after a session on the ice, and the few would get to be quite a few, and by closing time Robert would not be in very good shape to drive the eight miles back to the Holstein house. So if Marlene was not with him, the boys would find somebody sober to drive Robert's vehicle and someone else would follow in another car — or more likely a pickup — to bring that driver back, and they would get him home safely. Teaching — and those evenings in the pub are remembered by the guys as being laden with the most intriguing kind of teaching — was not a one-way matter. As he tried to engage them in the stuff that engaged him, he was being nourished in return. Marlene remembers that

he came home after an evening with the guys and he said,

"You know, Tim said something really interesting to me. He'd seen me working on something and he said, 'Do you really see all those colours in the trunk of a tree?'" He was really grateful for that question because that meant that Tim was really looking and it just sort of opened the floodgate for conversations about art.

It was the same with his friends in the art world. Av Isaacs says, "A lot of people became very attached to him because he had a very special mind and it didn't flow along normal predictable lines. He could cause you to really dig when you were talking to him."

As an art teacher he combined an almost evangelical eagerness to lead people to find joy in the investigation that line and form and colour constituted for him, and at the same time to provoke and tease and upset any predisposition they might have to take themselves and their work too seriously.

There is film from his days at the New School of Art, part of the Three Schools started by John Brown, of *Warrendale* fame. This was a school where the instructors were all young contemporary artists whose work was being shown in the city, and you didn't need a high school certificate to get in: if they liked your portfolio, that's all it took. A lot of the sometimes very intense teaching took place around the corner at the Brunswick Tavern. In the film, Robert is working with a young woman, telling her in that soft, crooning voice he dropped into when he wasn't barking at the students, that she was

trying to make the colour do something in terms of form. And also you're trying to design on the page. With one brush full of paint you're trying to do all those things.

Woman's Voice:
That's right. . . . Yeah, all those at once . . .

Markle:
You can't do it.

Rae Johnson, now on the faculty of OCA, was one of those early students.

I met Robert Markle when I started at the New School of Art in Toronto and it was a different kind of an art school run by artists. These were like the real McCoy. These were like the guys, the Isaacs guys. . . . I [still] hear him talking to me sometimes. I still remember the things he said just as if it was yesterday. And when I'm teaching my own class, I'm constantly reminiscing and coming up with Robert stories to tell people.

The very first class, we had the nude model. Robert walked in and said, "Okay, draw the model," and he left. And you know, he came back hours later and he stood up and he said to everybody, "Okay, I want you guys to take your drawings home tonight and look at them and try to figure out why they're all so shitty!" And he walked out and that was it.

His language was often rough, the F word popping up as often as ums and ahhs and other pause words and with not much more intent. "Asshole" might sound like a distressing dig at you, when he probably thought he was being affectionately critical. Rae Johnson says she almost slips into those modes sometimes, Robert being so much present when she teaches. But you can't get away with casual "sexual" references in this time of Political Correctness, she says.

The way it is now it's all kind of, you know, you have to be very namby-pamby and make nice and everything. Once in a while, a little bit of Robert kind of creeps in there and then I kind of hope nobody is going to go hire a lawyer or something.

But beneath the playful, verbally rough edges, there was the constant inquiry. Paul Young again,

We went to New York [together] several times. We were standing in the Metropolitan in the roomful of Rembrandts. We were looking at one of his self-portraits. I was looking at it thinking, that's a nice picture. I like that, I like that. And I asked Robert, "What do you think?" And he said, "Hmm, I'm trying to figure out what the fourth last mark is." I thought, what? He said, "Well you can see the last mark and then you can see the mark before the last mark and then you can see the marks that came before that. But what's the one before that?" He was literally taking the picture apart backwards. And most people, even artists, stand in front of something like a Rembrandt and they're just awestruck. But nobody ever actually takes one apart and tries to figure out what makes it go. And that's the way Markle thought about art.

Rembrandt's own life work he had interpreted as investigation, one he was intensely eager to share as far as he could. In 1974, when I was making my television series *Witness to Yesterday* (for Global, which in those days was trying to demonstrate a commitment to original Canadian programming), Robert called one day and proposed that he play Rembrandt — we wouldn't need a script; he knew Rembrandt's life story so intimately all I had to do was ask the questions a scholar or a journalist would ask the real person. His proposal had an imperative tone. I knew I would refuse at peril, but in fact it was an appealing idea, and I had no difficulty persuading my producer-director (and the series' originator) Arthur Voronka.

He had never acted, although he was certainly a performer, as his music and storytelling revealed, and his dancing — astonishingly light and graceful for a man who had become so heavy that one of his closest friends always referred to him as "The Fat Man," an echo from the dialogue of the Humphrey Bogart film *The Maltese Falcon*.[1] But if he was not a professional actor he was certainly a performer, and I was also counting on the drama of watching that probing, playfully inventive intelligence at work.

We partied irresponsibly the night before the shoot, and Robert was fearfully hung over when we got to the studio for his character makeup, which he mostly slept through as the makeup artist transformed him into an arresting version of one of the famous self-portraits. He walked painfully into the studio two hours later, waved away a proffered coffee and said plaintively, "Anybody got any speed?" — not as shocking a remark in those days as it might be now.

One of the stagehands said he was pretty sure he could get some nearby, and came back with it in minutes. Robert popped a couple and leaned back in his chair on the set with a dreary sigh. Arthur Voronka came over looking

1. The Fat Man in the film was played by Sydney Greenstreet.

not inappropriately very anxious. "Uhmm . . . is this going to be all right . . . ahh, should we ahh . . .?" Robert waved at him irritably and said, "Get on with it, man, get on with it." Voronka looked beseechingly at me. I gave him a wave that was more reassuring than I felt, he called the set to order, and we began.

We were shooting 16mm colour film in those days, 400-foot rolls, so there was a pause at least every ten minutes. The slate went up, the call for silence, the "Roll 'em" command — the clapper boy put in the slate, and I put the first question.

There was a pause. Robert leaned forward, frowned, and said, "I don't think that's a very interesting question. Listen. In my time . . ." and he was off, a Flemish painter struggling to make a name for himself four hundred years ago. He was looking for the issues basic to his work, and in a strong metaphorical and dramatic sense we all believed we were listening to Rembrandt van Rijn. At the first ten-minute pause the whole studio burst into spontaneous and sustained applause. Robert blinked, smiled a shy smile, and said, "I could take that coffee now." That episode of *Witness to Yesterday* remains one of the best in the whole canon of more than sixty programs. Paul Young said,

In terms of his own work, I think that's really what it was about. He was looking for the basic issue — why am I an artist in the first place and why do I care about this and why should I take all this trouble? What does it all mean?

"What does it mean?" was the question he asked more often than any other, and he expected answers from Marlene, from the priest who dropped in at the gallery, from the drunk at the bar, from his hockey mates at the Mount Royal — leading all of them, through his own radiant intensity about the central nature of *investigation* in the process of living, to feel the importance of that search in their own lives. It was, indeed, a question he often put in a despairing voice, sometimes overwhelmed by its elusiveness. At other times, over a just-completed painting or even just a stroke of the brush, he evinced a quiet sense of triumph: the investigation had arrived somewhere.

Another mode of investigation was music. Robert learned and played the tenor saxophone with highly individualistic gusto, and once said that anyone can criticize his art but "if they criticize my music I'll kill them." He had taken only a few lessons and had only a vague intellectual grasp of harmony, or chord and melodic structure. But he was — characteristically — a profound student. Jazz was his first taste, his tastes were wide-ranging, and he had great tolerance for experiment and the edges of the envelope. Where an Ornette Coleman would leave me wincing at what I heard only as resentful screeching, he would discern aural probings. And he too was always probing. Once, I came into the house to hear his great McIntosh sound system, cranked up high enough to make the windows shimmer, swarming with the rich viola and 'cello sonorities of some hypnotic medieval French music that he'd just discovered and was transported by. That particular music remained an almost daily favourite, and when I play the copy he made for me, he is suddenly sitting there in the room, nodding softly with a look of distant and profound understanding.

Gordon Rayner says unequivocally that music was even more important to Robert Markle than was his painting. They both played in the AJB, the Artists' Jazz Band: Rayner was a gifted natural on the drums and Coughtry (also untaught) was on trombone; what might have been acoustical chaos was given a spine and a coherence by the piano work of Michael Snow. Snow would later become famous for his *Walking Woman*, for his slow, sculptural, dreamy, prodigiously original films, for his flying geese at Toronto's Eaton Centre, and even more famous for the huge comic heads of baseball fans that decorate SkyDome's outside walls. Snow said,

None of them had any basic technical knowledge at all really. They just got instruments and started playing. So it's an interesting kind of representation of what they liked in the jazz that they admired. They didn't have the harmonic understanding or the chops to make exact imitations, but out of having a kind of aesthetic formal sense and just out of a pure passion and the substances, some truly amazing things would happen. The music was very, very good.

When he came to the Artists' Jazz Band, Michael Snow was already an accomplished painter, sculptor, and filmmaker and the only professional musician among them.

It was Christmas time and everybody decided to play — or it was suggested that we play a Christmas carol. And somebody said, "How about Joy to the World?*" It's just a scale. Da da da-da, da da da da. So we got all these guys, Graham on trombone and we started to play it. And nobody could play it. So you have this wonderful thing of going . . . (sound effects). It does descend sort of . . . (sound effects). It's amazing. The funny thing about that is that incompetence in a certain sense is a kind of way of making variations, because it's better than playing it right, in fact, what they did.*

In June 1978, the AJB was invited to play at the Canadian Cultural Centre in Paris, and to bring an exhibit of their art to be hung in that institution. Robert said he didn't want to go. "When I get more than twenty miles away from my studio my nose starts to bleed." Caroline, my wife-to-be, was living in Paris then and I was planning to spend most of the month there as well, so I more or less forced him to get a passport.

Gordon Rayner says that Robert tried to walk off the plane at Montreal. When he got to Paris, Caroline took a week off work to look after him. While he was still muttering, "Get me on the next plane home," she started to drive him around the city, just quietly letting him see all the stuff she knew would fascinate him visually — the ornate Metro stairway arches, the huge seventeenth-century buildings, the painted cast iron street urinals, the bars.

They stopped in a few bars she knew, including the one her mother ran, Casey's Irish Bar. He was wearing the denim suit that he had, for an Art Gallery of Ontario contest, decorated with exquisite needlework — nudes, of course — which had taken him a year to complete. The Parisians made a great fuss over him and the suit, and bought him drinks.

He withdrew his plea to be put back on the next plane, went off to Ibiza with the lads for a few days, came back in great spirits, and allowed himself to be bamboozled by Caroline and me into visiting the Louvre for which he had expressed a lofty contempt: "They're all tourists." Once in, we couldn't get him out till closing time at nine that night, and our photographs show him sometimes with his nose right up against the brush strokes of a ten-foot-high Géricault, sometimes posing beside a standing mummy case whose profile matched his, always staring with that look of penetrating inquiry.

The AJB concert at the Cultural Centre was a great success, and he felt by the end of the trip that it had all been glorious, crowned by making music for strangers in one of the world's greatest cities. "When he came back," Marlene says now,

he looked so young and smooth and — transported is the only word I can think to describe how he looked. It sort of reminded me of how he described his feelings when he first went to the reserve — that he'd just been so moved and thrilled and his eyes opened. His heart and his spirit opened to something he never suspected was there.

Making and listening to music were a constant part of the Markle investigation of meaning and of life. The central element of that catalogue of investigations was the sexual mystery. But in his forties another theme, almost as powerful, at first crept up him on like a hardly known visitor from his youth, and later became a motif that transformed the last years of his life: his Mohawk heritage.

I suspect he was drawn back to his roots in part by a new sense of the importance of heritage that this very urban-formed man had found when he and Marlene moved to the country northeast of Mount Forest, Ontario, in 1970. Somehow in those conversations at the pub the idea flowered of his doing something for the community of Mount Forest. Bill Koehler, then the manager of Freiburger's supermarket (now an IGA store), offered the eighty-foot-long stuccoed storefront as a surface Robert might work on. "He drew a sketch," Bill Koehler says, "and we seen this sketch. But I'll tell ya, it'd scare the hell out of you, okay . . . (chuckle). But anyway, he says, 'That's what I'll do.'"

It scared the hell out of them because it filled that whole eighty-foot wall, eight feet high, and would turn out to be one of the most intricate public murals in any small town in Canada. It is still there; you can't miss it if you drive down Main Street, although it is a bit faded and perhaps in need of a local philanthropist to provide the modest funds to restore and protect it. It is an intricate, narrative depiction of the woods and rivers, streets and birds, farms, old buildings on Main Street, and legends of the area, and it already contains hints of this next chapter in the artist's investigation of heritage.

It was soon after finishing the mural that Robert made the transforming visit to his parents' reserve at Tyendinaga. It was an opportunity to investigate another part of himself. "When he came back," Marlene says,

> he was really, really quiet, very, very still. And slowly it came out what the experience had been like. He walked onto the reserve, and not like there's a line there, but suddenly you're on the reserve. And he said, all the post boxes and all the signs on the stores were Maracle.

He told his sister Susan, "I saw people that looked like me and people that looked like you." And he said, "And it was such a good feeling." And he told Marlene that he suddenly felt at home and peaceful. "He wanted to move onto the reserve. If it had been possible, I think that's the direction we would have gone."

He took me down to Brantford and the Six Nations Woodland Cultural Centre to meet its director, a fellow Iroquois, the Onondaga teacher and curator Tom Hill. Tom Hill was helping Robert with a script for my *Heritage Minutes* dramatizing the creation of the Iroquois Confederacy.[2] The script was a daunting challenge, and he was still struggling with it when he died.

He also wanted to honour his township with a Mohawk theme; so, using traditional cedar split-rail fencing, he built a snaking structure in front of his and Marlene's house. The work is still there, seventy feet long and twelve or fourteen feet high. "You can only see it [properly] from an airplane," he said with a laugh (when we were shooting that pilot). "It's called the Great Horned Serpent of Egremont."

Around 1982, when Metro Toronto called for proposals for a mural in the then new Metro Convention Centre, he proposed a Mohawk-inspired piece, to be made of untraditional materials: coloured neon tubes, mirrored stainless steel. Some of it was painted, and every shape was drawn from the forms and traditions that had taken

2. Originally the League of the Five Nations (also known as the Iroquois Confederacy) included the linguistically related Cayuga, Onondaga, Mohawk, Oneida, and Seneca. It became the Six Nations when the Tuscarora joined the confederacy in the early eighteenth century. The original confederacy, whose constitution is one of the world's oldest, may have been formed as early as the fifteenth century.

on such significance in his life. His proposal was accepted. The fee was substantial, but he kept little for himself, spending almost every cent on materials and on the specialized crafts he had to engage to form the stainless steel and to bend the neon tubes into his Mohawk shapes. He called the work *Mohawk: Meeting*. It is an astonishing 160 feet long. You'll see it immediately as you begin to descend the escalator from the main entrance to the lower level at the Convention Centre, and you may want to stay and be with it for some time. He signed it Maracle.

◆　◆　◆

My wife Caroline Bamford and I saw a lot of Robert in the last months of his life. Together the three of us developed a television series in which he would ride a Harley (the company provided the bike) from town to town seeking out the microbreweries that were springing up. Robert had discovered Creemore Springs Lager, in the Dufferin County town of that name, and that was the brewery we chose for the pilot of the series that was to be called *Something Brewing*. CBC Television liked the proposal well enough to invest a crew and an editing suite for that pilot, and we went up to Creemore in June to shoot it.

With Caroline producing and me directing, Robert would ride the Hog into the microbrewery town. He'd spend as much time sketching the local architecture and chatting on camera with the weekly newspaper editor or a group of teachers in the local middle school as he did investigating the brewery and its products. And then the idea was that he'd stack his drawings on the back of the bike and ride off to the next episode and the next micro-brewery town. Sadly, he died only days after we finished editing the pilot.

It was a July evening in 1990. Robert had a beer with the Flyers at the Mount Royal, and set off for home on his own. He was fine, no need for anyone to drive him. Doug Kerr, known to the lads as Suds, was the last person to speak to him. "He said, 'See you tomorrow, Man,'" Suds recalled in the documentary, at a table at the Mount Royal, his eyes welling. But somehow, inexplicably, in that clear starry, moonlit night, Robert drove hard into the back of a tractor on the road, and that was it.

One of his friends said, "There is a big black hole in the universe now."

There is.

◆　◆　◆

The History Television documentary was written and direct-ed by Daniel Zuckerbrot.

◆ Part Three ◆

FRED ROSE
THE MEMBER FOR TREASON

Sometime in 1946 Soviet espionage agents working the Montreal area set up a meeting with a thirty-nine-year-old Canadian named Fred Rose. Rose was sympathetic to the Soviet cause. He was a card-carrying member of the Canadian Communist Party, and, like many Canadians in those first years after World War II, he still saw Stalin's Soviet Union as the great friend from the East who had helped bring down the Nazis. That was one reason he was proud to be a Communist. Probably the majority of Canadians then, whatever their political outlook, still thought of Stalin as the "Uncle Joe" they'd been taught about in school during the war, the benevolent head of an allied nation without whose help the democracies would almost certainly have lost. Some cooler heads had not lost sight of the dark essential centre of Soviet power; Winston Churchill had made his famous "Iron Curtain" speech on March 6th of that same year, but the phrase had not yet entered the popular vocabulary as the prime metaphor for the closed and cruel Soviet dictatorship. The Cold War had not really started.

It was about to do so.

The Russian agents wanted something from Fred Rose, of course, and they were very good at their job. They flattered him, but not too much. They responded with almost shy courtesy and dismissive gestures to his praise of their country's role in defeating Hitler. The gifts they proffered were pleasant but not extravagant. They had heard about a new explosive formula developed by a Canadian chemist, something called RDX. They were able to persuade Fred Rose that it was in the interests of International Socialism and World Peace that Russia have this RDX, about which their Canadian allies were being unreasonably secretive. Rose was able to find a chemist who knew RDX, and to pass the required information to the engaging Russian who, in his low-key but authoritative way, was clearly someone close to the levers of power, an insider.

The Soviet embassy in Ottawa had brought this man in as a "military attaché" from Mongolia. His name was Colonel Nikolai Zabotin, and Rose was pleased to be brought into the inner circle. He was excited when Zabotin gave him a code name and secret instructions for communicating with him. Zabotin was, in the parlance of the espionage professionals, "running" Fred Rose: Rose was his agent.

What makes this story much more extraordinary than it would have seemed had Rose been just another seducible member of the CCP, is that he was also the Member of Parliament for Montreal-Cartier. He was the first and only Communist ever elected to the Canadian Parliament, and even in the eyes of some of his political opponents, a pretty darn good MP.

Rose was Jewish. The Montreal community had been badly divided between Jewish anglophones and Catholic francophones in the years leading up to and well into the war. In those years there was, among some Quebeckers, what now seems an incomprehensible sympathy for the Nazi movement. Anti-Semitism was a normal undercurrent of the times, not only in Quebec but also across Canada and throughout the United States. Jews did not get elected to public office. It was hard to get into medical school if you were Jewish: there was a quota on Jewish admissions at McGill in Montreal and at the University of Toronto, never publicly acknowledged, but quietly firm and effective. If you wanted to teach in a public school in Ontario and were Jewish you'd just better forget about it. There were eminent Jewish law firms, as there are now, but in those days it was hard to get into such a firm if you were not Jewish, and hard for the Jewish firms to attract Gentile clients, next to impossible for a Jew to get into a non-Jewish firm.

But in Montreal for a while, layered on top of that "normal" undercurrent of anti-Semitism was a sympathy for the Nazis not unrelated to the fact that during World War I the issue of conscription had set off a huge conflict in Quebec. Most Quebeckers felt that they had no obligation to fight the British Empire's wars for them. Their reluctance to be roped into another seemingly irrelevant war allowed Fascism to take hold in Quebec more strongly than most places in prewar Canada. There were brown shirt marches in the streets of Montreal, with the famous straight-arm salute. The producer of our documentary on Fred Rose, Francine Pelletier, found a photograph of a Montreal mother tucking her baby into a cradle decorated with a swastika, beneath a photograph of a benign, avuncular-looking Adolf Hitler.

Montreal's Jews were, not surprisingly, very fearful about all this. They had heard the stories coming out of Germany. For many of them, the far left was the natural opposition to Fascism, and in those days a great many members of the CCP, the Canadian Communist Party, were Jewish.

But even fellow Communists close to Rose were deeply disturbed by what he did. For many, an important part of Fred's getting elected to Parliament had been the legitimization of the Party as a part of the Canadian democratic system. Probably very few members of the Party, even the deeply committed and ideological ones, had any idea how profoundly undemocratic the "Parent Company" was. When they went for visits to Moscow they didn't see the gulags, or the dissidents being tortured and shot in the head; they saw happy smiling faces and well-fed kids who had been paraded for their benefit. It was a good show, and they were taken in by it, as were many non-Communists — the British philosopher Bertrand Russell among them.

But this! This was a guy committing out-and-out treason, and not just any guy, but an MP who had taken a special oath of loyalty. It would hurt the country, and more important it would hurt the Party. Yet Rose was not alone. A younger Canadian Communist, Harry Gulkin, had also considered committing sabotage on behalf of the Soviet Union. In our documentary he tells the story, looking elderly and benign, with long flowing white hair and mustache. It is hard to believe that this is the same Harry Gulkin who once planned to blow up a freighter in

Montreal Harbour, the SS *Cliffside*, which was known to be carrying munitions to the Chiang Kai-shek's nationalist, anti-Communist Chinese. Chiang Kai-shek was technically an ally of the West in the war against Japan.

Gulkin says now that his pals had warned him: if his scheme was discovered it could destroy the hopes of Canadian labour. In the end, Harry Gulkin's commitment was to the workers more than it was to International Communism, so he did not go down to the SS *Cliffside* after all.

"We didn't think about the consequences through," Gulkin mused on camera. "I think Freddy could not have thought through the possible consequences of . . . that act."

Those consequences began to gather momentum. A man named Igor Gouzenko, a cipher clerk in the Soviet embassy in Ottawa, defected and went to the RCMP. Gouzenko was so terrified of what might happen if he were caught by his former bosses after he appeared in public to testify, or to be interviewed on television (once by Laurier Lapierre and me, for *This Hour Has Seven Days*) that he wore a pillowcase over his head with cutouts for his eyes. This gave an unfortunately comic colour to what was the extremely serious message Gouzenko had to convey.

He told the police and later the media about the enormous extent to which Russia had been spying not just on Ottawa but also on all its Western so-called allies. The news exploded. The Western world was scandalized. Canada was at the centre of the scandal, Russia went from friend to enemy, and the Cold War was on with a vengeance.

Colonel Zabotin's spy ring, Gouzenko revealed,

included military men, high-ranking bureaucrats, and scientists. Rose had been working Gordon Lunan, a captain in the Canadian army and a CCP member, and had tried to get him to bring Canadian scientists into the net.

All told there were twenty other CCP members nailed for collaborating with the Communists. Nineteen of them were, after all, "only Communists"; you could expect mischief from them. But Fred Rose was a Member of the Canadian Parliament, and what he did was explosive. There was a widespread demand to declare the Party illegal again, as it had been for a while in the 1930s. Captain Gordon Lunan, an officer of His Majesty's Armed Forces, was tried for treason, convicted, and given the surprisingly short sentence of five years. He would later write a very readable book about his experiences, *The Making of a Spy: A Political Odyssey* (1995), trying — with a measure of success — to exonerate or at least explain himself. Fred Rose also claimed innocence; cocky to the end, he said to reporters when he was charged, "If I was guilty, do you think I would have stuck around?" He never testified in his own defence. He got six years, which also seems surprisingly little.

The Party was not declared illegal, but the Rose case did lead to the RCMP's decision to set up Canada's first separate elite intelligence unit, the Security Service. And if Official Canada began to isolate Canadian Communists, the Canadian Communist Party also took steps to isolate the convicted members from the rest of the Party. Ironically, that was Fred Rose's idea. He insisted that none of the convicted group say anything to incriminate the CCP: they had acted on their own, that would be the myth.

Rose may have been foolhardy, but he was steadfastly loyal to the party — more so, as it turned out, than they would be to him.

In 1951, on his release from prison at the age of forty-four, Fred Rose died — not physically, but spiritually. The rest of his life was lived in a weird twilight, a state hard to reconcile with the irrepressible street fighter and outspoken parliamentarian he had once been, who had carried the banner for social justice, for universal tolerance, and for the rights of the downtrodden. Now he was just a shabby little traitor, and outside his family nobody wanted anything to do with him. When he got out of jail, his old comrades in the Party set him up in a small business selling lamps, and then told him to stay well away from them.

After RCMP agents began to appear, all wanting to buy lamps, the Party proposed that Fred think about moving abroad "to look after his health." Poland would be a good choice, they said. Poland was Fred's birthplace. He and his parents had immigrated to Canada when he was thirteen. Returning now, in his mid-forties, he could find little there to make it seem like home. His home was Canada, and he was an exile. The Polish Communists gave him and his wife and daughter a comfortable existence. The apartment near the *Staromiejski* (town square), once a grand bourgeois residence stripped and partitioned to make tiny workers' flats, was now restored to its original splendour and nicknamed "the movie set." The Party even provided tropical vacations. But for Rose it was still limbo. He had refused Polish citizenship and Canada had revoked his Canadian citizenship, so not only was he nowhere; he was, in a way, no one. Polish Party members might tell him what a hero he was, risking his life to spy for the cause, but it seemed to Fred as though they had put him in a case, in some kind of museum.

The ironies became more painful now. From his "museum case" he witnessed the beginnings of the collapse of Communism. It began with what seemed a roar to the West but was perhaps not much more than the whispering of what had been tacit but common knowledge inside the Soviet Union: Khrushchev's denunciation of Stalin. When the plump, humorous, gap-toothed Khrushchev made his way to the top position, he seemed to be ready to open some doors and strip away some of that absolute power that Lenin had established and Stalin had entrenched. Khrushchev said he would not agree to be "General Secretary," only "First Secretary," first among a small group of equals. He said that too much power invested in one leader led to problems, and he openly denounced in the twenty-first congress of the party the blood-soaked excesses by which Stalin had murdered so many millions of his own people and imprisoned millions more.

Bold though this seemed to the West, where the monolithic loyalty within Russia had seemed unbreachable, in fact, Stalin had already begun to appear as the monster he really was and the exposure of his regime as a black comedy made it easy to dissociate the dictator from "real Communism."

Rose was also a witness to Poland's growing rebellion against the authoritarian heart of Communism. In Canada his old friends had fallen away from the old Party one by one, but Fred had not. In Poland, even as food was rationed and martial law imposed, even as he and his wife watched in fear through the windows as riot police gassed the demonstrators, they kept the faith. What a sad picture it is in retrospect, the countryless little guy, once influential and applauded. He'd a big name in what he thought of as his real hometown, Montreal, and he was on his way to be a somebody in his adopted country. And now he was a nobody — a citizen of nowhere. He could dream and watch TV. One of his few pleasures was television, especially the broadcasts of big Soviet military parades. Those, he loved; they bespoke the old dream that he still clung to.

His nephew, one of the few who visited them in Poland, said that Rose was "trying to show that he was quite comfortable and quite on top of things." But of course things were not as they appeared. He was desperately lonely; all he had left were his memories. He treasured a recorded message from Paul Robeson, a recording he would play over and over, as if to keep him in another age. It was Robeson's endorsement of Rose's campaign for a seat in the Parliament of Canada, as a Communist.

By the time he turned sixty he was almost bald, and what was left of his hair was wispy and white: he looked naked and helpless. The old twinkle was gone from his eye. His daughter Laura tried without success to get permission from Ottawa for her parents to return. "He was so harmless by that time," Laura said. "How could they not allow him to go back?"

How could she not understand?

He turned seventy-six in 1969. Everything got slower

and slower. His heart stopped. The historian Pierre Anctil wrote, "He rode the wave to power and when the waters receded, he just drowned and was never seen again."

And indeed today, Fred Rose, once a name on the front pages of every newspaper across the country, is forgotten. When the story was proposed to History Television, almost nobody among that very historically alert group of programmers had heard the name. Our crew, canvassing Montreal streets with that device familiar in the biographical documentary — "Have you ever heard of a man called Fred Rose?" — found only one elderly francophone who had, in a working-class coffee shop: "A Communist, wasn't he? Didn't he go to jail or something?"

Of course, there may be more to that story than we know even now. The RCMP files on Rose, three bankers boxes, mostly of newspaper clippings, are still unavailable to historians. Maybe they contain the memoirs he left, which seem to have disappeared, unread, unpublished.

What is solidly documented is that Fred was born Fishel Rosenburg in Poland about 1907, the son of Jacob and Rachel Rosenburg. The family arrived in Montreal about 1920. They were part of the great influx of Eastern European Jews, a fact that would be decisive in Fred's political future. His daughter Laura said that the new life in Canada, even for their parents, was the real life. It was the first sense of security and the possibility of some kind of future that they had known.

The Rosenburgs settled in the Jewish neighbourhood around "The Main": Boulevard St. Laurent. And they probably had no idea that they would become part of a three-way political and cultural struggle. The old, deep-rooted conflict between the minority English-Canadian establishment and the French-Canadian majority was becoming tense again as the war fanned some old, never-quite-cooled embers. The largely Protestant anglophones had the money that ran the province, politically and industrially, and the francophone majority trusted too much in its true royalty, the hierarchy of Quebec's Roman Catholic clergy, who were grandiose, powerful, reactionary, and quietly in league with the powers in Ottawa to keep the Quebec French Canadians ignorant and in their place. "The white niggers of America," one writer would call them, a cheap supply of labour. Ripe for a revolution which, amazingly, when it came thirty-odd years later, was carried through almost without bloodshed, The Quiet Revolution it would be known as, *La révolution tranquille*.

But when Fred Rose was a young man in Quebec there were no professions open to the French Canadians except the law, whose Napoleonic Code was different from the English Common Law that prevailed in the rest of Canada; there were no schools of engineering, little chance of medical school at McGill — the best in the country, no chance on the upper floors of the business community unless you assimilated almost to the point of disguising your francophone origins.

If, in the midst of this ancient stress, the Jews were to become a new force of dissent, that was bound to send the temperature up. The Jews, many of whom had reached maturity in Europe, had lived through the revolutionary violence of 1917; many were intellectually inclined and most were on the political left. It was a recipe for conflict. The most radical elements among the Anglos and the French were hard right and xenophobic. Lots of young Jews joined the Communist Party, many of them hardly out of their adolescence. They felt it was part of their history, in their blood. Harry Gulkin was only eight years old when he signed up, Fred Rose seventeen. That youth brigade, The Young Pioneers, an enlistment device in Communist countries around the world, marched out in trademark caps and red neckerchiefs, proudly chanting, "One, two, three, pioneers are we. We're fighting for the working class, against the bourgeoisie." It was a world struggle; they sang it in several languages. Some of them, Rose and Gulkin among them, would get free trips to Russia and come back feeling elevated, justified, confirmed: they had seen paradise, and it worked.

When Rose was in his twenties the Communist Party was outlawed in Canada, and for a while in his early married years Rose was harassed by the government, occasionally jailed, and often publicly booed. He spent much of the time in hiding. His wife Fanny called him "the little man who wasn't there." Their daughter Laura had repeatedly to change schools as she and her mother moved from shabby rented room to shabby rented room.

By the time Rose was thirty the Spanish Civil war had begun to change some of these attitudes. It was the Communists who spearheaded the international volunteers in the fight against Franco's Fascists in Spain. Rose, now working as an electrician, was one of the organizers of the 1200-strong Mackenzie-Papineau Battalion, the

Canadian contingent assembling itself to go to Spain and fight the republican Franco. Rose helped to set up the system of blood supplies for the wounded anti-Franco forces. He worked on the organization of a ten thousand-strong rally in Mount Royal Arena for the Canadian Communist hero Norman Bethune. The charismatic surgeon was just back from the Spanish front. The mood at the rally was euphoric, and the threat of fascism had begun to return some respectability to the Canadian Communists.

The social values of our present age are so profoundly coloured, if not determined, by that motif of the advertising stranglehold on our culture whose prime message is that the good life is achieved by buying things and that shopping is a duty. It may be hard for people raised in this world devoid of appeals to common purpose and shared values, to understand what it meant to be a marching Communist. To those zealots, some scarcely bearded, others whose dark eyes remembered a dark Europe, the world seemed as though it could just be on the verge of a revolution, a glorious, long-dreamt-of revolution. The empty-spirited, socially purposeless bourgeoisie would be trampled by the unavoidable march of history, and the working class would finally come to its rightful heritage where real social justice would be universal.

It was only a matter of time — that seemed so clear, so inevitable — only a matter of time now, before a few gentle pushes in the right place would bring the whole rotten structure crashing down. One of those gentle pushes was getting someone elected to Parliament, to show the whole country that a Communist is a serious player. Join the party, help the Bolsheviks, destroy fascism, and infiltrate the bourgeois political structure. You argue it, and you hear it, and you believe it on the street corners, at the poulterer's, in the bakery, at home over dinner. This kind of faith is not easily distinguished from religious conversion.

And when Marxist Messianism was married to a messianic Jewish culture, you had something more than belief. It became indisputable knowledge, certainty. For many it was like a drug that carried you through each day, because the end was at last in sight, as it was for the evangelists who gathered on the hilltops every few years to hail the apocalyptic blaze of light that would signal the end of the world, the Millennium, the Apocalypse.

The Revolution, the Millennium, the Messiah, it was all the same. And it was already embodied in the Soviet Union, a massive working-class country, where everyone lived in contented equality, in perfect freedom. That's quite possibly the roseate illusion that drove Fred Rose. He'd been there; he'd seen and possibly believed the show (although there was a part of him that seemed more of a realist). It was certainly that kind of evangelical fervour that fired hundreds of his young comrades in the Party.

By the late 1930s, Fred Rose had developed formidable organizational skills, more than ever in demand as the conflicting forces coalesced around their ideologies. Quebec's hard-drinking premier and demagogue, Maurice Duplessis, had declared war on Communism. He brought in the infamous Padlock Law by which the possession of Communist literature was made a criminal offence, and he used it to attack the Jehovah's Witnesses. The attack turns out in the long run to be a mistake for Duplessis and a move forward in Canadian civil liberties when the poet and civil libertarian lawyer F.R. Scott wins the case for the Witnesses.

But in the meantime, the police, instructed to be suspicious of anything in a red cover — it could be Communist literature — confiscated, among other things, Bibles and a copy of George Eliot's *The Mill on the Floss*. This brought ridicule down on the traditional authorities, and it certainly did not hurt the Communists.

With the Great Depression into its seventh or eighth year, the class war seemed to the Communists to be arriving right on schedule. Now imagine this multisided nest of animosities in which anti-Communist populism mixes with Jewish Communism, Anglo-Protestantism, and French Catholicism, and then Nazism emerges on the eastern horizon, dark and angry and atavistic.

Nazism's Quebec counterpart, Adrien Arcand's Fascist Party, began to move against the Jews of Boulevard St. Laurent. The photos show the young converts crowded into a room with their dark shirts and slicked-down hair and a sea of arms in the Nazi salute. Anti-Semitic cartoons of the period show dark, big-nosed Jews leering over showers of gold coins. An old woman now recalls that it was better not to shop too far from St. Laurent or storekeepers might peg her as Jewish and give her trouble. Harry Gulkin remembers a mob of students from the university moving down the boulevard, shouting *"A bas les Juifs! Et les Communistes!"* (Down with the Jews and the Communists!). He remembers his father rounded up local Jewish storekeepers and set out after that same mob. Later, his father came home victorious, crowing with delight, with blood on his shirt. The formula for this animosity was as volatile as the RDX that would soon send Rose to jail. Catholicism, not least the French-Canadian kind, has a history of anti-Semitism. The compliance — or silence — of the Anglos did not help. It was born of the massive power of English Canada in Quebec: it was easy to just ignore the Jews. Meanwhile, the French Canadians — a useful majority, kept in their place by the Church — were on the same lower level as the Jews, and they often lost out in commercial competition with Jewish merchants and professionals. The Jews, after all, were not long out of the *Shtetl* where talents were honed and children disciplined with uncommon intensity. Marxists in the Jewish minority looked on the French majority as class enemies. And finally it was anti-Semitism that helped bring Rose to prominence. As he appealed to all these groups to fight it, he would be in the lead, and while the Gentile anglophones were the despised bourgeoisie, you could deal with them, perhaps even get close to them, get them to trust you even if you could obviously not trust them.

In 1941 the hero of the hour was Uncle Joe Stalin. The Stalin-Hitler pact, which had given pause to many a Communist, had finally been broken. Hitler had launched his disastrous march on Leningrad. Sustaining unthinkable losses, the Russians stood fast around the starving, beleaguered city, the Nazis retreated into a winter that killed almost as many of their soldiers as the Red Army had, and from now on that Red army would beat the Germans in victory after victory.

For the time being, Uncle Joe, benign, mustached, with a thick head of hair, a pipe, and a twinkle in his eye was adored on both sides of the world as a champion of freedom from Nazi oppression. In Canada, the Communist Party acquired a new legitimacy by changing its name to the Labour Progressive Party. Fred Rose was their number one organizer. The dream of World Revolution had now been replaced by the practical promise of better housing and wages for the working class, be it Jewish, French, or even English.

You only have to see the pictures of the wretched poverty in Quebec in those years — children nearly naked, in filthy slums — to get a sense of Labour Progressive's appeal. Out from under the stigma of the outlaw, they went vigorously public in an open, familiar, legitimate political campaign complete with glossy brochures. Fred Rose looked very much the man of his time, with an elegant pencil mustache. Everyone wore suits and hats: Fred's suit and fedora were unusually sharp. Fundraising was suddenly a piece of cake. Party members gave a percentage of their income; donations came from middle-class supporters moved by guilt or by the Party's announced humanism. The popularity of Stalin didn't hurt. Even Jacques Parizeau (destined, in half a century, to lead the Parti Québécois as premier of Quebec) lent help and advice, and met from time to time with Fred Rose.

In April 1942, Michel Chartrand and other Quebec nationalists who opposed the national policy of military conscription formed the Bloc Populaire. It was made up of people who were outraged that Ottawa broke its post–World War I promise to never again introduce compulsory military service. Their leader was the journalist Andre Laurendeau, who later became a commissioner on the Royal Commission on Bilingualism and Biculturalism, which would change the face of Canada. A fair-minded and rigorous journalist — long the editor of *Le Devoir* — his time in the Bloc would inevitably trouble him with that Party's taint of racism. One friend of Rose's said the Bloc Populaire was "not just anti-English, anti-American (and) anti-Canadian — (it was) anti-Semitic."

On the eve of the federal election of 1943, the riding of Montreal-Cartier was evenly split between French-Canadian and Jewish voters. The issues were explosive, calculated to set the two head to head. Foremost for the Jews was anti-Semitism. It faced them every day in Montreal and in the dreadful stories out of Europe. For the French Canadians, it was the newly announced policy of conscription and they were in a fury: Why should they sacrifice their lives in a war they didn't want, a war on behalf of the colonizer who had stripped them of their dignity? Why should they fight for a colonizer in whose language they'd had to live day to day, where all signs had to be English, where all transactions, business deals, and even the call-up notices were printed in English?

The Bloc Populaire blamed the anti-Semitism on street bullies, although they did observe that Jews had taken a dim view of the refusal of French Canadians to participate in the pro-war Berlin parade. The Jews wanted a united front against Nazism; Quebec did not. Sadly, many Québécois were still quietly sympathetic to Arcand's Fascists.

In that Montreal-Cartier by-election, the Liberals were primed to fight to the death for their long-held seat, but they hadn't a chance: the real battle was between the French-Canadian Paul Masse and the anglophone Jewish Communist Fred Rose. The fight became pretty sordid. One of Rose's acquaintances saw thugs rolling metal rods into newspapers to attack the drivers taking Rose's constituents to the polls. At election headquarters at 5 Mount Royal, Jack Shaw, a seaman's organizer, leaned out the window shouting out the results as they came in. He referred to Masse as "The Fascist." Rose won by the narrow majority of a hundred-odd votes. His mother's response seems almost prescient. When her son came home jubilant she said quietly, "My son, I hope some good will come of this."

By 1946 the rough style of the streetwise, subversive Jewish immigrant had worn off. Fred Rose had joined the mainstream of Canadian society as a Member of Parliament. To many, even passionate enemies of Communism, perhaps he represented a hoped-for end of the war between the working class and the ruling class: perhaps it was a sign of hope that one day there could be a government that would care about them. Rose built a reputation as an indefatigable worker and a politician who never forgot that he was a man of his constituency. He was a good MP who chatted with his parliamentary colleagues on both sides of the house, nodded wisely, and put in an appealing good word for the working people.

And that was when Colonel Zabotin made his move. It is likely that Fred Rose's guard was down, and his confidence up. Russia still had the affection of the public, and he was in a position of privilege. What could go wrong?

And yet he was not a stupid man: he must have known something of the risk. So why did he do it? Why did Fred Rose throw away the best years of his political life? Why did he do something that many, if not most, of those in the CCP would condemn?

Oddly, perhaps, Rose was sentimental, not a quality we commonly associate with the disciples of the Karl Marx who condemned sentimentality as a vice of the bourgeoisie. Rose tried to hide his sadness during his exile in Communist Poland, the land of his birth. But he longed for Canada and Quebec. He heard the song about the wandering Canadian, *"Un Canadien errant,"* and when the singer came to the words *Si tu vois mon pays, mon pays malheureux* he cried. When his mother died, he wept easily and he wept long. He loved schmaltzy music and waxed grateful when someone sent him records of love songs by Dinah Shore.

A complex little guy, our spy, our condemned traitor. An irrepressible charmer. Short but rakishly handsome, he had brilliant blue eyes, with a faintly distant look. He was a ladies' man and a flirt. He loved action and the lure of power. Altogether, he had a charisma that attracted even people like Jacques Parizeau.

But there is, along with this charm, a sense of Rose not having time for ordinary people or ordinary things. One contemporary remembers him as being abrupt. Another speaks of an oversized ego: "a little man . . . who would like to be a big man." And there seems to have been little doubt, among those who knew him, that he enjoyed power and publicity. He sang songs too, but his were always Communist songs with a theme for every occasion. His daughter Laura remembers that as sometimes grating — never a song just for the fun of it — a kind of relentless political moralizing.

She also speaks of the bitterness she felt as a girl in need of a father and a family life while Fred Rose devoted everything to the Party or to hiding from his persecutors. Ironically, it was only during their exile in Poland that family life took on some elements of the traditional. "It was the first time in my life, at the age of seventeen, that I lived in a house with my mother and my father, and my father went to work and my mother did the shopping and the cooking."

The life stories of many famous spies get a little elusive when it comes to explaining their betrayal. Ideology is rarely the reason. Some, such as Kim Philby, were merely arrogant. They wanted to be sort of daring supermen. Indeed, many British spies were from the aristocracy; Oxford was a KGB recruiting pool. Few if any British spies came from the working class. American spies, such as Aldrich Ames, were seduced by money. Some Russian spies must have done it from boredom and a hunger to get out of their interminably drab home country. In many cases and in many countries, the act of treachery was the most colourful and the most decisive thing a spy ever did.

Perhaps we can even say that Rose was more sincere than most. Of course he would claim a transcendent loyalty to the Revolution and its progenitor, the Soviet Union. He would call what he did an act of principle, a supreme gesture of loyalty. But you can't help feeling that behind it all there was something vainglorious. Something of the ladies' man and the charmer, the hero who had little time for his daughter but all the time in the world for the Revolution. Maybe that's what his mother was thinking about when she said ironically, "My son, I hope some good will come of this."

◆   ◆   ◆

The History Television documentary was written and directed by Francine Pelletier.

Part Four

BROTHER XII
PROPHET OR FRAUD?

This is the bizarre story of Edward Arthur Wilson. It is a story that has been difficult to piece together. Wilson himself took elaborate steps to disguise, conceal, and erase his history. There are few living witnesses, and not much documentation, so there are gaps that invite a good deal of speculation. But there is enough evidence to considerably frustrate Wilson's intention to disappear without a trace. The story is layered with appearances and disappearances: an intriguing labyrinth out of which emerges a portrait of a man who seems to have been one of the most unlikely scoundrels ever to tread the Canadian scene.

For much of his life Wilson was a British sea captain. He was small of build, soft-spoken, but with a commanding presence. For purely narrative or dramatic reasons it is tempting to jump in at the point where Captain Wilson was personally going to choose the next vice-president of the United States of America. He told his followers it was time to strike. There would be a presidential election in 1928, and Wilson declared that the election would set off a war between Protestants and Catholics. He would travel to Washington, DC, from the Aquarian Foundation headquarters in the Gulf Islands of British Columbia, to make contact with James Heflin, the Washington spokesman for the Ku Klux Klan and also the US Senator from Alabama. Heflin led a strong anti-Catholic faction in Congress.

Wilson would convince Heflin of the equally dangerous threat revealed in the book *The Protocols of the Elders of Zion*, and that these two evil forces would have their way paved for them by what he predicted would be a massive financial crisis triggered by an imminent crash of the stock market. He said the stock market was on the edge of collapse because of insane margins, dangerously overinflated stock values, and out-of-control speculators. The ensuing Depression, he said, compounded with the inevitable religious wars, would lead to a worldwide cataclysm. He, Wilson, would be the world's saviour.

He announced all of this in the November 1927 inaugural edition of *The Chalice*. Published out of Nanaimo, British Columbia, *The Chalice* was the newsletter of Wilson's newly formed organization. It was no ordinary newsletter, nor was the Aquarian Foundation just another charitable institution or service club like the Rotary or the Lion's. It was an instrument of Wilson's own version of Theosophy, the movement founded in New York in 1875 by — among others — Madame Blavatsky. Helena Petrovna Blavatsky — H.P.B., as her followers often called her — said that she was in touch with the Accredited Masters, who did not apparently live in the same world as the rest of us, though there was something about a secret place in the Himalayas to which H.P.B. was able to travel by some kind of spiritual means.

We know that E.A. Wilson joined the Theosophical Society in 1912, giving an address in California, and that he stayed with it for several years. The movement is still active. There are thousands of enthusiastic pages to be found on the Web that describe it in language like that of one of Blavatsky's co-founders, W.Q. Judge:

[An] ocean of knowledge which spreads from shore to shore of the evolution of sentient beings; unfathomable in its deepest parts, it gives the greatest minds their fullest scope, yet, shallow enough at its shores, it will not over-whelm the understanding of a child. . . . Embracing both the scientific and the religious, Theosophy is a scientific religion and a religious science.

A tough-minded investigative journalist named Colonel Henry Steel Olcott had gone to one of Madame Blavatsky's seances with the intention of exposing her, and was so impressed with her apparent ability to contact the spirits of the dead that he moved in with her and helped found and finance the movement. Despite reams of scientific material exposing the fraudulence of Blavatsky's occultism, the movement survives today, although Wilson's Aquarian Foundation, inspired by Blavatsky, is long since defunct.

Wilson also declared his belief in the theory, then much in circulation, of an international Jewish conspiracy. This theory held that world finance, elections, executive decisions and government, whether monarchy or republi-can, were all secretly controlled by a small, shadowy group of Jewish financiers. The proof lay in a viciously anti-Semitic book entitled *The Protocols of the Elders of Zion*. It has long ago been demonstrated to be a hoax as fraudulent as Blavatsky's interviews with spirits, but it is still quoted by anti-Semites. In Wilson's time it had not yet been exposed, and was credited by a surprising number of influ-ential people. Wilson said that the Jewish conspiracy in fact intended to so control the whole of the world's governance and capital that it would achieve its goal of a world dictatorship led from Paris by a member of the Rothschild family. Wilson's views of Catholics, Jews, and others whose beliefs he deplored, were, in addition to being focused and nourished by such works as *The Protocols*, a rich and educated mixture of an enormous range of the world's religions, ancient and modern. He was a diligent student of the legends of the Egyptian gods Horus and Osiris, and other exotic texts including the *Bhagavad-Gita*, and the *Upanishads*. He talked with apparently great understanding and conviction about Karma, the Great Christian mysteries, and the unity of all things. And even when he carried out his final disappearing act (if indeed he did carry it out), it still seemed possible that in some measure he believed in his own extravagantly self-aggrandizing sermons, and in the reality of the special role in the history of the world that he believed he would play.

By the fall of that year, 1927, the most promising candidate for the leadership of the American Democratic Party was a Roman Catholic named Al Smith. If Smith ever won a federal election, Wilson said, it would be the end of Protestantism. He said that since the Republican candidate, Herbert Hoover, was under the control of World Jewry, there would have to be a third party. As an agent and founder of that third party, Wilson would save Protestantism, which meant saving the world. He said he had been told by the voices of his spiritual Masters that he had to slip into the White House by acting as a sort of elder adviser; and thence, by controlling the choice of both the next president and the vice-president, to save the world from perdition.

Curiously, his failure to penetrate the White House as announced, and thus to save the world, like the unfulfilment of most of his prophecies, did not seem to disenchant his followers. The man, like his inspiration Madame Blavatsky, had charisma.

In July 1928, the year of the election, Wilson convened a gathering of Aquarians from all over North America at Cedar-by-the-Sea, a few miles from Nanaimo. He then left by train for Chicago via Seattle. Travelling with him was an Ontario-born woman named Myrtle Baumgartner from Clifton Springs, New York, where her husband had been practising medicine. A few years earlier Dr. Baumgartner had been permanently disabled in a car accident, and the marriage had begun to disintegrate. In her distress Myrtle had a dream that seemed to point to a new direction for her life. In the dream she was crossing a dangerous, fragile bridge and on the other side of it a man stood waiting for her, a saviour. Later she had another version of the same dream, this one set in ancient Egypt. When she met Wilson, she recognized him from the dreams. It was later alleged by his enemies in the Aquarian Foundation that he told her she was the reincarnation of the Egyptian goddess Isis, and he of Osiris. He said they would have a child who would be the Horus of the New Age, that they had worked together in past ages and on "inner planes," and that the time had come when they must work as one in the real and outward world. By the time they got to Chicago, she was pregnant.

It was clear now that she had to wind things up with her husband Ed and move to Cedar-by-the-Sea. She headed East to settle her affairs. Meanwhile, in Chicago, Wilson was organizing the founding convention of that messianic Third Party. This was a gathering of a number of formerly separate fringe parties, who, realizing that they had a common bond in their militant Protestantism, were now trying to become the political saviours of America. The idea of a mystical Protestant crusade had come to Wilson in the form of a spiritually communicated instruction from a group of wise ones. Like H.P.B's mentors, Wilson's were known as the "Masters," were also hidden somewhere in the Himalayas, and were, perhaps, not exactly human. It was the Masters who had given Wilson his predictions. None of those predictions came true, except for the stock market crash and the Great Depression that followed. By then, the Third Party had been dismissed by the press as a national joke, and the movement had fallen apart.

E.A. Wilson was born in England in 1878. His father had built a metal bedstead manufactory into a substantial enterprise, thanked the Good Lord for his success, and took his family into an evangelical Protestant sect called the Catholic Apostolic Church. This was a millennial church whose members believed in the imminent Second Coming and required children to study the Bible and memorize vast passages to help insure their salvation.

Wilson would later say that as a child he not only knew the Bible inside out, but he had also had direct contact with the world of seraphim and angels. But the sect's evangelical fervour did not at first seem to be able to maintain its hold on him, nor did his father's authority, and in his teens he went off to sea as a trainee on a British Navy windjammer. He then took his skills into the merchant navy, worked hard, and acquired a command at an early age. In fact, although he had abandoned his family and his active membership in the Catholic Apostolic Church, that early training was always quietly at work in his inner being, as he travelled the world, and stood alone at the wheel during the long night watches. The author Colin Wilson[1] (no relation) specializes in self-styled prophets like E.A. Wilson — spiritual frauds and other misfits and criminals. He finds that many prophetically inclined people often feel like outsiders, reject the tribal magnetism of family and sect, and characteristically go through a long wandering period. Wilson tried to settle down in New Zealand, and even married and started a family. But he later abandoned them and they never saw him again. His later letters to colleagues and followers reflect on the almost continual sense of spiritual quest that accompanied his years at sea.

Wilson's uneven course, which included a lot of serious illness, continued for much of his life. But the bumps in the road seldom slowed him down. Colin Wilson studies suggest to him that this continual sense of being on the outside can lead to despair, suicide, even a fatal wasting away with this lack of direction, which can come to be, effectively, a lack of the will to live. But if the outsiders begin to feel they understand the reason for their spiritual or existential hunger, that's when destiny may appear.

It happened to Wilson in October 1924 when he was in

---

1. *The Outsider, The Spider World Trilogy, The Strange Story of Modern Philosophy*

the south of France. He said that he was sick in bed one night, lit a candle, and got up to get a glass of milk. But before he could move from his bedside, a cross with the head in the form of a loop, appeared to him. He recognized it: the Ankh, the Egyptian symbol of life. Then the room seemed to dissolve in an explosion of light. An Egyptian temple materialized before him, he wrote later. Wilson himself was standing in a colonnade whose pillars went on for infinity. A great echoing voice addressed him as the Pharaoh: "Thou who hast worn the crown of Upper and Lower Egypt."

Certain that he was in touch with one of the Masters or Brothers of the Great White Lodge, a hidden spiritual committee which, in Theosophy, controlled the world, he took the name of the invisible brother to whom he had spoken, Brother XII. A generous assessment of his legacy might credit him with inventing the Age of Aquarius and with developing much of the semi-evangelical and occult theory and practice that we now call New Age. True to his Catholic Apostolic education, he preached that the millennium, a great spiritual and cataclysmic revolution, was at hand and that everyone had to prepare for it. The chosen, he said, would pass into the New Age, namely the Age of Aquarius, which would reach fulfillment in the year 2000. We are saying he was "certain," and that he "believed" these things, as a convenient way for recounting the next part of the story. To the student critical of this man's strange career, it is not clear how much he believed and how much was an invention convenient to his plans and ambitions. As the story unfolds there does appear to have been a period of genuine seeking and inspiration, which may have been contaminated

— even destroyed — by the wealth and power that suddenly came within his grasp.

The First World War and the great influenza epidemic of 1918–19 was followed in Britain, America, and much of Europe, by an economic boom and a new spirit of excess. The flapper girls, the automobile, the rage for dance, drink, and sexual adventure among the affluent young — these phenomena had disillusioned conservative-minded people who had felt there were real lessons of moral and social consequence to take from the War and from the epidemic. It was to those people that Brother XII came with his message about the New Age. The Masters had told him to begin in England, where his leadership would be eagerly welcomed; and so, in England, he wrote and published *A Message from the Masters of the Wisdom in 1926*. With a table of contents framed in a classical arch supported by two Doric columns, the work purported to be an epistle from the Brothers of the Great White Lodge, addressed to all those alienated by twentieth-century materialism. It invited them to reject self-indulgence in favour of the wisdom of a universal brotherhood. The work had a strong millenarian flavour, predicting the collapse of the social order:

In the near future, existing institutions will be destroyed and practically all religious and philosophical teachings will be blotted out. Therefore the Masters, foreseeing these things which are soon to come on the earth, have prepared the present work. The message is everything; the personality of the messenger is nothing.

The messenger, of course, was Brother XII. Soon another article of his appeared in *The Occult Review*, over the pseudonym Chaylor. *Chela* is the Theosophical word for a special messenger of the Masters, and in British speech the two words can sound exactly alike. "Chaylor" wrote that there was an unusual centrifugal pressure from astral forces, or beings, pushing out into the normal world. Some of this pressure was benign, and some was composed of unprecedented evil. *The Occult Review*'s editor praised the author to his readers. Wilson began to receive masses of correspondence, and soon was signing up members for his Aquarian Foundation. Among them was a soft-spoken, fairly prosperous middle-class couple, Alfred and Annie Barley, who were astrologers. When they came to visit the Messenger in Southampton he read them a letter that he said had been dictated by the Brothers of the Great White Lodge:

> *This people is shortly to pass through a great tribulation, and warning is given so that those who heed it may remove to a place of safety. A small settlement is to be prepared in British Columbia. You should act now and save what you can. Remember that the existing order is about to disappear. You and yours . . . will almost certainly disappear with it.*

British Columbia would be the centre not only of the new Spiritual Age, but also the development of a "sixth sub-race." Money would be needed, of course, and the Barleys began selling their possessions. Brother XII allegedly became friends with some very influential Britons: Oliver Lodge, Arthur Eddington, Neville Chamberlain, and others. He was soon able to write to all of his new Aquarian members to say that he was about to fulfill the command of the

Brothers of the Great White Lodge by building the Aquarian Foundation colony in North America.

Early in 1927, Brother XII took passage across the Atlantic and up the St. Lawrence, and proceeded forthwith to visit the Theosophical lodges of eastern Canada on a mission of proselytization and recruitment. Most of the members had read *A Message* and were breathless with anticipation at seeing the great Brother XII in the flesh.

They were not disappointed. His photograph shows a good-looking man always in a shirt and tie, with a rakish goatee and intense black eyes at once foreboding and mischievous. He was more articulate, persuasive, and inspiring than they had imagined. A good number of these Theosophists began to sign up with the Aquarian Foundation, many offering to establish chapters in their home communities. These were not the innocent or the despairing so often seduced by cults: on the whole they were intelligent and sophisticated. Many were quite well off. They had already accepted the idea of the extraordinary spiritual accomplishments of Madame Blavatsky; now they were face to face with the one who might just be her successor.

Certainly there is ambivalence here: beliefs developed over fifty years, esoteric ideas and yet allied with a sort of hucksterism. G.K. Chesterton wrote that there was definitely an extraordinary power involved in the movement, but — diabolic or celestial — it did tell lies about matters of the spirit. At this stage, however, it would have been hard for anyone to see exactly where the lies were. To the disciples it seemed as though the entire future was theirs, promised by the — up to now — totally credible and powerfully charismatic Brother XII. People began to head for Cedar-by-the-Sea, on Vancouver Island, seven miles from Nanaimo, which was already a prosperous coal town, with its curving, busy, and crowded main street. The Masters had instructed Brother XII that this was one of the few parts of the world in which it would be possible for believers to survive the coming millennial cataclysms.

Brother XII got an eminent Vancouver lawyer by the name of Ed Lucas to incorporate the colony under the Societies Act of British Columbia. This was concluded in May 1927. The group arrived — Brother XII, his common-law wife Elma, the Barleys, and two more Englishmen who had also sold everything for the Aquarian life. They created a board of governors that took on added weight when the German-American novelist, astrologer, and wealthy entrepreneur, Will Levington Comfort became a member at Brother XII's invitation. A distinguished Vancouver publisher also joined the group. There was more than enough money from donations to buy the land at Cedar-by-the Sea. Then as today it was a surprisingly tame wilderness, a flat serene coastline, intensely verdant, forested with old cedar and backed by distant, misted purple mountains. Then as today its waters were often still as glass.

It all seemed to happen overnight. Ten months before, Brother XII had been unknown. Now, on the wilds of the British Columbia coast, he held the first meeting of the board of governors under a large tree. And you can see them still in the group photograph: a gathering of middle-class patriarchs, elderly and middle-aged, mostly in shirts, ties, and vests, standing and seated in the shade of a great cedar. It was Brother XII's forty-ninth birthday.

The place seemed to grow under its own power. First, as the colonists cleared the land, there were only tents. Then they began to build houses exactly like the trim, clapboard cottages of the 1920s that are all across Canada. The houses were spread out a mile apart, perhaps to ensure privacy, perhaps because Brother XII felt he could control things if people were not close together.

Lumber and supplies came from the co-op in Nanaimo; the father of one member, Mervyn Wilkinson, was the treasurer of the co-op. Construction went on day and night. In a matter of months it was done. A picture of about eight or ten colonists shows them looking like farmers of the period in overalls and dungarees, broad grins on their sunburned faces. Brother XII is in the background lounging on a veranda in hat and tie, separate in space and in style.

Soon, as if the settlement had always been there, there were social evenings. There is still no sign of the devious, whimsically cruel person who will so enrage his once-devoted followers that the whole enterprise will soon break down. In his recollection of the colony, Wilkinson's son Mervyn, lively today and in his eighties, gives us an insight into the personality of Brother XII who, in the following exchange, isn't quite the demagogue one might imagine. Not yet thirteen, Mervyn was doing his homework when Brother XII was visiting. The visionary asked if he could watch Mervyn and after doing so, remarked, "It's very good. You're doing well. You keep at it." And then he added, "One thing, Mervyn, yeah, remember that there is so much to learn that none of us have the time to know it all." And before leaving, he said, "Carry on, you're doing well . . ." And then what Mervyn felt: "That was my first meeting with Brother XII, which for a boy of twelve, he talked *to* me. He didn't talk down." Brother XII, as we will have to remind ourselves, was a very likeable, appealing, sensitive man. At this point.

Before long the Aquarian Foundation had about 125 chapters of ten members each around North America. It was also now that Brother XII revealed the bigotry at the heart of his mystical teachings and attempted to apply it to politics in the Third Party movement.

As we have suggested, the spectacular failure of the Third Party only revealed another side to this driven personality. After the founding convention in Chicago (which was after the Isis-Osiris generative train trip with Myrtle Baumgartner), Brother XII went to Toronto to meet Mary Connally, a wealthy woman from Asheville, North Carolina. She had written him to ask for the meeting, and the letter was particularly appealing since it contained a cheque for $2000. Somewhat softened and spoiled by her wealthy family, Connally was twice divorced. She had almost lost her only son to pneumonia at the age of thirteen. Connally was likely as desperate as she was unquestioning: perfect material for Brother XII. In any case, she — like so many others — had found sudden meaning and hope in his writings, and had been smitten with the idea that she had a role to play in The Work.

I was convinced (she later wrote) that this was The Work which I was going to do in the world. It was as if different architects had offered you a plan for a great building or a temple. I accepted his drawings. . . . I then realized that he was to be the contractor as well as the architect, and that he, alone, could carry out these plans.

When she met Brother XII in the lobby of the King Edward Hotel, his electric presence confirmed to her that The Message and The Work were indeed the meaningful directions she was so in need of. She wrote him out a second cheque, this time for $25,000, the biggest single donation the Foundation had yet received.

Back at Cedar-by-the-Sea, when the other new female adept, Myrtle Baumgartner, arrived she was not made very welcome by the colonists, including the board of directors. Not surprisingly, Brother XII's common-law wife Elma was outraged, and many of the colonists were on her side; what was this outrageous flouting of fidelity. Wilson/XII elaborated a complex proposition about the divine imperative of certain unions, which had no element of sexual gratification within them but were solely intended to bring into the world a new life to carry on The Work. Some members who were, like Brother XII, familiar with the Egyptian legends, were prepared to accept that the begetting of a Horus was only a metaphor for Brother XII's successor. Brother XII said that the divinely appointed child would begin his work in 1975, and would lead the Aquarians into the new millennium. But others speculated about an extension of that metaphor, which they thought was displayed in the central hieroglyphs of the Osiris story. In that schema, while Osiris actually faces toward Isis, his body is turned toward Nephthys, the Goddess who ultimately causes his death. Who then, they wondered, would Nephthys be?

The colony was no hit-and-miss do-your-own-thing sixties commune. The board of governors looked like a group 1920s bankers on vacation. As they considered the Myrtle Baumgartner incident, with Brother XII's convenient explanations about the spiritual imperative of The Succession and his contradictory abandonment of Elma, they began to wonder aloud whether or not The Messenger was, in fact, losing his mind.

When they confronted him he continued to insist that this was the sacred but temporary union of two higher natures. When Myrtle had a miscarriage, some took it as evidence against him. One said, "It seems Horus has slipped his moorings."

Then there was an incident involving Mary Connally. The board found out that Wilson had deposited her $25,000 cheque to his own personal account instead of to the Foundation's. "Enough!" they said, called the lawyers, and formally had him charged with misappropriating the money for his personal use. The preliminary hearing was a circus. The trial proper unfolded like a plot. At its crisis, reporter Bruce McKelvie wrote in the *Province,*

> The dingy courtroom of Magistrate C.H. Beevor-Potts
> Thursday would have made an admirable setting for a
> movie drama or a scene for one of the old-time plays of the
> coal-oil circuit where, at the crucial moment of the trial of
> the hero, the heroine, blonde and blue-eyed, bursts into the
> group of serious-faced officials, lawyers and spectators, to
> proclaim the innocence of the accused.

Remarkably, the judge believed her, and the accused was acquitted. But his troubles were not over. News came that the provincial government intended to investigate the Aquarian Foundation. In the meantime, Brother XII — who by now was beginning to quite dictatorially tell members of the colony what they could and could not do — confined Myrtle to the "House of Mystery," his place of meditation. She had a second miscarriage and then a nervous breakdown. He decided to send her home. Her dream of being consort to the Egyptian God Osiris was at an end. She sent a pathetic telegram to her paralyzed husband: "If you will have me back, may I come, heart sore and weary?" Dr. Baumgartner saw no reason to forgive his ex-wife for what must have appeared to him to be demented wanderings, and so Myrtle's story ended with a final plea to the doctor to expedite the divorce.

At the end of 1929, it might have seemed that the tragicomedies of the Third Party and the scandals of Myrtle, Mary, and the trial would have finished Brother XII. But we have to remember he was widely known to Aquarian groups scattered all over, people who knew little first-hand of the squalid goings-on. Immediately after the trial, Brother XII sent out letters inviting yet more Aquarians to the colony to be the next generation. And indeed they came.

Now, using Mary Connally's money, Brother XII bought the De Courcy group of three islands totalling close to seven hundred acres. Suitably lined with rock cliffs, De Courcy Island was to be the "inner sanctum" of the colony. Before long, an elite of the most zealous and still loyal colonists arrived to take up residence off the mainland. A couple named Herbert and Dora Jefferson converted their life's savings into gold and handed it all over to Brother XII. The preferred currency for donations was the gold American Eagle. The splendid coins were packed into mason jars, and hot wax was poured over them, as if they were preserves. The jars were then packed forty-three to a box and hidden on De Courcy Island. This would keep the gold safe from intruders, Brother XII told the colonists. But then secretly, at night, he would dig up the boxes and move them to different hiding places. And then compulsively, like some sweating miser, he would move them to discourage theft.

In early 1929, things got stranger yet. A peculiar woman named Mabel Skottowe arrived with the man whose mistress she was, the wild, bearded Roger Painter. He was the Poultry King of Florida and had made a contribution of $90,000. Brother XII was fascinated with Mabel, the sense of power in that cold, forbidding eye, her mouth stern with decision and hostility. Perhaps this was Osiris's other woman, Nephthys, his dark destroyer of the hieroglyphics. The god dressed as a pharaoh has his body turned to his right but his face is directed towards a second goddess on his left.

Roger Painter was named Brother IX. Mabel became Brother III. But Mabel had another name as well; they called her "Madame Zee." Madame Zee, with a lofty disdain for conjugal prudence, left Mr. Painter and went to live with Brother XII in his new house on a promontory overlooking the De Courcy Island anchorage. At this point we do not hear anything more about poor Elma. Mabel's new status as Madame Zee gave her an authority that she seemed to relish. She issued commands to the disciples, berating them, once even using a horsewhip. Snapshots were popular at the colony, but not with Madame Zee. It was speculated that she was on the run from the police.

But even then, there was a measure of harmony. The colonists were hard at work clearing and cultivating the land on De Courcy to grow enough food to make the island and the colony at Cedar self-sufficient. They succeeded. The ground was lush, the weather benign, the trees bore fruit and nuts, and there was a healthy dairy herd. Perhaps, some hoped, the unbalanced behaviour of Brother XII and the ranting of his mistress would pass. There seemed to be some promise that the colony could indeed spawn the New Age.

But Brother XII got worse. When the police came out to De Courcy to investigate some of the bizarre stories about buried gold and strange practices, The Messenger got the message: it was time to think about writing another chapter in this long, complicated novel that was his life. He and Mabel decided they needed time away from the colony. They spent part of the year in England, in Brixham, a pretty south coastal town of almost Mediterranean aspect, its crooked streets of bright buildings crowding down a steep incline to the water. He put his seamanship to work and bought a yacht that had once been a fishing trawler — a long, low, sleek seaworthy vessel with many doors and windows. They called it the *Lady Royal*. Together they sailed her to the Caribbean and there they docked for repairs.

Brother XII had a fight with the shipyard owner and sailed away without paying. Much later, Wilson would discover that a huge steel bar had been driven through the keel, the shipyard owner's revenge presumably. The bar gathered kelp, and the boat mysteriously got more and more sluggish; they went ponderously through the Panama Canal and up the coast of Mexico where they were hit by a hurricane. Taken far out to sea, they ended up becalmed and out of drinking water, parched, close to death (and wishing for it, they said afterwards) until a passing ship heard their dog bark in the night, and they were saved.

When Wilson returned to De Courcy in December 1930, the disciples gathered to watch him remove packets wrapped in black oilskin, all the time muttering wildly to himself. He began to bury the packets around the island, as he had buried the colonists' gold years before. Because of Brother XII's erratic behaviour and the subsequent strange business of headlights flashing from the mainland and secret boat trips back and forth, the colonists began to talk about drugs.

Things deteriorated fast. When Mary Connally's money dried up, she was put to work at exhausting manual tasks and completely cut off from the man to whom she had been so dramatically loyal. It was her money — yet another donation, $10,000 this time — that had bought De Courcy, but now she had to chop wood and carry heavy loads on her back. "It is a test," he said and when in his judgment she failed, she was given another, ploughing and cultivating a three-acre field, a test she also failed.

The colony was now arranged in a distinct hierarchy

with De Courcy at the top and Valdes Island at the bottom. Mary Connally was sent to Valdes. Brother XII forced everyone into a game of "musical houses" by which residents were moved from house to house. Soon they were freezing cold and eating poorly as they worked to exhaustion, terrorized and submitted to new extremes of humiliation at the hands of Madame Zee. As Roger Painter put it later, "We thought we were in the brotherhood of love. We found out we were in the brotherhood of hell."

There is no doubt that total control was at the heart of the cruelty. And by this time it probably wasn't even a means of enforcing the faith. Colin Wilson suggests that Brother XII had grown tired of his religion and his only real goal was to eliminate any possibility of anyone contacting the authorities or looking for the hidden wealth. When all was under control, he might escape with Madame Zee, a free and a rich man. But there is another explanation, and that is that he was syphilitic — which would explain his weekly trips to Nanaimo. A couple of doctors from a clinic there would claim in the future that a certain Dr. Hall had treated Brother XII for syphilis.

Sometime in 1931 the names of Edward A. Wilson and Mabel Skottowe were legally changed, his to Amiel de Valdes and hers to Zura de Valdes.

When immigration officers turned up one day in 1932 to investigate a reported violation, Brother XII began to talk paranoically about attacks by government agents. He set about stocking firearms and fortifying the De Courcy area. You can still see the sniper nests, small, one-person forts of boulders rolled together where the sentries —

exclusively women — watched out for interlopers. They did four-hour shifts, moving from nest to nest. Sometimes they fired shots in the air when boats came too close.

Then came the breaking point. Madame Zee ordered a seventy-eight-year-old schoolteacher to drown herself so that she could attain everlasting life. When the old woman tried several times and failed to carry out the order, Madame Zee terrorized her until the woman broke down. The De Courcy colonists were not yet so brainwashed that they could accept such an outrage. They confronted Brother XII. He responded coolly and systematically, ignoring the complaint, by quietly getting them off the island in twos and threes until everyone except for two determined loyalists was moved to Cedar. Only then did they realize what he was doing to them. They launched a legal action.

Mary Connally and Alfred Barley were the ones who brought that suit, technically to recover some of the money they had put into the colony. In a sensational deposition, the betrayed lover Roger Painter, once the Poultry King of Florida, declared that Brother XII and Madame Zee had seriously tried to kill their enemies in the colony with black magic rituals held at midnight in the cabin of the *Lady Royal.*

In the end the judgment went against Brother XII, but not in time to stop his escape. He and Madame Zee moved quickly, destroying many of the buildings on De Courcy. They sank the yacht, dug up the gold — maybe half a million dollars' worth — and disappeared. The courts awarded the De Courcy property to Mary Connally.

The fugitives reappeared briefly in Devonshire, where Brother XII made out his will, leaving all his wealth to Madame Zee. In 1934, they move abruptly to Neuchâtel in Switzerland. Brother XII had heart problems (perhaps a cover for syphilis) and was treated at the luxurious Clinique du Chanet, with its *Deuxième Empire* Mansard roofs and gallery verandas on every floor. At sunset on November 7 of that year, in the idyllic setting of an apartment with a wrought-iron balcony overlooking the lake, Brother XII died, perhaps of a heart attack.

Or did he? Colin Wilson offers another version. The one-time visionary had been reduced to the empty, bitter, and evil-tempered Mr. Wilson. Mabel, bored and fed up, deliberately terrorized him to bring about an end by which she could only profit. Perhaps it was a subtle and undetectable murder. In any case, she had him quickly cremated, and disappeared with an amount equal, in today's money, to at least ten million dollars.

And then there is another version, and in this atmosphere of paranoia it has a hell of an appeal. Did Brother XII, or E.A. Wilson, perhaps fake his death? Donald Cunliffe, the son of Wilson's Nanaimo lawyer Frank Cunliffe, says that in 1936 he travelled to California with his father. He saw Frank meet a mysterious man on a yacht in San Francisco Bay and hand him a briefcase full of money. The man was all in white — shoes, hat, everything. He had gleaming eyes and a powerful presence. Colin Wilson dismisses this, and says he thinks murder is much more likely. But in 1937, Donald Cunliffe said, his father got a call from Gibraltar from a man the operator called Mr. Wilson, and the lawyer afterwards confirmed to his son that it was the man on the yacht, Edward Arthur Wilson.

Whatever the truth, the wildest speculation only inflates the myth. Even the embittered colonists were not so alienated as to leave De Courcy Island despite the horrible associations. They stayed on for several years. Mary Connally, once forced to be a beast of burden, was the last to leave, in 1944. She told her lawyer: "For the old Brother I'd give that much money again, if I had it to give." Even journalists and historians are ambivalent about the man, some inclined to read in his early writings a deep and sincere inquiry into the human condition, an inspired if romantic vision of how that condition might be transformed, and then a transformation of the man himself from a benign leader into a crazed despot. The speculation about syphilis contributes to this almost forgiving view.

Hundreds of people have combed the island looking for gold that might have been forgotten or left behind in that hasty final departure, but the old caches have turned up nothing, except one hidden vault in the basement of a colony bunkhouse, empty but for a handwritten note: "For fools and traitors, nothing!"

If there is a Brother XII spirit looking down on it all, he must love the story about the man in white on a yacht in San Francisco Bay.

◆ ◆ ◆

The History Television documentary was written and directed by David Cherniak.

Part Five

JOHN WARE
The Fame of a Good Man

During the dreadful winter of 1882–83 an American cowboy named John Ware came north with the drive, and hired on with the Alberta rancher to whom he had helped deliver the cattle. That winter was brutal even for Alberta. Ware had never seen anything like it; where he came from all that happened after November was that some leaves fell off the sycamores, and the nights got a little cooler. But that first winter in Alberta, one day when the herd disappeared and the boys had to ride out looking for them, there were places out on the range, far from the few trees around the ranch house, where it felt like — and probably was — forty degrees below zero.

The other cowboys gave it up and beat it for the bunkhouse, but John Ware had somehow determined he would find that missing herd — he had, after all, driven them all the way from Montana. The wind brought tears to his eyes; he later said he thought they had frozen. He lost his hat. He said that he'd been afraid to move his fingers in his thin woollen gloves for fear they'd break off. He went so far into that white hell looking for those cattle that he had to go four nights without sleep before he got back. He knew that if he and his horse stopped moving they would die, and in fact when he reappeared at the ranch he had been given up for dead.

His boss found the man's stamina uncanny. Not only

had he seen few if any come through an ordeal like that, but once warmed up the cowboy appeared to be in great spirits: "Happy as a woman with a new hat," the boss said.

But he had not found any of the cattle, and no one else had either. When the wind stopped a few days later, and they all went out on the search, eight thousand head lay piled in the river bottoms, hard as rocks. But for all that, as we will see, there were good reasons for John Ware to be happy in this barren land, this white hell, as he called it.

You do not hear a lot about Canadian cowboys, but John went on to live most of his working life as a Canadian cattle hand and then as a rancher, and earned such renown and admiration that his funeral in Calgary in 1905 was the largest the town had ever seen. And when they began to write about him, it was not so much his achievements as his character that shaped what became the John Ware legend. Not so much because of what he did as what he was, and to know how that character was shaped we have to back up a bit. There had been a lot of adversity, in the shaping of that character, and some of it was very recent.

In Montana, that summer of 1882, John Ware had been hired on as night herder, the lowest and most trying position on a drive of three thousand cattle. The destination was Highwood, up in the territory of Alberta, which was still twenty-three years away from becoming a province. That would happen the year that John Ware died.

The Montana stockman was a man called Tom Lynch, and it seems that he had not wanted to hire Ware. Perhaps Ware's size — over six feet and 230 pounds — had something to do with it, a lot to feed and heavy on a horse.

Lynch liked his boys lithe and light. But there was probably another reason, a reason that has a little bit to do with Ware's fame, which we will come to later.

The hand whom Tom Lynch really wanted for that drive was a good-natured cowboy named Bill Moodie. But Moodie was a close friend of John Ware. He told Lynch that he'd come only if Ware came too. The blackmail worked. Ware was hired on. But there may have been a residue of resentment in Lynch's mind.

In any case, from the beginning Ware sensed that he'd better conceal his own resentment at being the low man on the drive. He was, and he knew it, a better cowboy than the others. But life up till then had given him a lot of practice at lying low, and had given him a talent for irony and modest indirection. When he wanted a better horse than the old nag they'd fobbed off on him, he would say something like, "I wouldn't mind a worse horse . . . if you got one." The gang decided there might be some fun here, so they brought out the worst-tempered horse they had. It may have been a routine initiation, or it may have been part of that other aspect of Ware's life that we'll come to presently.

At any rate they put him on this mean critter, and the horse bucked, reared, jounced, jolted and swung the cowboy's massive bulk around the fence-line for twenty minutes, while John Ware hung on spectacularly, and the other cowboys had to concede that the guy they'd been trying to humiliate was a gifted bronco rider. The unassuming, slow-spoken, ruefully smiling John Ware had won their respect, a reluctant respect perhaps, but genuine; the guy was really good.

He went onto the day crew, and things began to get better.

They were driving those three thousand head north for Fred Stimson, the manager of the Bar U Ranch in Alberta, the same man for whom Ware would endure the blizzard later that same year. After the three thousand head and their drivers had crossed into Canada and signed off the herd, Stimson hired Ware at twenty dollars a month. It was on the recommendation of Lynch, the man who had not wanted Ware in the first place.

It is true that some people would not have hired Ware on sight, but Alberta was virgin cattle country, there was a huge demand for cowhands, and Stimson didn't look twice when he found a man who could do the job and came with a top recommendation from Tom Lynch. Winter arrived; the blizzard came and went. Stimson lost the cattle, but by then he knew that Ware was a man he wouldn't want to see the back of.

The hands liked Ware too, and thought they knew him well, but after a while they began to notice some idiosyncrasies. Cowboys were not an educated lot; they tended to have certain odd beliefs and rituals. But by comparison with the profoundly superstitious John Ware the others were models of rationality. He could brave blizzards and stampedes, but he believed — among other things — that snakes were inhabited by Satan. One night the other members of the crew coiled up a rope and placed it in the foot of his bedroll so that it was just like a sleeping rattler. What they expected to happen, happened. Ware lost control and went into a monumental rage. Whether or not the big man actually hurt any of his mates is not recorded, and maybe it was, again, a matter of character that when he calmed down he regretted his display of temper and left the Bar U ranch.

Here we ask the reader to forgive the "we'll-get-to-that-later" device above; it seemed to be a way of communicating some of the surprise that accompanies the John Ware legend, without giving it away all at once. It is sometimes hard to believe this whole story because this was the 1880s and John Ware was not white; he was black. He was a black cowboy. Because he was good at what he did and lived in a cut-and-dried world of casual manners and unending work, it is difficult to tell whether or not there was an element of racism in his treatment in Alberta. We are not told. In Montana it may have been the reason for Lynch's reluctance to hire him, or for the low position they gave him when he started. The legend doesn't say. But it does seem unlikely that it could have been absent from the practical jokes with the bronco and the rope snake.

John Ware had survived a lot of horrors in his young life, and surmounted most of them. His fear of snakes came from his childhood and adolescence as a slave in South Carolina. He said that a dead snake had been used to whip him when he was young. On the range, his memories travelled with him:

I have often been awakened by the most heart-rending shrieks of an aunt of mine. The slave holder used to tie her up to a joist . . . and whip upon her naked back till she was literally covered with blood. He would whip her to make her scream and whip her to make her hush . . . and not

until overcome with fatigue, would he cease to swing the
blood-clotted cow skin.

That plantation was near Georgetown, South
Carolina. In the documentary, the slaves do not look as different and separate from the white world as we might
imagine. The ancient photographs usually show them in
the cast-off clothes of their employers, dark and tattered
shadows of the larger society. Even at work in the cotton,
they are in the same breeches and doublets and vests, the
long dresses and shawls, the frock coats, although now
these old garments are filthy and ragged. Pictures taken
outside of work hours show men, women, and children
anonymous in their grimy surroundings with nothing to
do. The black faces seem to hide something, perhaps the
last shreds of dreams, or hopes that their children at least
might still make something of themselves. Or maybe there
were no dreams at all, just numb habits of concealment,
hidden rage, and grief.

For Ware, the time came — as it must have come for
every slave at least once — when he got fed up. One day
he saw Chauncey, his overseer, beating his sister. Ware
spoke out, and for his trouble he too was whipped without
mercy. It was at this time that the American Civil War
broke out and wore on four long years. There was not
much change to the slaves' lives during the war, but at its
end, General Sherman's march had, in a great firestorm,
wrecked the whole plantation system that had held slavery
in place. Ware couldn't leave without having a last word
with Chauncey. He found him not far from the whipping
tree. He pinned Chauncey to it and told him he could

finish with him then and there, but just to show his spirit was nobler than that of his ex-overseer, he let him go. He was lucky not to be shot in the back.

The slaves left the plantations in groups to pursue a future in a world that was only nominally free and probably more dangerous than the plantation, where they had at least held the status of valuable property. Even if they had ever been allowed to know anything about the world outside, they must still have wanted to get away from plantation territory, and about fifty thousand did manage to leave the South. But the majority stayed on, south of the Mason-Dixon line, as hired labour, often itinerant, still in poverty, still in cast-offs from their former owners now "employers," still barred from participating in the reinvigorated Republic that had freed them.

John Ware travelled farther than most. He worked his way south and west to Texas and then back into Oklahoma where he came upon the legendary Chisholm Trail. James Horan and Paul Sann, in their *Pictorial History of the American West,* tell how the defeated confederate veterans came back to Texas after the civil war and "found their ranches in ruins, and the entire state running wild with unbranded longhorns, the tough, ugly-tempered steers descended from the herds imported earlier from England and Ireland."

They would not have been steers, which are castrated. So when these authors tell us that a steer got five bucks a head in Texas and fifty dollars in Chicago, they probably mean cows as well. In any case the saying was that any Texan with a pencil and paper knew where his future lay.

So instead of trying to reconstitute the old cattle ranches, they drove north with the first 260 thousand head in 1866. The first big drive. By the time John Ware got there the three-and-a-half million wild cattle that had been grazing all over central and west Texas were slowly being gathered up. They must have looked like a walking gold mine. The idea was to claim and brand as many as you could and drive them north along the Chisholm Trail from Fort Worth to Abilene, Kansas, and eventually to the rail head whence they would be shipped up to the stock yards of Chicago.

At that point John Ware was no cowboy. The only beast he had ever ridden, as he put it, "was a buckin' mule." But when he saw the open range, something slipped into place in his mind. He never looked back. He neither saw nor heard from any of his family ever again.

John Ware's decision here was uncommon, and what made him different from so many of his fellow former slaves is not clear. Like Ware, most ex-slaves had the mobility that went with their transient labour. But the majority of them seemed to be locked in a kind of paradox. Fear caused them to stay in the place where there was, in fact, the most to fear: in the reconstructed South, or in the confinement of factories and farms in the north. They had drifted into other forms of bondage, perhaps less inhumane than what they had known as slaves on the plantations, but virtually as inescapable.

We know there were blacks who drifted into roping and handling and herding, but mostly in groups, in a few all-black cowboy outfits. The lone black freelance cowboy was a rarity.

But John Ware moved on alone working his way around the Southwest until he had picked up enough of the craft to be able to handle cattle on horseback. And now he kept moving until he found a life better than the one he would have had back across the Mississippi or in a Chicago sweatshop. Somehow he was able to climb out of whatever it was that had immobilized so many of his people. To them what he decided to go for might have seemed wildly improbable, but he thought it was just common sense, plain logic. It would actually be better for a black man to go where there were fewer people, more money, and such a rush to hire able bodies that colour didn't matter. All you needed was ambition and a steady eye on the horizon.

You can see it in the few and extraordinary photographs of him that survive. Above the closed lapels of an old flannel suit jacket there is a big and pleasant face with a thick goatee. But the eyes are startling. In each picture they have a light in them: the gaze is unmistakably distant and yet burning with reproach, of pride, as if to say, "Nobody can stop me."

Cattle trails branched out and spread quickly like a pattern of veins on the skin, until, by the late 1870s, there wasn't enough grass left in the southwestern states. Now it was the grasslands of Wyoming and Montana that beckoned, and there was word of a growing cattle business up north in some place called Canada. By 1879, pressure from the ranchers persuaded the government to open the northwest to the cattlemen.

It was this spreading growth of the trails that gave John Ware his opportunity. Somewhere, probably in Texas, he signed on as drag man to a herd of twenty-four hundred Texas Longhorns headed for Montana. Ware couldn't read or write, his horsemanship was still only half-developed, but he was strong and willing, and the stockmen needed anyone they could get.

As drag man, Ware was slotted at the "back end push." The job was considered to be a notch above night herder. Nobody wanted to be night herder. It was boring; you had to sing the cattle to sleep. You had to watch for rustlers and you had to keep things quiet. A sudden noise could waken the cattle and start a stampede that could kill you or anyone else, and — worse from the stockman's point of view — kill some cattle as well.

Drag man was a better job than that, but it was the dirtiest job. The drag men rode behind the herd and got all the dust day after day for maybe a thousand miles. It was in that slot that Ware met Moodie, the man who would stick up for him, later, with Tom Lynch. Ware and Moodie were both new, both drag men. You rose in the hierarchy as you moved forward in the herd. There were men on the flanks and two men at the front and finally the man ahead of them who "rode point" and was the most experienced of all. Ware rode back there with Moodie, and dreamed of moving forward in the herd, and then moving forward beyond the herd, and then beyond the horizon and beyond that too. Moving as far as he humanly could from the past.

Whether being black was any obstacle to his moving forward, Ware doesn't tell us. Perhaps on the frontier there actually was a greater respect for individuals and for talent, just as the myths and the movies suggest. Ware survived all the physical hazards of the ride. He got to the other side of the dangerous Brazo River in Texas where cow pokes often drowned during the crossings. He survived the outrage of the Indian tribes whose grasslands the herds crossed, and he was lucky to miss out on the gunslinging thieves who sometimes ambushed a lone rider, after his pay if he was carrying any, or his watch if he had one, or even a few cattle.

Ware travelled through the middle of the Wild West just before 1880. It was at its height and at its dirtiest. The herd no doubt rested at the notorious Dodge City, marshalled by Wyatt Earp and Bat Masterson. They provided order in a world where there was almost none. Maybe Ware and another hand walked down its streets to get provisions, or maybe the entire crew felt it best to stay clear and stop somewhere else.

The myths and the movies have not, in fact, captured much of that West, the real one that John Ware saw. The old still photographs convey more of the tone of that life, the spirit, the mood. You sense a too-fast, impatient adventure over a huge distance in an extremely short time. The vistas are flat, blasted, and bleak. Almost everything built on that landscape ends up small, ugly, and quick, little more than an infrastructure minimally needed for the movement of beasts and money, more a construction site than a building. Nothing seems finished. Stores and hotels are half tents, half rough boards. Everything is dirty. What looks like faded cloth or wood in the old photographs of dresses, old coats and trousers, saloon floors and coaches, is really the bleached look of mud and filth dried to dust. Genuinely bad men seemed to rise out of that dirt, like Orcs in a fantasy film, stupid-looking, gaunt, underfed, instinctively brutal. It is all freakish; neither city nor country, its habits are neither east nor west. Even in the few faded shots of Ware facing the camera or at work, there is no cowboy wear, in Western Movie terms, no chaps or bandannas or Stetsons. Like everyone else on the crew, he wears city clothes — or their remnants. Like everything else in this makeshift, short-lived world, the wardrobe is mixed and in flux and unexpected, a sort of shabby variety. And perhaps, in this free and chaotic confusion, a solitary black cowhand like Ware, passing through on a big drive, would not look at all out of place, since everything was out of place.

When the heaving ocean of grass that was Montana appeared ahead in the distance over the dusty backs of those thousands of cattle, it must have seemed nearly primeval, virgin, a good place to stop and create a new life. But Ware's old drag-mate Moodie wanted to go farther. He persuaded Ware that they should go on, to Canada. He had heard about the Canada thing, even more untouched than Montana, a sort of Promised Land for American cattlemen who had begun to settle southern Alberta when there were still only a handful of non-native Canadians there.

The Hudson's Bay Company, moving in from the East, had collided with some of those northern-bound pistol-toting Americans. The Native peoples, whose lands these were, were in between. The whisky trade, the systematic depredation of the Native peoples, and the mad slaughter of the buffalo were threatening such chaos and lawlessness that in 1874 the government of the seven-year-old Confederation created the Royal Northwest Mounted Police.

Some historians say that one reason there is less violence in Canada than in the United States, despite the commonality of the two countries' origins, is that the Canadians put the law on the land before the people got there. The RNWMP moved into southern Alberta from their base at Fort McLeod. The white settlement followed the Mounties, and soon there was a market for ranchers and cattlemen.

In Montana, what Ware and Moodie had probably heard about was the heart of this paradise, the Alberta foothills: well watered, sheltered, and kept relatively free of snow by the warm westerly Chinooks. They had to get there some way, and Lynch's drive seemed to be the way. They crossed the border and henceforward Canada would be Ware's home. Some time afterward, after the blizzard and after the prank with the coiled rope, he decided that he wanted to be on his own again, at least away from trail gangs, running things, not being run.

That was when life began to look up for Ware. A serene reward for his adventure was in sight. So far he had had no trouble making a living. His skill was already getting known. And for someone so long on the trail, he was remarkably obliging. What he wanted more than anything was the chance to do a thing that was primordial and universal, a thing which, in the world that he had come from, he couldn't hope to do. He began to think of owning a piece of land, and some cattle, and a house to settle down in, and maybe even a family. A disciplined man, he saved every cent he could, and by the mid-1880s he had enough money to go into the land registry office in Calgary to sign for a property.

And things continued to go well, although there were some surprises. Calgary was a surprise. Calgary was young and wild but it was also a city. In Canada, it was the city that was more likely to harbour racial prejudice than was the country. There had already been a murder or two, and the latest one was traced to a culprit who happened to be black; so all black males were under suspicion. On his way into town, to that registry office, he saw how they were looking at him. Somebody must have told him what it was about, but all we really know is that he never made it to the registry office that day, he just turned around and left town. He planned to winter that year, at Stimson's Bar U Ranch, and perhaps the racial tension eased off, or perhaps Fred Stimson took the application in for him. In any case he got his land that same autumn, and he cut and squared timbers for a cabin, and dragged them three miles by hand by tying them to a rope around his waist. But he didn't have enough time to finish building before the snow flew, and Stimson gladly took him in.

While Ware was at the Bar U, Stimson signed him up in the rancher's own local militia. The experience and the contacts would be useful in the future, and the pay would get him back to his half-built cabin. One can only speculate on his feelings, if any, at being something like an Indian scout for the white man. There had been trouble in the northern territory. The Second Rebellion of Louis Riel's Métis had sent alarming rumours through the hills. There had been the now famous battles at Batoche and Duck

Lake. Soldiers and cowboys were mobilized to defend the settlements. Now no one knew what the Blackfoot would do, whether or not they might join Riel and substantially change the balance of power. What Ware and the other militiamen had been assigned to do was watch their movements on the plains.

Did Ware see in the Métis a people a situation similar to that of his own people — free but with few effective rights? What was more, many of the ranchers commanding the militia had an upper-class British or Canadian military background. From what can be pieced together out of the slim documentation, it seems that Ware understood himself in no special way as a black man with a mission in a white world, nor indeed was he assimilated to the larger white world. He referred to himself as a man who had made his own destiny and had a duty to continue to do so — beholden to no one except by his own good will.

The rebellion didn't last, and the peaceful spring brought with it opportunities for raising cattle. We know that on May 25th, 1885, John Ware walked into the office of CED Wood, recorder of brands, and registered the number 9. It was just a practical thing: 9 was the number of cattle he could afford to start with, and with a flourish he stamped it on each of them four times: Brand 9999. This was exuberance, but it was not a legal brand. A few years later, when he finally had the money, he officially bought brand 999 and settled for three nines instead of four.

He had his house up by now, rough and unfinished but livable, in that Sheep Creek area in the foothills. We are told that when he moved in, his neighbours were at first uncomfortable with this "nigger in the neighborhood," but he won their acceptance before long. He would walk right up to people and ask if they needed a hand. They'd seen him handling cattle with as much deftness, speed, and horsemanship as the best. He took part in the local roundup and its communal spirit, and the way the story is still told in Alberta, if there had been any tetchiness about that "nigger in the neighbourhood," John Ware soon put it to sleep and was accepted as a citizen. He had adapted to Canada in three years and risen to the top of his trade in five.

All the same, John Ware's small farm and few cattle were not enough for a living and not enough to fill his time. He went to see John J. Barter, previously of the Hudson's Bay Company, who now had the Quorn horse ranch, raising thoroughbreds for the English gentry of the Leicestershire Hunt Club. Barter tried him out and made him foreman in charge of the ranch's saddle ponies. It was a step up, and it was serious business. Thoroughbreds were a kind of power centre in the colonial hierarchy. The Quorn Ranch set out to supply mounts for the British cavalry; in return various earls and marquises seem to have invested in the ranch while their sons worked there. If Ware was a foreman, Ware had their respect.

Now he had a position, but for all his work, little he could call his own. The unfinished hill cabin and the herd, now grown to seventy-five head, were still not enough. He needed land that would produce what he needed to make him fully independent. Then he would be ready to marry. It was 1886; he was thirty-seven. It would be hard enough to find a wife.

Another bad winter tested everyone on the prairie. The round hooves of horses could paw through the ice and snow for stubble pasture, but the cloven hooves of cattle could not. John Ware lost half his herd. He needed a better job. When Fred Stimson and John Barter decided to put the two best men in the region against each other in a round of bronco riding, they put John Ware against a man called Frank Ricks, and gave them the deadliest unbroken beasts they had. Ware easily won, and the High River Horse Ranch people were impressed and took him on at a better salary than Barter had paid: fifty-five dollars a month. He would be able to finish his cabin and set up properly on Sheep Creek, but he was still alone. It had become clear that citizen or not, champion bronco rider, admired professional, all the friends and admirers notwithstanding, the colour bar had never really vanished, and he was never going to marry a white woman.

So when John Barter told him that a Negro family by the name of Lewis had moved into Calgary and that they had a daughter named Mildred who was not yet twenty, he obviously had to see her. He must also have been embarrassed, even angry that all eyes were on him and presuming a match just because they were both black. He was a man who made up his own mind; this might be an opportunity, but he would not have people think it simply inevitable. Nonetheless, he walked with dignity into the dry goods store where the meeting had been set up, and Mildred liked him. He was invited to Sunday dinner with her family. Soon he and Mildred settled down to a careful round of what was for John Ware an all-too-public courtship.

By the spring of 1891, John Ware was a rancher. He had finished the house. It had a fine front porch and several rooms. There were two hundred cattle branded with the now legal 999. But his land was unfenced, and crop farmers started to trickle in buying up land, encroaching on the ranchers. Had he thought about it, he might have sensed danger, but he seems not to have foreseen what was coming. Fall had come and he was thinking about marriage. For the first time he had what he needed to support a family and the prospect of another hard winter alone was not attractive. He had to propose, now or never. He spent Christmas with the Lewises. The story is that he finally showed her a photograph of the house, and said, "It's an awful nice house and if you ever think you'd like to be an old cowman's missus and have that house, I'd sure like to know." She must already have made up her mind because she answered, "Yes John." They were married on February 29, 1892.

When the newlyweds went up to John Ware's house that night they paused; there was candlelight in the window. The trespassers turned out to be the neighbours, gathered to bid the new couple a happy future. For a while that seemed to be finally possible. Ware's lucky number 9 turned up again. On March 9, 1893, Mildred gave birth to a baby girl whom they named Jeanette. All he needed now was for everything to stay as it was. That would prove to be the hardest part of all.

The early 1890s were dry. Instead of riding out the droughts like most ranchers — or being ridden down by them, John dug an irrigation ditch that led in from the creek and watered the meadow where he was growing hay for the winter. The farming was going well, but Mildred hated John's long absences out on the range. She hated the cold and the hard work. But the bonds were still stronger than the differences and in November 1894, Mildred gave birth to a son Robert.

So often the beginning of the end of something remains imperceptible. For John Ware that beginning seems to have been a mild discomfort at the arrival of an unexpected burgeoning population where he had always counted on open space and the long divides that make good neighbours. The crop farmers were finally getting their way. The government was selling the good grazing land right up to the backcountry. Encouraged by good land prices and the search for larger pastures, the ranchers were moving out. Ware drove his three hundred cattle eastward to better grazing. He sold Sheep Creek, and then he and Mildred loaded the children and everything they had into a wagon and moved ninety miles east to cheaper land on the Red Deer River.

From there things took a different course that must have seemed relentless and without cause. The landscape itself seemed a kind of warning: low, marshy, dreary, melancholy. Mildred's next child died shortly after birth. The labour had been difficult and left her permanently weakened. Cattle mange swept across the territory like a plague. The sores ate ruinously into the hides of the cattle, herds were quarantined, and the entire trade came to a stop.

For John Ware everything became a fight now. He

tried to fight Mildred's increasing illnesses, to fight the vicissitudes of raising cattle, to fight the inhospitable land. He tried to raise his children at the same time. His daughter Jeanette recalled a stream over which her father had placed a hut where he kept the milk fresh and cool. And in that stream they were not allowed to play. She said her father caught young Robert playing there, seized him by the ankle, and dipped the boy into the chilling water several times just to scare him a little and teach him.

But this was only a moment in a train of sorrows that seemed to increase. In 1902, the river, of which that creek was a tributary, burst its banks and carried off the Wares' entire house (ironically, the tributary is now named Ware Creek). When winter arrived, Mildred came down with pneumonia. Ware rode off to get medicine but his return was slowed down for hours by a blizzard. He must have remembered the futility of his search for Fred Stimson's cattle in that blizzard years before. When he finally got home, Mildred was all but gone. It was March 1905. When she died he sent the children away to their grandmother and stayed alone for a while, in the desperately empty cabin.

Freedom at its best is a condition of possibility, not of perfection. The dreamed-of destination of his life, of honourable self-sufficiency, work, and marriage turned out to be a place of hardship and heartbreak. Floods, disease, and death are as indifferent to freedom as they are to talent and hard work. Still, he said, it was better to suffer in liberty than to be born without hope. And indeed he kept the facts of his past from his own children.

Five months after Mildred's death, when his son

Robert was ten and Ware himself only fifty-six, they were out riding together when his horse stepped into a gopher hole, threw John Ware, and killed him. He had ridden half a million miles, up to then.

His epitaph said that the purity and fineness of his colour reflected the purity of his soul. His story came down to us in the tales of aged ranchers and cowboys, and those few photographs, and a couple of newspaper accounts. The ranchers and the cowboys told it because they recognized it. In a way it was about them, and — like them — both ordinary and remarkable. They told it because he was a man who rose out of a nightmare they could only guess at, came to their land, did the kind of work they did, and did it with courage, skill, and honesty beyond what was required. What they did not talk about so much, although they knew it with that kind of unspoken social common sense of people of the open spaces, is that one person of a different colour is more likely to be accepted than is an entire community. When you are alone, the colour of your skin is a pigment and nothing else, and your abilities are free to develop so that you can show yourself for who you really are.

In the end, in those tales from those ranchers and cowboys, John Ware's fame is of a rare and amazing kind; it is for being a good man.

◆　◆　◆

The History Television documentary was written and directed by Brian Dooley.

Part Six

SAMUEL CUNARD
THE MAN WHO INVENTED THE ATLANTIC

In the minds of millions of people around the globe, the image of the classic ocean liner used to conjure up the romance of a sophisticated passage between New York and Southampton, dressing for dinner, dancing with a handsome stranger to the strains of a white-coated orchestra, flirtations and more on the starlit afterdeck. Hundreds of movies — most spectacularly the 1998 *Titanic* — have entrenched all these clichés, perhaps to the point where they have become archetypes. The great liner also bespeaks another kind of romance, one sometimes triggered by desperation, sometimes by great hopes: in the darker lower levels and crowded decks there travelled millions of players in the great drama of immigration to the New World.

For most of us the prototype for the classic age of transatlantic travel, roughly from 1900 until 1950, is the Cunard Line's first *Queen Elizabeth*. Launched not long before the start of World War II, she seems to us now almost timeless, not especially modern, not old-fashioned, simply *the* ocean liner, inheritor of her predecessor's style, the *Queen Mary*. It is not easy to imagine a world without those *Queens,* as big as floating cities, yet with a regal grace in their soaring prows, the black hulls and towering funnels over the white superstructure, the bright red strip of the waterline. The three erect funnels of *Queen Mary* become a swept-back pair on the *QE One*, then a graceful single stack on *QE II*. When *Queen Mary II* comes down the ways on which she is taking shape in France, she too will have a single stack, broad as a wing and utterly distinctive, but she'll still be unmistakably a member of the same royal family.

Although the preposterous, towering, pregnant bulges of the Mediterranean and Caribbean cruise ships may have overtaken the *Queens* according to purely commercial criteria, the great liners still bespeak a vision, and the first incarnation of that vision was built by a man from Nova Scotia named Samuel Cunard.

He was born in Halifax in 1787. Halifax is a city created by wars, a major mustering and supply centre for British naval strategy from the moment of its founding in 1749 by Colonel Edward Cornwallis. The Seven Years' War (1756–63) established the port's strategic importance. Towards the end of the eighteenth century when George III's son Prince Edward,[1] the Duke of Kent, moved there as Commander in Chief of the British forces in North America, he built parts of it to resemble a tony aristocratic British city. When Charles Dickens visited in 1842 he said that looking at Halifax was a bit like looking at Westminster through the wrong end of a telescope.

Samuel Cunard's father had been a successful shipbuilder in Pennsylvania, but his loyalty to the British cause, which brought him to Canada after the 1776 American War of Independence, also forced him to abandon everything he

---

1. The colony called The Island of St. John was re-named Prince Edward Island for him in 1798.

owned, and he arrived penniless in Nova Scotia. When his son Samuel was born, Abraham was working as a foreman-carpenter for the British Naval garrison in Halifax. The boy would show a sharp entrepreneurial sense early on, would go on to build a substantial industrial empire, and die Sir Samuel Cunard, in London, in 1865, by then the owner and builder of the great and seminal Cunard Steamship Lines. Long before that company would bring into being the above-mentioned archetypes, its founder would have made and lost millions, and set his name in stone, wood, and paint all over Halifax, to mark his many and various enterprises.

Much admired today by those historians of business for whom competition and private enterprise are the great values in life, Samuel Cunard was, in fact, one of the first great industrial beneficiaries of massive state subsidies. His steamship line exploded from a modest coastal enterprise into the world's greatest transoceanic service when tapped into the British Treasury by persuading the British admiralty that his ships would be at the disposal of the Empire in time of war.

And indeed they did serve in times of conflict, carrying troops overseas in all of Britain's subsequent wars. It was a Cunarder, the *Lusitania*, whose sinking helped propel America into World War I. On May 1, 1915, the *Lusitania* left New York for Southampton, carrying a good number of Americans, including the famous millionaire Alfred Vanderbilt and the noted theatre producer Charles Frohman. On May 7, with the coast of Ireland in sight, a German submarine, the U-20, torpedoed the *Lusitania*. She sank in eighteen minutes taking 1,195 lives — 123 of them American. Although America did not actually declare war until April 1917, it is generally agreed that the *Lusitania*'s sinking contributed to the turning of the tide of American public opinion against Germany and led the United States to join the Allied cause. The outrageous suggestion that British officials, including Winston Churchill, were complicit in setting the ship up for this disaster in order to arouse America has been taken seriously by many historians, challenged by others, and is still not completely dead.

At a cursory glance, Samuel Cunard is remarkable for an apparently unending string of successes, each greater than the last. But when you look at it closely, the successes are interspersed with an almost equal number of failures, bankruptcies, and staggering periods of seemingly ineradicable debt. Samuel Cunard's failures tell you something about the man: he seems to have learned little from them, except to try harder.

He is a little like Napoleon in that way. As a military strategist, Napoleon was nicknamed "the scrambler." Cunard too, always seemed to begin in chaos and then formulate some rapid, almost too-clever head-on plan that would get him out of it. Like Napoleon, he was a small man. He had a reputation for rushing everywhere as if he could never quite pause long enough to organize his day. He was a devout Christian. His last communication — a letter written from his deathbed — is a glad exclamation of thanks to God for a full and satisfying life.

As a young man during the War of 1812, he was beginning to succeed as a merchant when peace came, and with it a recession that all but wiped him out. A few years later he decided to invest in whaling. Some whaling outfits were making huge fortunes, but those old prints of whaling skiffs being tossed in the air by angry blunt-nosed sperm whales give you some idea of the prodigious risks. With characteristic haste, Cunard appears to have greedily over-looked the need to keep his investors happy, and proceed-ed to build and outfit the big ships at a speed that suggests he had either forgotten or ignored the certainty that there would be no return on the investment for at least three years. All he seemed to know was that when it paid, it paid in showers of gold.

But when three improvident whaling trips drove him deep into debt he had to quit. It should be remembered that the idea of a public company of limited liability was a new-fangled American idea at that time; it had not caught on in Canada. Sam Cunard, both legally and by the standards of honour of the time, was personally liable to his investors, and his whaling caper looked as though it was going to wreck him permanently. This does not seem a promising start for a man who is going to build a maritime empire.

In the 1830s he embarked on the fulfillment of a Nova Scotia dream that must have been as old as it seemed impossible. It took a week to sail around Nova Scotia. The logical thing, people had said for years as they studied their maps, would be to be to build a thirty-mile canal right across the colony, linking the Dartmouth Lakes to the east end of the Bay of Fundy along the old Mi'kmaq Indian trail. Cunard got some partners together and decided to actually do what had long been speculated. They put the locks in first, great stonewalls with heavy wooden doors. But soon after they began the actual digging and dredging, the tidal bore of the Shubenacadie River drove in with such force that it washed out the locks, and an eighty-five-thousand-pound investment was washed away with them. Cunard's canal company was bankrupt. The canal was actually finished, almost half a century later, not long before Cunard's death. It ran for about a decade, but could not compete with the railways. Ironically, it was Samuel Cunard who financed the first railway in Nova Scotia.[2]

Astoundingly, given the outcome of the first venture, the man had another go at whaling, this time in the South Pacific. And with it came something that would become a motif in his life: a hint of conflict of interest. The South Pacific adventure was started with a government subsidy arranged by a politician who just happened to be a good pal of Cunard's. It was no more successful than the first. Within a few months, although the event was never satisfactorily explained, it appeared that his crew had inexplicably deserted ship off New Zealand.

Then, around the same time this apparently luckless but indefatigably persuasive man managed to borrow enough to invest in the Halifax and Quebec Steam Navigation Company which sent the very first paddle steamer, the *Royal William*, across the Atlantic. It was to be the start of a new kind of shipping, but the other investors were not impressed with that first voyage, and pulled out, and once again Sam Cunard was up to his ears in debt.

We have been a bit unfair to Cunard so far, stressing

2. It was Sandford Fleming who built it for him (see Part Fourteen).

this one theme, the almost continual failures, and the growing mountains of debt. He obviously had his share of good luck too, and added to that driving, restless enterprise, were his indisputable brilliance, an ability to argue compellingly for his visions, the good ones as well as the feckless ones, and talent for making and keeping influential friends.

One of these was Lord Dalhousie, the lieutenant-governor. Around 1815 Cunard had persuaded Dalhousie to give him an exclusive contract for the vice-regal official boat tours around the colony. A few years later he got out of the whaling fiasco by landing a maritime mail contract. Then he was saved from the canal project by his shipping company. When the South Pacific Whaling project's demise was followed hard by the cancellation of the Atlantic steamer service, Cunard used the latter's technology to start local steamboat and ferry runs. He survived a much later financial crisis — in 1842 — by marshalling family, in-laws, and a grudging bank into working with him.

So Samuel Cunard's life is more than just being knocked down and getting up again. There was a generous helping of good luck in it, and there were some simply stupendous, inventive, and genuine accomplishments, nourished by zeal, diligence, and daring.

Samuel Cunard's father, Abraham, had been an enterprising and successful shipbuilder in Philadelphia. Loyal to the cause of the Crown, he fled Philadelphia after the thirteen colonies declared their independence, and arrived in Halifax with nothing. Abraham's ancestors may have been Huguenots, business-minded Protestant refugees who had fled persecution in Catholic France, some heading for America. Now, ironically, Abraham himself became a refugee, fleeing Republican America for the Royalist Canadian colonies.

Much as his son would have to do time and again, Abraham Cunard had to start all over when he got to Nova Scotia, at first as a foreman carpenter in a shipyard. He married Margaret Murphy, a young woman he had met on his way north from Philadelphia, to whom he proposed as soon as he had established himself securely in Halifax. They had nine children; Sam was the second. A childhood portrait shows little Sam with a sly expression; a later photograph shows the short and energetic man with bushy sideburns, high collar, and that bright gaze that led someone to say he had the look of a furiously energetic rodent.

Period prints show most of Halifax as little more than a village, although with a few stern and somewhat grander houses, men in knee breeches and tricornes, an uneasy mixture of small luxury and much shabbiness that seemed part of the city until after World War II. The sea was a constant presence. From the big windows of his father's tall Brunswick Street house, the wharves, the forests of square-rigged cargo boats, the ships-of-the-line, and the provenance of trade and naval and military business were seldom out of sight as the boy grew up. Scarcely past puberty, Sam found his entrepreneurial feet, and took advantage of the busy port by buying spices and coffee right off the ships and carrying them up to the town where he sold them door-to-door. He peddled vegetables, ran errands for anybody who'd give him a penny, and carried messages as well.

He was haunted by an urge to regain his father's fortune, and so when Abraham decided to build a wharf at the foot of Brunswick Street and go into business for himself, Sam dropped everything else and put himself at the disposal of what soon became A. Cunard and Son. Before long they were doing very well, primarily shipping fish, salt, and timber to the West Indies and to Europe. Sam's craft and cunning got them through the boom and bust of the War of 1812. Much of it was a cash business. There were no banks. Sam carried so much currency on his person that he took to walking around Halifax with a guard armed with a club.

On February 4, 1815, he married Susan Duffus, the daughter of a tailor who had the Halifax contract for British military uniforms. With the marriage and the Dalhousie connections he now had a substantial social position. The children began to arrive. He built a fine house next door to his parents' house, and took a respectable family pew in St. George's Anglican Church. The pew is still there, marked by a discreet brass plaque. Samuel Cunard had entered the Halifax establishment.

Misfortune and good fortune are often coupled in the story of Samuel Cunard. It was the recession after the war that brought him the first of his powerful British contacts. The lieutenant-governor, Lord Dalhousie, had asked him to set up a soup kitchen for Halifax's sudden crowd of destitute men, women, and children. His reward would be that contract to take Dalhousie on official tours. He used his hundred-ton brig, the *Chebucto*.

When Abraham died, Samuel changed the name of the

company to S. Cunard and Sons. He had already been given control by his father. The company negotiated an international tea contract that soon began to write down the debt. The man he beat out for that contract, Enos Collins (who would be known as the richest man in Canada when he died) was angry at Cunard as a result and shunned him for a while. But this was a small world where it did not pay to make long-term enemies. Cunard and Collins buried the hatchet and, among other things, decided to eliminate the need for armed guards by founding the Halifax Banking Company. The original building is still there, and the company would grow, acquire, spread, and finally turn into the Canadian Imperial Bank of Commerce. By 1827, Samuel Cunard was a millionaire. His company had forty ships. He was quietly invited to join "the Club," the compact that ran Nova Scotia. He became a close friend of the editor and future statesman Joseph Howe, who helped him open offices in London, Glasgow, and Liverpool. S. Cunard and Sons was on its way to becoming one of the first vertically integrated multinational corporations, its enterprise diversifying as it grew.

Samuel Cunard's wife, Susan, died in 1828, and for years afterwards Haligonians who had attended the funeral at St. George's spoke of the devastation in the small man's face that day. But he was soon energetically back at work, perhaps displacing his grief with hard work.

By 1835 his vision, this time correctly, had led him to embrace the newest shipping technology and launch the first of what would become a whole fleet of steamships. Steam needed coal; Cunard took over most of the Nova

Scotia mining industry. He acquired a huge piece of Prince Edward Island to ensure a steady supply of lumber. He retailed the surplus coal out of Halifax, delivering it from the S. Cunard Coal Company in horse-drawn wagons. He started a coast-to-coast pony express mail service across Nova Scotia and up into Quebec. He bought the first steam locomotive in the colony, and built a railway in Pictou.

His fifty-first year was marked by his crowning achievement. In 1838 Cunard's friend Joseph Howe happened to be in London with Judge Haliburton (the author of the popular Sam Slick stories) when they learned that the admiralty was inviting tenders for a transatlantic mail contract. Ocean travel was still painfully slow, and it took two and a half months for Cunard's friends to get the news back to him in Halifax, but as soon as they did Cunard commandeered one of his own ships, made his first steam crossing, and arrived after the deadline had passed. He went straight to the admiralty and found a sympathetic contact, a senior officer whom he convinced that with his sources of coal and lumber he could make the most attractive bid, and he successfully secured an extension of the deadline.

That admiralty contact promised to help, but Cunard knew he was fighting some highly placed competition. He needed contacts, and set out on a round of socializing that led to a certain Caroline Norton who found the irrepressibly optimistic Canadian completely charming. He told her about his scheme for the transatlantic mail, and how his resources and experience made him the very best of all the contenders if Britain seriously wanted an effective and secure service, better than those Milords and Sirs who might have many friends at court but nothing like Cunard's own hardware, supplies, and track record. Caroline Norton said that she quite agreed, and would do what she could. Cunard would say later that he had no idea at the time that she was Prime Minister Melbourne's mistress, a connection that led to the biggest single coup of his career.

S. Cunard and Sons began to build steamships in Scotland. First the *Britannia* slid down the ways, to make her maiden Liverpool-Halifax-Boston mail crossing in 1840. *Britannia* was followed by the *Acadia*, the *Colombia*, and then the *Caledonia*. All the ships' names, Cunard decided, would end in "ia" — it would become the brand. Compared to their queenly liner descendants they were an odd-looking hybrid kind of a vessel, but to Samuel Cunard they were jewels of undeniable beauty. Their hulls, long and low in the water, were roughly interrupted by the hub and cowling of the paddle wheel. They still had three masts with both square-rigged and fore-and-aft sails, but they *were* steamers nonetheless. They made the crossing faster than had ever been possible, and reliably on schedule. Soon, with more ships coming out of Boston as well, Cunard was delivering millions of letters on each vessel, on both sides of the Atlantic in a steady stream of literally tons of mail.

The effect of this traffic on both Halifax and Boston was marked: both cities had fought to be chosen the North American destination. Halifax encouraged the building of several hotels to accommodate the expected Cunard Line passengers. Boston did better, putting on a huge parade in his honour and bringing an impressive cohort of dignitaries to persuade Cunard, successfully, that their city was the better business opportunity. The next year was spectacular. In the depths of the winter Boston cut a seven-mile channel through the harbour ice to get the Cunard ships into port. In that single year Boston's take from international trade doubled. They gave Cunard a massive silver trophy in his honour, and it is said that he received two thousand dinner invitations.

There were to be more financial ups and downs, but the mail service and the rapidly growing passenger traffic soon produced a cash flow strong enough to discharge all the loans and mortgages, and the steamship service continued to grow.

He was a pioneer in transnational finance. In a way, the Atlantic Ocean was more his home than anywhere on land. He was one of the first to recognize the Atlantic as a self-contained unit of trade, a kind of continent with terminals on either side in which there were fortunes to be made. And as other enterprising colonials began to set their sights on transatlantic business opportunities, this seemingly hit-and-miss guy was always a bit ahead of them. When he heard that his fellow Haligonian Enos Collins was planning a trip to England to negotiate what would be, in effect, a monopoly in the tea trade, Cunard did not hesitate or plan. He just took the fastest ship he could find, beat Collins to London, and got his foot in the door with the famous East India Company, which effectively controlled the world's tea trade. Soon he was delivering the first ever shipload of tea to arrive in Halifax from China.

He played the intrigues of the British aristocracy as if he had written the scripts. To secure those Nova Scotia coalmines that he needed for his steamships, he had to get the coal-mining rights in the colony, which were a royal prerogative. Cunard learned that the King had rescued the Prince of Wales from his gambling debts by selling those mining rights to the jewellers to the Crown, Rundle and Rundle. Cunard understood that a London jeweller wouldn't have the faintest idea of what to do with mining rights in Nova Scotia, wherever the hell that was, and he knew from his gossip connections that the Rundles themselves were serious gamblers and seriously short of cash. He simply made them an offer, and the relieved jewellers were happy to accept.

Now he had to find the money. He had started building ships in Scotland, and wrote to his daughter Mary: "I had to go to Scotland to contract the building of my steamboats and so have to pay another visit to see how they are progressing." It was here, oddly enough, in the land of canny thrift and caution, that Cunard found people willing to make up the balance after he had invested his own money. The Scots shipbuilders saw that coal and steamships were a perfect fit. They had already been interested in railroads. It was a Scot after all, James Watt, who had seen the promise of steam to begin with. Cunard told his Scottish friends that the Atlantic was better than a railroad, because "we have no tunnels to drive, no cuttings to make. No roadbeds to prepare. We need only build our ships and start them to work." The base for his new company would not be Halifax or Boston, but the busy port of Liverpool.

With the heavy penalties imposed by the Royal Mail for failure to adhere to the timetable, it would not have been surprising had Cunard made fast crossings his top priority, but he did not. He was convinced that reliability was the better virtue, and reliability meant safety. A reputation for safe crossings would help put more passengers in the tiny cabins on his mail ships.

His decision was dramatically justified by the activities of his first major American competitor, another Collins, Edward this time, who went to the US government when he heard of Cunard's fat 275,000 pounds sterling subsidy from the British admiralty. Edward Collins persuaded Washington that the US could become the prime mail carrier because he would build ships that were bigger and faster than anything on the Atlantic, and — like Cunard's — would be an asset in time of war. He got an initial $350,000 subsidy, which grew to nearly a million dollars before he was through. While Cunard was skimping on his furnishings and hammering home to his captains that safety was everything, Collins built colossal ships twice the size of Cunard's. He supplied heated private cabins, made the interiors of his vessels like Bavarian palaces, and had one dining room designed to look like an opera house.

Collins told his captains that breaking the speed records was what it was all about, and for a while he stole a lot of business from the Cunard line. Then, in 1854, off the coast of Newfoundland, Collins' flagship the *Arctic* collided with another vessel. Three hundred and twenty-two lives were lost, among them Collins' wife and children. Ships of other careless and aggressive Cunard competitors met similar misfortunes. For Edward Collins, the vicissitudes of haste included mechanical failure and a disenchanted US government, who, after the Newfoundland tragedy, soon decided that the annual $875,000 subsidy was not helping the country, and stopped it. Collins filed for bankruptcy in 1858.

Cunard had laughed at Collins' gimmicks, which he dismissed as "trying to break our windows by throwing sovereigns at us." His fleet grew to eight ships, each built for simplicity. What was lost in luxury and speed was made up for in safety and punctuality. Passengers grumbled about the accommodations. Charles Dickens described his Cunard passenger cabin as a hearse with windows. "Retired to my bed," he wrote, "somewhat smaller than a coffin, read to this day I know not what. Reeled on deck. Drank cold brandy with unspeakable disgust. And ate hard biscuits perseveringly. Not ill, but going to be. The cow bellowing moodily in the fog." But Dickens had chosen Cunard, and so did tens of thousands more, because they felt safe.

When a Cunard vessel ran aground near Seal Island off the Nova Scotia coast — the only accident of substance during his whole career — Cunard personally took charge, sailing out to the wreck, and supervising the successful rescue of every passenger.

It may have been an earlier shipwreck that had set the issue of maritime safety firmly in the young Cunard's mind. There were no lighthouses around Nova Scotia when he was a boy, and one night the frigate *La Tribune* sailed blindly into the harbour and was wrecked with the loss of 240 men, women, and children. Young Samuel saw the funeral and the masses of coffins and never forgot them. In the 1830s he was on his way to being a magnate when he became commissioner of lighthouses, and erected the towers with their warning lamps along the dangerous shoreline. And collected their fees as well.

The present-day Michigan Institute for Public Policy, a hard-nosed centre for free-enterprise rhetoric, scolds Edward Collins for his subsidies and praises Cunard for his private enterprise, apparently forgetting that his spartanly furnished mail ships not only collected $200 from each passenger — roughly equivalent to about $10,000 today (although those comparisons are fraught with irrelevancies), plus 24¢ per letter (say $10, with the same proviso), but that he also had that 275,000 pounds sterling annual subsidy from the admiralty, and kept on collecting it because he did indeed deliver on his promise of safety and punctuality.

But it was not all diligence, luck, prudence, virtue, and hard work. There are traces in the story of "sharp practice," that nineteenth-century euphemism for dealings not quite above board. What, for example, was this special permit, early in his career, for trading with the New England States during the War of 1812? Working from a British colony, surely Cunard was, at least technically, trading with the enemy. The money from his 1831 tea contract enabled him to buy up a seventh of Prince Edward Island for lumber.

That land grab and his Nova Scotia coal rights amounted to sole possession, and Cunard's flair for cornering markets and developing monopolies was not quite in tune with the best traditions of fair and free competition.

His lucrative position as commissioner of lighthouses came from political connections. When he went after a government subsidy for his second whaling expedition even his friend Joseph Howe accused him of corruption. How indeed did he get the contact with the king's jeweller to secure the mining rights? It was not just his gossipy London connections: he had already persuaded Lieutenant-Governor Lord Dalhousie to make him Nova Scotia's commissioner of mines, a position that facilitated what we might now call insider trading.

And who was the man in the Admiralty Office in London who actually stretched the deadline that day in 1838, so that Cunard could put in his own tender for the transatlantic mail? He was Sir Edward Perry, a one-time Nova Scotia midshipman, an old family friend who had been a regular at Cunard parties in Halifax. And are we to believe the story that the socially alert Cunard really had *no idea* that Caroline Norton was the Prime Minister's mistress? He seemed to know everything else that was going on in London.

In 1842, when he learned that the British banks decided to foreclose on their Cunard loans, he was working out of his Liverpool offices. To buy time he skipped town, had himself secretly rowed out to one of his own ships, raced back to Nova Scotia for help, and got it. The Bank of Nova Scotia, which just happened to have his brother-in-law on its board, guaranteed the needed loan. Connections, connections, connections.

The family connection was the strongest of all. Samuel's son Edward went to England to manage the shipping trade so that Cunard himself could put matters in order at home, the bank having bound him to stay in Nova Scotia until the loan was discharged. The family had backed him in his times of need, and now he showed that he would give as good as he got. His brother Joseph, a lumber baron on the Miramichi River, came to Cunard in desperation: he was nearly broke. Sam took on his debts, and spent twenty years paying them off. When he finally returned to England to handle investment matters and contracts, he put his younger son William in charge of the entire concern, S. Cunard and Company, and then, when he turned seventy-four in 1861, he made his elder son Edward the senior partner in the company, and retired.

As with the city of Halifax itself, war has a lot to do with the Cunard story. In 1811 Cunard was all of twenty-four when he sensed hostilities coming between Britain and America and obtained a special permit to trade essential goods to the New England states. He captured his first fortune in the boom that followed. In mid-century, troops and supplies had to be rushed to the Crimea. Once there was a whole shipload of army boots, all for the left foot. True to his promise to the Admiralty, Cunard volunteered his vessels to be "STUFT": Ships Taken Up From Trade. Among the more tragic passengers his fourteen STUFT ships were to carry, were those doomed cavalrymen destined to be immortalized by Alfred Lord Tennyson in his poem *The Charge of the Light Brigade*.

In time Samuel Cunard beat out every one of his competitors. In 1863 he retired as Sir Samuel Cunard with a mansion in Halifax and a fine address in Kensington, Number 26 Princess Garden. In April, two years later, he came down with bronchitis on a cold trip back from Canada (he kept up this vigorous transatlantic mobility to the end). He took Holy Communion a few hours before he died, going off happily, his son reported to the family, "trusting in Jesus Christ and him alone."

Throughout that long and productive life — and the age of seventy-eight was very old a century and a half ago — not only was there the almost constant dance of success and failure, huge revenues and huge debts, but there were two apparently similar contradictory aspects of his character: an almost obsessive concern for safety, and a love of risk. Again Napoleon comes to mind; flagrantly ambitious designs for campaigns bristling with risk, and the insurance of an enormous army with high morale and crack training. With Cunard it was a willingness to move far afield in search of contacts and investment, always mediated by a scrupulous concern for the physical safety of his ships and passengers.

By the time of the next war, the First World War, and with Sam long dead, Sam's grandson Ernest was running the company, and Cunard ships were once more being STUFT. The line bore its share of losses. Ten were sunk by the Germans, including the Cunard flagship the *Lusitania*. Winston Churchill said that the great twentieth-century

Cunarders, the *Queen Mary* and the *Queen Elizabeth*, shortened World War II by a year. The *Queen Mary* was stripped of all her trimmings, until she was nearly an empty shell of compartments. In one aerial photograph the decks and superstructure are almost invisible. The topsides look like a teeming ant colony — solid humanity. On one crossing the *Queen Mary* carried more than sixteen thousand soldiers, the greatest number of passengers ever carried by a sea-going vessel. Forty years later a Cunard vessel assisted in the Falklands War. In about eight days it too was stripped down and converted into an armed floating barracks, with helicopter pads placed fore and aft.

It was Cunard ships that brought the masses of immigrants to Canada early in the twenty-first century. If we include the US immigration of both centuries, Cunard vessels delivered over two and a half million immigrants to North America.

The company was characterized by resilience, adventure, and mobility, always tempered by that commitment to safety rather than speed. They built an empire on land and at sea. But no enterprise, no empire, no work of genius can ever quite outlast its founder. The elder Cunard son, Sir Edward, was less astute than his father, and in the late nineteenth century the keystone of the company, its mail service, lost business. When Edward died, his younger brother William took over a company that was now up against powerful competitors who had learned a lot both from Cunard and its earlier failed rivals. William finally took it public and put it on the London stock exchange.

It was Samuel Cunard's grandson Ernest who took the

Cunard Lines into World War I, and by then the ships began to resemble the ships of today, their hulls high in the water, smooth stretches of riveted steel, the white above, the black below, the four tall funnels that would become three, then two, then one.

Ernest's death in 1922 marked the end of the Cunard family as directors of the Cunard Steamship Lines. The great twentieth-century liners were launched. The first of the great liners was to be called the *Victoria*. Her keel was laid at the John Brown shipyards in Glasgow in 1930 as "Hull #534." When the Cunard chairman went to see King George V to seek the royal permission necessary to use His Majesty's grandmother's name in this way, he neglected to tell the king in advance what it was about.

When the opening formalities were over, the chairman said, so the story goes, "Sir, we are about to launch the greatest ocean liner the world has ever seen, and we have come to ask your permission to name it after England's most remarkable Queen." To which His Majesty replied, "My wife will be so pleased." And so that was the end of Samuel Cunard's brand-name "ia" endings. In 1934 Queen Mary swung the champagne bottle against the prow of Hull #534, launched her, and named her after herself. A few years later the *Queen Mary* would be followed by the *Queen Elizabeth*.

Although most of Samuel Cunard's papers were burned in a dockside fire at the turn of the century, his great-great-grandson Hugh Paton still has a few of the original letters. They include the one to his daughter about the shipyards in Glasgow, the one from son William about the old man's devout last hours, and the founder's original leather-bound passport. You can see the writing kit on which he signed the admiralty mail contract on display in the Cunard museum in the original *Queen Mary*, which no longer sails, and is a dockside hotel and tourist attraction in California.

But there is still a Cunard heritage on the Atlantic. The conventional wisdom now says that the jetliner spelled the end of transoceanic travel as a commercial norm. But for those who see that ocean not as an obstacle to be overflown but as a splendid part of the world to be enjoyed for its raw beauty, the liner is still the way to go. The new *Queen Mary* demonstrates that the founder's vision, though much modified, is not dead. The real presence of Samuel Cunard's hand is in that mastery of the Atlantic, the drawing together of Europe and America, and in the millions of immigrants who came to the New World in Cunard ships.

◆ ◆ ◆

The History Television documentary was written and directed by Peter Rowe.

◆ Part Seven ◆

SIR WILLIAM OSLER
THE ENLIGHTENER

In the fall of 1919, at Oxford, Sir William Osler was stricken, along with millions more around the world, by the great influenza epidemic. Before long he knew he was dying. The attending doctor tried to be encouraging, but Osler said, "You lunatic, I've been watching this case for over two months and I'm sorry I shan't see the post-mortem." A few weeks later on December 28 he was dead.

Osler's death seemed not to interest him much, nor did death in general. But life certainly did. And this is a clue, if a small one, to his enigma. He founded no great institution; he made no startling scientific discoveries. Yet he stands with Paracelsus, Hippocrates, Galen, and Pasteur as one of the giants of Western medicine. To say that he was not much taken by death will at first seem contradictory as the images unfold in a documentary film, so many stained, grainy old black-and-white photographs of him gesturing over a cadaver on a table, to a crowd of intrigued students. The cadavers often seem more than dead with their skin partially flayed and what remains blackening with time, with parts missing, tendons and organs exposed, manifestly much handled. But it was not the death in the corpse that intrigued Osler; it was the implication of life and the suggestions for healing and the relief of suffering that teased at him from every fibre, every fragment of diseased tissue, every sign of where something had gone wrong that might have been prevented or healed.

In the end he became famous for something discreet and rather surprising, and it is interesting that as significant an authority as the *Dictionary of Canadian Biography* isn't much help in getting to know this monumental figure. It says, simply, "He published numerous monographs and essays on medical subjects," and proceeds with a list of rather uninteresting titles. Nothing much on the reason for the reverence with which he is still held by the profession. Nothing on the interesting speculations we could easily make about what this great generalist's views of medicine might be now, were he to see it from the grave. Would he shudder at our specialization and industrialization, at the shortage of general practitioners, the obsolescence of house calls and other humane elements of the practice of medicine to which he devoted his life?

Or perhaps he would just shrug it off, and get on with whatever he was doing: he wasn't really a moral or social critic. Perhaps it is best to look at what he did in terms of the state of medicine around the time of his birth in the mid-nineteenth century. Medical practice was a loose and quiet anarchy, full of speculation and quackery, fatalism, and vain and damaging remedies. Patients were treated like broken machines. The causes of disease were largely unknown. Louis Pasteur was only then discovering that bacteria lay at the root of so many of them, but his drastically important discovery had not yet persuaded surgeons to wash their hands before operating.

Cell theory and microbiology did not exist. Surgical patients were strapped to the table so they wouldn't writhe too much, and the only anesthesia in common use was still a bottle of whisky, although Queen Victoria was pioneering and would soon help popularize the use of "Twilight Sleep" — nitrous oxide or laughing gas — in childbirth. That was a practice many disapproved of, as the pain of childbirth was thought to be morally improving.

Theory still eclipsed practice. In medical schools, everything was done in the classroom; a student almost never saw a patient until he graduated and actually went to work. House calls were not a significant element of the practice. The emotional state of patients was still decades from being understood as a critical component of disease and healing.

Death — we begin with death. Death was not simply the cessation of vital processes, it was encased in religious and mythic baggage, a sacrosanct and desired release from the miseries of life, and at the same time a mysterious terror to be resisted until the end. Life after death was taken for granted and generally thought to be a desired and wondrous state, and the terminally ill were often tendered respect and deference.

The actual study of dead bodies as a way of understanding disease was little used. There was no general consensus on therapeutic techniques. The practice of medicine had, to a large extent, developed haphazardly, and on the whole it was still a poorly defined somewhat mysterious profession.

And here is where we find the essence of Osler's contribution to medicine, and the reason why he is still honoured around the world. While it is true in a strictly technical sense that he did not, as we said at the outset, make any great scientific discoveries, what he did accomplish, working out of the heart of this chaotic, unsystematized, and largely intuitive or even guess-based profession, was to *invent* medical practice as we know it in the modern world, a set of methods organized around commonly agreed principles, like engineering — or indeed, like science itself. The British scientist, historian, and popularizer of science, John Ziman, argues convincingly in his definitive book *Real Science* that at the heart of it is a social or communitarian principle of consensus about what constitutes science, a social convention that is more important than mathematics, experiment, theorizing, rationality, or any of the other elements commonly seen as central to science. Osler brought the same idea to medicine, and to do so he worked from a base of humanitarian common sense, in which seeing patients and examining the fabric of the human body was right at the centre of things. Everyone in the profession would agree.

He committed his learning and his ideas and principles to print. His seminal thousand-page *The Principles and Practice of Medicine* has gone through countless editions. Written out of his own experience, it summarized the proven and agreed-on knowledge of the day and also rigorously listed all that was obsolete.

His own collection of medical works, the *Bibliotheca Osleriana*, is his largest material legacy to the world. It is a massive collection of books and other documents on the history of medicine that fills several rooms. Osler had read them all and written many of them.

What he accomplished seems to have grown out of an attitude, perhaps an attitude to the whole question of existence, in which he saw life, as the poet said, "steadily and saw it whole." In an age when doctor, patient, disease and sufferer, student and hospital were seen as separate entities, Osler realized that in fact they were all just aspects of a single, interdependent organ. He conceptualized that which had been haphazard, made it into a system. And in doing so he made medicine humane, simply by making it into a single, agreed-on system. It was no longer detached, its problems isolated like auto mechanics. He said, "Treat the patient not the disease" only to take it further, expounding above all on the doctor-patient relationship. And then of course the medical student had to learn from a real live — or even dead — patient as well. Osler gave the Americans the idea of interns and internships for novice doctors. He gave Canada's first course in histology, the microscopic study of the body. He gave North America's first course on post-mortems. At the Medical School of Philadelphia he used his own money to set up an autopsy lab since no one in America took autopsies seriously. His classes were so crowded that some students attended by looking through the skylight. His humour made people desperate to perform autopsies. When a student blundered, he congratulated him roundly; he praised mistakes because they were the way people learned.

In the process of defining what it was the profession could agree on, Osler also raised what had often been a thankless study, its practitioners often the butt of contemptuous humour, into a rewarding art.

Attitude appears to be the key to this man's character. As important as system and agreement were to him, so was the emotional bearing and deportment of the practitioner. While defeat in the face of unconquerable death had traditionally produced either panic or resignation, Osler saw a better way. Metaphysical panic, hair-tearing, or sleeplessness were not, after all, going to help. Nor was throwing up your hands in resignation and trusting in the Almighty. If there was anything approaching a Bible in the armamentarium of this utterly practical and undoctrinaire man, it would have been Thomas Browne's *Religio Medici* (1643) on the pragmatic reconciliation of religious belief with reason. With Browne in hand, Osler seemed to say, "You can have nothing before you but the problem." And out of this attitude grew the principle that is still attached to his name, still cited as the deportmental and even spiritual aim of the best practitioner, the resolute calm in the face of other people's storms, which Osler called *Aequanimitas*.

So Osler is theory, practice, and *attitude*. If he is not the Descartes or the Leibnitz of medicine, he is very much like the age that followed them. He opened up, systematized, and criticized; he removed superstition and prejudice. He procured agreement. Osler was an Enlightenment.

But as with all rich and complex personalities, there is still a world of contradiction and enigma in the compact frame of William Osler. There is no *gravitas*. There is not much of the stormy impatience we might expect from a man who saw early and saw clearly that the profession he had chosen needed an overhaul so prodigious that one lifetime might be insufficient. And there is a certain lack of dignity for one so universally acknowledged to be a Great Man.

In fact, he was — all his life — as much a prankster as a serious professional and a teacher. That part of him shows up early. At the age of eight he locked all his fellow students' desks in an attic and filled the classroom with geese. At nineteen he barricaded an unpopular teacher in her classroom, and then fed in the fumes of burning sulphur and molasses. (Was this intended as an admonitory metaphor? Sulphur and molasses were a common spring tonic and mythic remedy for constipation.)

When he was twenty and studying to be an Anglican priest (a brief digression before he settled on the field that apparently already intrigued him), he swiped a fetus from the school of medicine and left it in the divinity school. The joke became a parting gesture, since he was expelled for it.

Later, when he was at McGill and visiting his Montreal cousins Marian and Jeannette and their family, he brought all the children over to a friend's house. The friend was William Molson, son of the great brewer. Molson was giving a big party that night and when the main course had been served and taken away, the servants were flabbergasted to find that all the desserts had disappeared. Osler had given them to his cousins' children.

As he matured, so did the style and character of his irrepressible mischief. On the threshold of fame he took a prodigious risk by posing as the non-existent "Dr. Egerton Y. Davis," the author of a deadpan letter to the editor of the pompous *Medical News*. The letter was about the phenomenon known as "Vaginismus," the entrapment of the male's penis by constriction in a vagina, popularly said to be common among dogs. Osler invented a fictitious human case that ended in a laborious separation by a surgeon, during which the man sustained some serious injury. Of course it was all to embarrass the self-important and, Osler thought, slow-nodding fools who ran the *Medical News*. The jape worked. They published it, whereupon he unmasked himself — and somehow got away with it.

But another joke was so broad and so profane, that even today it would separate the literal-minded majority from the rest. It was 1905. In his farewell address to Johns Hopkins — of which institution much more later — he offered, for the university's consideration, some thoughts about how long a professional person should continue with this moving on from one post to another, as he was about to do. Perhaps, he suggested, in order to open things up for new people and new ideas . . . perhaps, in the medical profession where people were no longer superstitious about death . . . perhaps, we could deploy euthanasia as a form of retirement. After all, old age was not only an obstacle to the advance of society — it was also a dreadful burden to the old themselves. They should be chloroformed.

Scandalized, people took it seriously as a cruel proposal for the extermination of the aged. Of course he had only been making fun of useless hand-wringing about old age. Many discerning editorialists got the joke and exposed it, but somehow the world did not, and the tremors lasted for years. Osler was asked again and again if he had been serious. The thing even turned up in James Joyce's *Finnegan's Wake* with "The ogry Osler will oxmaul us all," an environment where it was probably understood as the joke that it was meant to be.

Perhaps genius can never be entirely serious. It takes a talent for mischief to break rules and make connections that no one else would. Certainly there is nothing in Osler of the unsmiling moral mission. In his early education he became enamoured of the classics. His instincts were artistic and literary — which we take to be a good sign in anyone, including mechanics.

And so we are tempted to draw a picture of a man producing inner synaptic fireworks while doing handstands on the street corner, or booby-trapping doorways with cans of water while conceiving the idea of internships, or realizing the true value of cadavers at a production of Aristophanes' comedy *The Clouds*. And then — in what *may* have been a very different state of mind — Osler proposed the idea of the "day-tight compartment," a mental work space in which, having only the problem before you, you were supposed to rigorously exclude regrets for past mistakes — and perhaps rejoice in successes — and certainly exclude anxieties about the future. You would have only the problem before you. This was not a neurotic or psychologically self-defensive withdrawal; it was a technique for achieving that essential *Aequanimitas*. But it is doubtful that the compartment was really watertight, even as he practised it. He always had his mischief and his art with him, in whatever space he was working. They were part of the *Aequanimitas*.

And could he work! When Grace Revere Gross refused his proposal of marriage as long as he was lost in the composition of what was to become his thousand-page *Principles and Practice of Medicine,* he cranked up the pressure on himself and finished the book in seven months.

The marriage was superbly happy and Grace's first pregnancy a blessing. Osler's fondness for his young son knew no bounds. They swam and fished together. When the boy was sick, Osler found it hard to treat him; he lost the equanimity for which the outside world knew him. Again, when the child needed discipline, the doctor was something of a softy. In many ways he preferred the company of children to that of adults. He entertained them. It was his capacity to entertain that made him loved by strangers.

It seems likely that some of his humour was connected to his dry sense of practicality. For example, at the time when Osler was just beginning to teach at Johns Hopkins, the medical school found itself strapped for funds. It needed a benefactor. There appeared a committee of women in Baltimore who undertook to raise the necessary money, on condition that Johns Hopkins would open its doors to women. The male directors were red in the face. At first Osler shared their prejudice, but it must have been a sense of the ridiculous that made him see the idiotic pomposity of sticking to the principle at the cost of an entire medical school.

And anyway, he couldn't see any practical reason to deny women the study of medicine. Surely this was also an example of *Aequanimitas,* and he said so, and publicly agreed with the women. But the other men held out. They raised the target from a hundred thousand to a whopping five hundred thousand dollars — probably more to block female enrolment than to build the wing. Of course the women called their bluff and raised the half million. Due to Osler, if only in part, Johns Hopkins became one of the first medical schools in the world to admit women.

This sort of leavened genius had uncertain beginnings. He was born in the bush, in Ontario, in 1849. His first school was the grammar school in Dundas, Ontario, the one where, at age eight he had filled a classroom with geese. For that he was expelled. He was sent to Trinity College School up in Weston, where, despite the usual colourful behaviour he began to apply himself and was made prefect. In that school there was a microscope, a rarity even in a university in those days, an instrument that transformed the commonplace world into an entirely different sort of universe. It was the headmaster who had blessed his students with this treasure: in the half-cleared bush it was a piece of technology that would have been far ahead of its time in many a city school. And that particular microscope, for all its scratches, may have changed history when the young Osler saw the minute moving structures that lay within what had seemed to be the clear and empty water of ponds, the familiar surface of a leaf. He saw the miraculous components of blood, and was enchanted.

That enlightened headmaster, E.A. Johnson, introduced the young Osler to Dr. James Bovell who taught at the Toronto School of Medicine. Still a student, Osler walked with Bovell and Johnson through the bush and river valleys as Johnson sketched and Bovell collected specimens of insects and plants. Johnson spoke little but demonstrated much: the motion of the heavens alongside the micro cosmos of a drop of pond water.

It was 1867, Osler was eighteen, and surprisingly, given the path his life would soon take, his first choice for advanced study was divinity, at Trinity College in Toronto. We have to speculate here, since he did not leave us an account of what happened. But the maturing mind would soon move far away from the authoritative mythology of the Bible, and it may have been the smug, self-satisfied dogmatism of his ecclesiastical teachers that helped him turn the corner. While those divines were vesting every-thing in the authority of scripture and of the hierarchies, Dr. Bovell was inviting him to look into Browne's *Religio Medici*, a book of inquiry in which the author, himself a physician, was struggling to reconcile faith and reason. This was more appealing than doctrine; it seemed to touch a real world; the givens of the divinity school mentality began to smell like superstition. Only someone deeply con-temptuous of the institution he was enrolled in could have played that genuinely tasteless and offensive joke with the fetus, and he got his hands on that fetus only because a teacher very different from the Trinity clerics — Dr. Bovell — had been quietly and unofficially opening the labs at the medical school to his young friend.

This is not to suggest that Bovell's inquiring and experimental mind was characteristic of the institution in which he taught. Bovell, like his young apprentice, was an exception at the Medical School of Toronto where Osler now moved, and where he spent the next two disappoint-ing years. The faculty doctors taught by lecturing. The students saw no patients, no corpses, no diseases in action. They were not allowed professional access to the Toronto General Hospital. This at a time when Pasteur was studying harmful bacteria, Rudolf Vierchow was exploring the complex world of putrefaction, and cell theory and microbiology had made it into the scientific curricula at last. Toronto was not an advanced school, but it was not so backward that his teachers didn't recognize that the young man had genuine talent, and someone suggested that he turn to what had become one of the premier medical schools in North America.

The McGill University Medical School, in Montreal, gave him the luxury of studying the dead. He trained at the Montreal General Hospital, which he said had two great advantages. It was old and full of infection, disease, and rats; and it had talented teachers.

At the time autopsies were still at the frontier of medical practice and not taken entirely seriously. But young Osler seemed almost obsessed, and some of his fellow students thought him genuinely eccentric with his endless dissecting, extracting specimens, fragments of diseased livers, collapsed hearts. Some of his specimens are still on view, almost unidentifiable cloudy and diaphanous tissues, grey or salmon-coloured lobes of organs waving gently in their great jars of formaldehyde. He became, literally, the pioneer of the dead house. Pathology, the study of the causes of disease and death, usually from dissected corpses, was his prowess. He had the genius to grasp its full significance. It was a talent rare enough to bring him fame.

This knack for the practical, for getting straight to the heart of the matter, for turning medicine towards root causes, culminated in a brilliant dissertation that earned him his MD and Master of Surgery at the precocious age of twenty-two. Well ahead of provincial Canada now, he was able to finish his studies in London, Berlin, and Vienna.

It has been said that when he returned to McGill, where his obsession with the microscope and minute organisms and the process of infection and decay were still a curiosity, he next had to bring the university up to his own standards. McGill had been wise and generous enough to teach him but not quick enough to catch up to him. Autopsies were still marginal, and this premier medical school, like the prep school back in the bush in Ontario, still had only a few microscopes. And so Osler and the medical dons George Ross, and Francis Shepherd set about something that now seems laughably obvious: they decided to bring more science into the curriculum, beginning with more microscopes.

But in those days at McGill a skyrocketing reputation as a teacher and prolific writer were not enough to pay the bills. He still had to trudge over to the Montreal General Hospital to earn a decent salary. What might have been a fatal stroke of bad luck only brought him closer to the medical concerns that would become his major field of endeavour. It was 1878, the year of Montreal's first dreadful epidemic of smallpox. It is difficult to give an idea of what the young pathologist had to face. That smallpox could exterminate entire peoples among North American Natives was bad enough. It was also a spectacularly raging disaster to which the grand and powerful courts of seventeenth- and eighteenth-century Europe had been as vulnerable as a peasant village or an urban slum. Contemporary descriptions of the appearance of ailing kings and queens only hint at the almost indescribably repulsive expression of the disease in its advanced stages.

We have almost forgotten smallpox. It occasionally surfaces in the public awareness with news stories about the risk of its use now by bio-terrorists, and the proposal by some politicians, discouraged by scientists, that we return to mass vaccination of the population. Mass vaccination is the reason we no longer know what smallpox is. The virtually universal vaccination program is one of the world's great success stories. The last "natural" case of the disease was in 1976, and while mass vaccination now would almost certainly kill more people than a terrorist attack (the virus is very difficult to spread artificially), the result of the vaccination program is that the only known stores of the virus are in laboratories in Florida and Siberia.

The disease began with headaches and pains in the belly. After three or four days those pains became excruciating. The rash of encrusted sores would start to appear around the tenth day, and death could follow any time in the next two weeks, often sooner rather than later. Once the rash appeared, death was more likely than recovery.

It was not just the patient's cheeks or arms or forehead that showed sores, but rather the whole head. In the worst cases the entire body became a pustular, undifferentiated mass of sores. For a physician to venture onto the ground and try to treat this contagion was to play Russian roulette with his own life. And here we must stop abruptly. Because Osler too must at least have paused. He must have realized he had to concentrate on the problem, not its effects — which might well include his own infection. Perhaps he just concentrated on the patient as a person, and not simply the pathology. Or maybe he did not; maybe that's what he learned in the course of treating eighty-one appalling cases. For this focus on the person came to be the central point of what he taught.

He must certainly have applied the principle of detachment to himself; he had to because he caught the disease and got over it. Ironically, at almost the same time smallpox killed Osler's much-loved mentor, the schoolmaster W.A. Johnson, who probably was infected by a sick student.

When he recovered, Osler was rewarded with the position of attending physician at the hospital. But in the late nineteenth century the medical doctor was not, as he is today in most countries in the West, one of the best paid of all professionals. Here was a man with great good looks and superb professional prestige, but at this time he was simply not earning enough to marry and raise a family. He doggedly kept on though, deciding to take some time away from teaching, visit some of his old colleagues abroad, see what he could learn in Berlin and Leipzig and London. While he was in Britain his name somehow came to the attention of the medical school at the University of Pennsylvania. That was the largest training ground for doctors in the whole United States. It needed a professor of clinical medicine. The faculty heads liked what they had heard about Osler's methods at McGill, and sent him an offer. McGill heard about it and sent a counteroffer. Osler is said to have flipped a coin, and taken a ship for Pennsylvania.

Before long that institution found itself with its first autopsy lab. For five years he lectured on, and popularized the use of cadavers. He became admired, even loved, and certainly listened to, as he had been at McGill. He published without stop.

Not far away, in Baltimore, Maryland, there was a new university, Johns Hopkins, that would before long become one of the most important educational institutions in the United States. Johns Hopkins needed a physician-in-chief and professor of medicine. The university and medical school were all new; the medical school itself was already the most advanced in America. Osler made his decision; before long he delivered his farewell speech at Pennsylvania. This was the speech in which he first publicly developed the idea of the doctor's *Aequanimitas*.

We have said that William Osler made no spectacular scientific discoveries, but perhaps that's not quite true. Strange as it seems now, the idea of teaching at the hospital bedside of a real, live patient instead of in a lecture room was sufficiently revolutionary to deserve the term *scientific discovery*. At the new university in Baltimore, Osler took American medical students to the hospital wards for the first time. He had introduced internships to the United States. It was at Johns Hopkins that he wrote and published *The Principles and Practice of Medicine*. Here again he was innovative, for Osler gave credit where it was due when he could easily have claimed certain discoveries for himself. Plagiarism of that kind was not unknown in the profession; the rigours of publication in the scientific society had not made that practice as impossible as it is now, and Osler's honesty was exemplary.

In Johns Hopkins, Osler found an institution his own equal if only because he and the new university actually made one another into what they became. Married, prestigious, well paid, and generally loved, he could not go much further than this. It was his apogee. At forty-five he became a father and began a semi-retirement by increasing the proportion of speeches, articles, and addresses to classroom and laboratory work. His private practice blossomed. It was said you couldn't die respectably unless Osler had gently sent you on your way.

It was at Hopkins that he gained his worldwide renown. His practical philosophy for approaching medicine became a world standard. It was still an age when doctors from San Francisco to Berlin went into the field knowing anatomy and perhaps even what they wanted to achieve, but they did not know how to achieve it or how to question what they were doing. With the teachings of Doctor Osler there now stood beside them a spectral figure who provided a relation between themselves and their craft, between doctor and patient.

What was there left to do? Where could he go but to some position more august, more serene, but also less demanding and better for his health? Seldom short of luck, he was offered the Regius Chair of Medicine at Oxford. Fully confident but a little jaded, perhaps, by the eager worship of his vast audience, it was in his farewell address to Johns Hopkins that he offered the notorious "euthanasia" proposal.

In 1905 he took his family to England. As Regius professor at Oxford, even though he was now in a position of unchallenged authority and prestige, there was little change in the routine of his days. At the "Open Arms," which he called his house, he received visitors and carried on his profession as before. He maintained an enormous practice, and his hospital routine wore out the young interns. He was fifty-six. Life has rarely been so good to anyone for so long. Wealthy, serene, balanced. Presently a Knighthood. An age of equanimity.

That period between the Boer War and the Great War was perhaps the closest to a "normal" time the Western World has ever known: neither hectic boom nor frantic bust; no war, no insane progress, no revolutions, social or otherwise. Blissfully unaware, it lay in the shadow of doom. As did Osler himself. Britain's declaration of war on August 4, 1914, startled him.

He must have had very mixed feelings when his only son, Revere Osler, enlisted at nineteen. At first Osler managed to keep him away from the action by getting him placed in the McGill Hospital unit. But young Revere wanted to be at the front, and got himself transferred to a field unit. At twenty-one he wrote to his family from the muddy squalor of the trenches that he was gambling on getting a "blighty": a wound just grave enough to send him home. But on August 29, 1917, in the middle of the terrible Passchendael campaign, Revere Osler was splattered with shrapnel from an exploding shell. They carried him a couple of miles by stretcher to a dressing station. A friend of his father's from the McGill days was on duty there and tried his best to save him, but Revere died a day later, and was buried on the devastated, shell-pitted field.

Who knows how Osler felt during his last two years, as he busied himself building the *Bibliotheca Osleriana*? Some say his son's death crushed him, that the Oslers had felt its approach from the beginning of the war, as the world began to fall apart. Others say his resort to building a library was only a living demonstration of his principle of *Aequanimita*s.

Beneath the exterior near cliché of The Good Doctor, there was certainly this rich combination of determination and humour, and a confidence in his own capacities that he certainly shared with his siblings. Inherited or learned? That is one of those continuing vexations in the scientific world: nature versus nurture. But certainly that Osler family was spectacular. The boy grew up with the unsubtleties of the frontier bush, but in an atmosphere of religion and learning. His father, Featherstone Osler, had once been a naval officer but had become an Anglican priest and circuit preacher. William Osler's mother, Ellen Picton Osler, bore William, their last son, in 1849. They lived in a leaky, drafty house in the hamlet of Bond Head, now a sleeper suburb of Toronto. He was the youngest of eight children. His brothers became masters in their professions, one a great judge, one a great lawyer, another a great financier. As far as we know, William's sense of mischief that, so strangely for a man of such sensitivity and compassion, could descend to demeaning pranks and genuinely hurtful jokes was not shared.

His death from influenza in 1919 was mercifully speedy, and not particularly different from the millions of such deaths that swept around the world that year and the year before, his particular case in no way instructive. Sir William would probably have been quite disappointed in the post-mortem.

◆　◆　◆

The History Television documentary was written and directed by Roberto Verdecchia.

◆ Part Eight ◆
MA MURRAY
THE FASTEST PEN IN THE YUKON

The state of politics in Canada is as low as a snake's belly in Arkansas.
But a snake there would never go so low that he didn't have a pit to hiss in.
– Margaret (Ma) Murray

In the town if Lillooet, British Columbia, in the 1930s, there was a weekly newspaper called the *Bridge River-Lillooet News*. Lillooet was a mining and lumber town, big enough to have some delicate issues and small enough to have a few local egos. That was normal. But as soon as a woman by the name of Margaret Murray took over the editorship of *The News*, the complaints — both from the egos and about the delicacies, came unusually fast, many of them on lawyers' letterheads: "Dear Mrs. Murray, I would like to advise you that my client is not a crooked horse trader and he is not a gypsy." Or, "Madam, I have been instructed by my client to demand a full apology — and a retraction." And one that almost looks as though she'd written herself, as a spoof: "I have the highest regard for our volunteer fire department, and must point out they are not all wet."

In 1935, Margaret Murray, or just plain "Ma" as she was by then known, had been left to run the paper while her husband, the editor, George Murray, took his seat in the BC legislature down in Victoria. Ma Murray had her way of doing things. She had only a grade three education, a pretty raunchy approach to self-expression, a lot of strong opinions, many of them unpopular, and only a dim notion of the concept of libel. Although she had nominally replaced her husband when he left for the legislature, being The Editor meant that she would write the paper most of the time and nobody would edit what she had written. The traditional restraints and cautions of George's blue pencil may have gone to Victoria with her husband; they certainly didn't show up much at *The News* any more, once he'd left it in her hands.

Libellous, bawdy, plebeian, infuriating, and colourful, Margaret Murray was, in fact, a very good fit for a rollicking frontier town. Lillooet was not the sort of place that would care a whole lot about spelling, punctuation, and grammar. When some complaints did arrive about the absence of periods and commas in *The News*, Ma ran a front-page box in the next issue completely filled with punctuation marks and told her readers they could put them in themselves if they felt the need.

While much of Margaret Murray's style was wisdom in the rough, sometimes she was just plain indecipherable. Most of her readers loved it; perhaps it made them feel part of things. And once she got her children working for her, she didn't object when they followed her style. Her daughter Georgina wrote about a fire reported by a miner named Ollie. And it proceeded: "Ollie had just completed the first two hours of his afternoon shit." "Shift" was the intended word, but as we've said the blue pencil was not getting much use. The readers were delighted. Ollie was known to spend quite a bit of his work time in the privy, and Georgina also noted that he was said to have evacuated the town as well.

That story about Ollie helped cement the paper's *succès de scandale* and the issue that it appeared in became sufficiently notorious that it sold for five dollars apiece — the price of a year's subscription. By then the *Bridge River-Lillooet News* was selling almost 2000 copies a week, although "selling" is not quite the right word, Ma being not very much focused on money matters. She would barter the paper to those who couldn't pay cash — for an issue or subscription. One small enterprise paid for the paper with raisin pies, of which the Murray kids later said, "We had them coming out of our ears." Chickens, vegetables, before long the newspaper was bringing in pretty well all their groceries without the usual intervention of cash.

Ma was a supporter of her husband George's political career and she was tireless in attacking other politicians, not just his opponents, but also his superiors in the Liberal Party. In one editorial she called George's boss, the premier, a "paragon of senile decay." George would write home, "In the name of reason, what are you trying to do to me?" But Ma didn't care. Embarrassing her husband had become an old habit which for her didn't mean much since, as we will see, she loved him more than she loved anything and she thought he ought to be able to put up with a bit of fun.

But this playful and mischievous journalist was nonetheless a powerful presence. In her photographs she seems imperious, even menacing, despite the huge smile adorned with fairly irregular teeth. It is a smile declaring that she has something great to offer and doesn't give a damn what anyone thinks.

Once someone made the mistake of asking Ma to introduce George at a political event; she accepted with enthusiasm and opened by saying that the north was filled with good men, "none better than my husband. . . . And as you all know, when a good woman gets under a man he moves." The characteristic dour probity in Depression British Columbia hadn't a chance. The room collapsed in howls of laughter.

"Well," she continued, "we like to grow 'em big up north." Whereupon she puffed out her great forty-four-inch bust. A button popped and ricocheted with a ping off a wineglass and the decorum of the house was destroyed for good. Now it was George's turn. He stepped up and took, quite appropriately, a long pause. He said that he now understood why the American President Franklin Roosevelt was reputed to pray that his wife Eleanor would wake up more tired than when she'd gone to sleep.

Ma's wordplay would not even be roped in by the protocols surrounding royalty. The Murrays had been invited to meet the King and Queen on the royal prewar tour of Canada. Ma wrote afterward in her lead editorial that she hadn't known whether to curtsey to the king or give him a big kiss. She told them in a later issue that what she finally did was to hold his hand "'til his little sword rattled."

Behind that perfectly genuine façade of playfulness there was a woman of great practicality. In 1937, George was sent to China on a trade mission. A photograph shows the two of them in Shanghai looking like a rich Western couple in a rickshaw. When a Japanese battleship began bombarding the city, they had to make their way through the chaotic streets, strewn with mangled corpses, to the British troop ship that was to evacuate them. The refugee-laden ship was teeming with chaos and desperation. The Murrays had an elegant suite of staterooms since Ma had managed to let people think George was the premier of BC. She could easily have sought refuge in those staterooms and disappeared and rested up after the ordeal of escaping from a city under siege. Instead, when she learned that another refugee was in labour, and there was no doctor or midwife to be found, Ma delivered the baby.

But there was a contradictory and sometimes hateful side to this uncommonly generous-spirited woman. During World War II thousands of Japanese-Canadians were moved from their coastal homes lest they help their Japanese relatives carry out an invasion of Canada — it was one of the major injustices of the war. Lillooet was far enough inland that the authorities considered it a safe stopping point for some 4000 of these internees, and most of Lillooet thought the sudden increase in the population both good for business and a useful supply of low-cost labour. Not Ma Murray. Her editorials bristled with racist vituperation. Perhaps she was surprised to find out how unpopular these editorials were; she made herself unpopular with everyone, Japanese-Canadian or not. The Murrays left Lillooet. Ma said it was because the town was getting overcrowded.

By this time Ma's pictures show her on the far side of

middle age, more formidable-looking than ever. Scouting for a town that needed a paper, she looked almost as far east as Edmonton and finally settled for Fort St. John where there were wooden sidewalks and weather that got to sixty-below. Ma and George and the family moved into a log house. Ten thousand US troops were building the 450-mile Alcan Military Road from Edmonton to the Yukon. George had long championed such a road and decided it was time to start a new paper, *The Alaska Highway News,* and try to keep the Lillooet paper running from a distance. *The Highway News* wasn't going to sell many copies; the Lillooet paper would have to subsidize it for a while. Ma didn't think much about that side. She had a new paper to help run and that kept her going.

Now if Ma Murray had little financial ambition for herself, she was completely against any sort of welfare for anyone else. In the documentary we see her in a late interview polemically declaring, "Nothing is worth a damn in this world unless you've earned it. And that's the reason why your socialism won't work. It won't work for anybody, because something you get for nothing isn't worth any more than you paid for it." She was not one for the velvet glove; you can hear the hostility, the finger-shaking menace in her voice. Curiously, the only political party she could stand was Social Credit, which had been founded on the principle of giving a subsistence income to every citizen. However, by the time Ma Murray became involved with it, it had become *the* right-wing party in Western Canada. When her husband George's Liberals formed a coalition with the provincial Conservatives, George disliked the Tories so much that he ran as a lone independent. Ma ran for Social Credit, against her husband. Her son Dan, then editing the Lillooet paper, used the front page to warn readers that Margaret Murray was related to the family only by blood.

Ma may have had strong opinions but she wasn't big on details. It was doubtful that such a dogged individualist could ever have really been a party person, and in any case she didn't seem to care what policies her party stood for: this was just an opportunity for some more polemical fun and a chance to play at George's game. Campaigning she would just duck questions about policy. Her son Dan, unlike her husband, was not amused. Rebelliously serious and fastidious, Dan wrote another *Highway News* editorial that said, "Mrs. Margaret Murray has nothing whatsoever to do with the editorial policy of this newspaper." The election was a disaster for both Ma and her husband. They both lost, miserably.

Dan's editorials against his mother are characteristic of family life among the Murrays. They all fought among themselves and the battle lines were usually around Ma. Dan himself had his own family now and the family wars hadn't abated. It is not clear whether Ma's robust delight in conflict and mayhem made her oblivious to what people outside the circle might feel, like Ma's daughter-in-law, Dan's wife. Dan's daughter Bridget said of her mother,

Mom would be so upset when they'd come for . . . Christmas. This was when we'd always have the big arguments, and there'd be a great hoo-ha over something or other — great, great debate. And Mom would be just

destroyed because there would be, you know, foul lan-
guage and shouting and raging and a lot of unhappiness.
And yet I'd say, "Mom, it's just the way they relax, the
Murrays. It's just how they go through this Gethsemane
of arguments and discussions."

Ma's daughter-in-law would simply never understand how a disagreement about Canada's new maple leaf flag versus the old red ensign could ignite an outright screaming quarrel full of personal invective. Even less could she comprehend the speed at which they returned to normal before they left, and maybe young Bridget was right, maybe the whole thing really was just some form of family pastime.

In any case, all that receded for a while when George went into federal politics, got himself elected federal MP for Cariboo, and he and Ma went off to Ottawa. Left with both the *Lillooet* and the *Highway News*, Dan worked to make them solvent, serious, grammatical, efficient, and businesslike, exactly the sort of papers his mother hated. But even at a distance Ma managed to interfere, and in the end Dan gave up, sold the Lillooet paper, and left. Ma came back to Fort St. John and took over, doing what she had always wanted to do.

Within a few issues, *The Alaska Highway News* was back to its old, raucous, faintly scatological self. There was a water shortage. Ma quite reasonably determined that the single most extravagant use of water in the town was the flush toilet. She wrote an editorial about it, saying that it was simple: "Never flush for number one, just for number two."

"Only flush for number two" was the phrase that

would stick to Ma Murray for the rest of her life. At the time it was delightfully picked up by newspapers and broadcasts all over North America. It made Ma Murray famous. It may not have had the sonorous glory of "Ask not what your country can do for you . . ." or "The lights are going out all over Europe . . ." but it said a great deal about a persistent ecological issue and about a crusty, determined, and practical-minded interventionist editor. And it stuck and spread and endured. In Whitehorse today, half a century later, they still say, "If it's yellow, let it mellow; if it's brown, flush it down."

In 1959 Ma had had enough of Fort St. John. The *Bridge River-Lillooet News* had been idle since Dan dropped it, and Ma decided to get it going again. She was past seventy, amazingly high-spirited, and unsinkable as ever, but she would soon have to draw on all the character and experience that had carried her this far, and it is probably appropriate here that we back up a little to look at how that character was formed and what those experiences had brought her.

The woman we remember as Ma Murray grew up poor in rural Kansas; she had been christened Margaret Lally in Kansas City in 1888, the seventh of nine children. Her mother and father had been Irish immigrants, poor enough that one winter the family had nothing to eat but turnips. She was working as a housemaid at the age of thirteen. Then she got some office training that led to a job in a saddle factory that supplied cowboys in Alberta. That's where she conceived her first dream: to marry an Alberta cowboy. Cowboys she knew only in their romanticized incarnation by Zane Grey and the other dime novelists of the era. She and the other girls who worked in the saddle factory used to slip notes into the finished saddles with their names and addresses. Nobody ever wrote back, but the lure of the Northwest was still strong; so Margaret and her sister Bess decided to work their way west, arriving in Vancouver via Seattle sometime in 1912. By then they had run out of money. Margaret was twenty-four.

Around the same time, George Murray was using some family money to start a newspaper in South Vancouver, a new suburb being hacked out of the forest. The big Vancouver papers like the *Daily World*, were put together in varnished offices downtown — you've seen them in old photographs: six or seven stories of West Coast rococo, massive and hazy from the dusty streets. A new man with some new ideas, Murray took rooms at 30th and Main out in the sticks, and announced his new venture, *The Chinook*, which he declared would advertise neither tobacco nor liquor.

As soon as two days' worth of papers had been sold, Murray advertised for a bookkeeper at twelve dollars a week. Margaret Lally applied. On the way to her interview she stumbled badly on the crude plank sidewalk, breaking her heel. But she limped on painfully to the *Chinook* office, and said, "George Murray, you live at the end of the line." George said, "Margaret, I like to think of it as the beginning of the line." And she was hired.

Margaret, as we have already seen, was not one to beat around the bush and no sooner did she walk in the door for her first day than she asked for a raise to fifteen dollars a week. All it took was a little verbal bluff to convince George Murray that Margaret Lally was worth it. She got the increase, and she got down to work.

It did not take this down-to-earth, hard-nosed practical woman long to realize that her employer often had his head in the clouds, and that much of what he did was backwards and impractical. She wrote home that his *Chinook* was the "dinkiest little paper that you ever saw." But already she felt herself falling for the distracted, muddling, occasionally infuriating George Murray, cowboy though he definitely was not. His photographs show a man of middling good looks with a bit of a distant narrowing of the eyes, nothing that looks like vanity, a sense of stolidity. But still, even though she was intrigued, and had a pretty good time keeping him laughing at her earthy language and sharp observations, George remained hard to figure out.

If George Murray was the type who delayed or failed to notice or maybe was just too dumbstruck by a woman who was as subtle as a locomotive, Margaret was the kind to run out of patience. She hadn't entirely given up on the romantic notion of an Alberta cowboy. So she submitted her resignation. George, more than a little taken aback, nonetheless gave her a fine fountain pen as a parting gift. "You take it," he said. "Think about us and write us some time."

Whether Margaret Lally actually ever met any Alberta cowboys is not recorded. But it seems that she soon found herself missing the *Chinook,* and it is not unlikely that she was even playing a bit of a game anyway, taking a risk in order to let George see what he'd be missing. In any case, she was back to Vancouver five days later, and the scheme, if it was a scheme, seemed to have worked because George was there to meet her at the train. And George even managed to keep focused long enough to say right out that it hadn't been the same without her and would she marry him. Having finally got the question she wanted, Margaret gave the answer she'd been saving. They were married before the week was out.

He consented to be wed by a Catholic priest and knew enough not to invite his Protestant family. For a while they didn't speak to him, but they soon relented. An uncle of George's let them have an apartment in a building he owned, and before Margaret knew it, she, a poor, Kansas, Irish-Catholic girl, had become a member of the Vancouver middle class.

Perhaps it was some of those differences that made the marriage so rewarding. He came from an established, well-heeled Presbyterian family and she from a poor brood of Irish Roman Catholics. In the photographs, he's modest, quietly cheerful, and well dressed but sombre. In almost all her photos, from youth onwards, she has a grin and wears hats, often sombrero-like and wide enough to be pretentious. Both were dutifully observant, she going to early mass, George going at a more reasonable hour to the United Church service (after the Presbyterians and Methodists merged in June 1925 to create that uniquely Canadian almost secular denomination).

That early leap upward was followed by a couple of dips, although still well within the middle class. The

Chinook was struggling at best. Margaret had given birth to their first child, and financial difficulties drove them to look for new ways to pay the rent. George learned that the government was handing out free land an hour and a half by boat up the Burrard Inlet. He borrowed the ten-dollar registration fee and suggested to Margaret that country life would be good for their new young family.

But the face of Burrard Inlet was not much like what we see today: it was high country, clothed in dense conifer forest descending steeply to the water. They found what someone called a stump ranch — a dark, wet, and dreary landscape made up of what the lumber companies had left behind. You get a sense from the letters that, disappointed as Margaret may have been, she was undaunted. Some of the stumps were gigantic. In one photograph lumberjacks are posing in front of one as big as two Volkswagens. George and Margaret set about burning and blasting them to open up some land for cultivation.

The prewar Depression of 1913 didn't help, but coming from the poverty she had known as a kid, Margaret was less affected by it than George or probably most other people. All her life she took pleasure from simple things. She said once, "We had bread lines . . . we had soup kitchens, we did everything to get along, but my goodness alive, beans were the nicest thing that there ever was. I'd even trade a good plate of beans for the best porterhouse steak you ever had." They were saved from the far-reaching family tragedies of World War I. Since Margaret was on the way to giving birth to their second child, the Dan we've already met, George was exempted from military service.

But it was a tough time. They lived by subsistence work, both at the newspaper and their small ventures into agriculture. George did the writing, and Margaret tended a vegetable garden. Together they raised chickens and bought a cow and a couple of goats. It was Margaret who cut the heads off the chickens and coaxed a crop of vegetables out of what had been stump-strewn, rocky, weed-laden soil. George would dream, and Margaret would get on with it.

After the war the economy improved spectacularly. George was able to sell the *Chinook* and move into the position of managing editor at the *Vancouver Sun*. But he and his wife shared a dislike of working for someone else and he only lasted a year at the *Sun*. Nevertheless, he used his new connections to keep moving. Modest and conservative George may have appeared, but he also had the nerves of a gambler. It is said that he invested his last ten dollars in a lunch meeting with the lumber magnate, H.R. MacMillan, and soon had the money to start up two new journals — the *Western Lumberman* and *Country Life in B.C.* Patrician though the name might sound, Margaret got involved in *Country Life,* and made sure it was a magazine for pioneering farm women. Instead of hunt club news there were instructions for salting and preserving. She got George to publish the club reports for the BC Women's Institute, an institution that was helping farm women to find some sense of common purpose and solidarity. Now her rough-hewn practicality found fertile soil, and from the start her stuff was marked with a kind of cheerful country-style eccentricity. In one column she explained how to make a yellow dye that worked well in wool. It was composed of goldenrod flowers steeped in horse urine. Margaret made a wool suit to try it out, and modelled it herself.

And so almost without thinking about it much she had become a newspaperwoman. She would hammer all this out non-stop on the typewriter without regard for the conformities of punctuation, capitalization, and accepted spellings. George would do his best with the blue pencil, when he could find the time, but it seems likely that Margaret enjoyed the teasing her typographical eccentricities earned her. In any case, she never did conform and apparently he did not insist.

And so the twenties rolled on pretty happily. There would never be another war; everybody knew that. Margaret had time to take the kids to the beach and George began to think about being in the legislature instead of just telling it what to do in his papers. There are photos of her in those summer days in a black dress with an enormous black hat (still bigger than a sombrero); maybe she's telling the kids their father was "on the verge of the verge of getting into politics."

But before George had made up his mind, they were hit by the Depression and their advertising revenue dried up. Once again they were back to something close to the subsistence level, and the garden and livestock were essential. One of the daughters was at St. Anne's Boarding School, and they didn't want to have to give that up. One day the girl saw her father coming across the St. Anne's courtyard with her tuition payment on his back, in the form of a pig. But through those hard times, indeed fuelled by them, George kept his sights set firmly on politics. In 1933 the Liberal Party asked him to run provincially. That's when he and Margaret first heard of Lillooet, 250 miles away, which was having a by-election. The party gave George three hundred dollars for three months of campaigning, and the family packed up and headed north.

Lillooet was a rough little frontier town, mining and logging. Everything was primitive from the hand-cranked telephones to the mud streets, the omnipresence of horse-drawn wagons and buggies and the near-absence of law and order.

The Murrays arrived on a Saturday evening. The miners had just got off work and were headed for wherever they get something to drink. There are photographs of that Lillooet, and of those men, dirty under vests, suspenders, vast unruly mustaches, and seemingly very long arms and big hands. That first night, as George and Margaret were talking in a room they had rented above a tavern, there was a terrible snarling down below where a gang of these guys were pounding the hell out of each other, staggering, falling into the muddy road and making a huge row.

Margaret opened the window, stepped out onto a ledge, and bellowed down, "Will you stop making so much damn noise!" They did not. She came back inside for the washstand's pitcher of water, went back out, and dowsed as many as she could. Her reputation was getting under way.

This was not a place she very much wanted to stay in, but she stuck it. George hit the road with the official Liberal platform modified by his own somewhat visionary and less-than-well-thought-out proposals. He told the voters that if he were elected the farmers in the Peace River country would get wealth and commerce from an extension of the Eastern Pacific Railway. He probably honestly believed in the outlandish idea that a highway to Alaska, for trucks and motor cars, could be built with enough votes and goodwill, and he promised to do what he could to make it happen. And he topped it off with a promise to fight the expansion of bureaucracy. Visionary though they may have been, impractical and imprudent though George Murray often was, he kept his promises when he could, and the one about the bureaucracy was the only promise of the three that wasn't kept.

Margaret, meanwhile, ran a parallel campaign in support of George and her promise was to move the family permanently to Lillooet — and to start a town newspaper if he won the election. And if that happened, she told them, "This town will never be the same again."

She was getting stronger, more confident, certainly not mellower. Photos of the time show a woman in early middle age. The rather homely Kansas girl with large opaque eyes and rimless spectacles had grown into an imposing iron-jawed, no-nonsense matriarch, the kind you might be a bit afraid of, even in a photo, if she weren't always smiling.

George won Lillooet, and Margaret launched the newspaper. There wasn't a printing press to be found within two hundred miles; so she got a Vancouver printer to do the production, sold the ads, and wrote the stuff herself, and got her first advertising revenue in from the local Chinese businesses.

She cheerfully used the *Bridge River-Lillooet News* to boost her husband's reputation. Again and again the lead editorial and even the news would feature George Murray stories. She unabashedly promoted his plan for shipping Lillooet pears to Vancouver and his fairly advanced ideas for trade with Asia.

It's hard to say with precision exactly when it was that she became "Ma Murray." But her soon-to-become-famous editorial style was established almost from the start, and before long they were able to order a printing press shipped up from the city, and buy a building on the Main Street, where Ma ran the paper while George was more and more over in Victoria at the legislature.

At the beginning of this narrative, we followed this unlikely and intriguing couple up to their leaving Fort St. John and the *Alaska Highway News,* and making their way back to Lillooet again, in 1959. They were both hugely enjoying the rough and tumble of it all, and Ma was a woman who could carry her curmudgeonly style as well as anyone. She'd been through a lot, and now she was where she wanted to be, and things were just fine. And then George Murray, seldom sick in his life, died painlessly of natural causes.

It was 1961. Ma was stopped in her tracks. George was gone. He had whispered near the end that he wanted to convert, finally; so she was able to have him buried in consecrated ground, which gave her some comfort. As their children later observed, they had not appeared on the surface to be an especially close couple. There were lots of rows, and he was away a great deal. But those two may have been spiritually closer than anyone knew. For a long time after his death she was still running upstairs to call out, "George, I've got to tell you something." George's hat and coat remained hanging where they had always been, and Ma didn't want to hear anyone say anything about that.

One of her daughters saw her do something after George died that she had never done before, as far as anyone knew. As she was writing her husband's obituary she picked up a dictionary, something George had been after her about for years.

Like many, Ma countered grief with work, probably working even harder than she had at any time since George Murray had hired her forty-eight years before. There is a poignant photo from this time, taken through the windows of the editorial office at night, and Ma Murray is in there alone, typing, typing, typing. She hired her kids as reporters and columnists, rewrote a lot of their copy with an ironic eye, and made sure that they were "overpaid or underworked."

She was politically active too. Once she was speaking at a meeting in the BC interior, now attacking Social Credit and especially the Social Credit premier, W.A.C. Bennett. Ridiculing the famous premier's shameless oratorical style she said, "You know, at the right time, if you can just jerk a little tear and have it trickle down, that's when you know that you've really got things going your way." Upon which the audience gave her a standing ovation. Then suddenly Bennett himself appeared and jumped up on the stage and kissed her. The crowd cheered all the louder.

Not long afterward, Ma remarked, "Did you see that? He's a smart politician. I had them right in the palm of my hand and that old son of a B, he jumped up and gave me a hug and a kiss and he swung them all back just like that. It was all for naught." In her editorial she was quick to say that he may have kissed her but she had not kissed him back.

By now, Ma was a national figure. There is really no twilight to her story: it just seems to get bigger as she gets older. The wonderfully comic Eric Nicol wrote a very successful play about her, starring the irrepressible Joy Coghill. It toured all across the West. When the tour got to Lillooet, a special performance was given for Ma, and she arrived in the theatre, all dressed up with her hair done, and there was a standing ovation. Afterwards she went backstage and sat and held the actress's hand for a while, and she said, "You know, you're good. I can't hear a goddamned thing, you know, but I could see them all laughing around me. We should form a company, and we'll go East. We'll go to Toronto and all those places and we'll make a lot of money."

In the world that Ma lived in, of newspapers and barn-burning outdoor speeches, it is hard to remember that this had been the age of radio and was now the golden age of television. Elderly as she was, television seemed made for her. Her big smile and steadfast iron jaw had become a trademark. Assertive glasses with heavy black rims replaced the old rimless spectacles. She and the networks were an excellent fit: they knew exactly how to use one another: one minute she'd be interviewed and knocking over the audience with one of her famous slips: "Well, women — women hold men right in the palm of their hand. I always held my husband right in the palm of his hand." And the next she'd be alongside Sophia Loren or appearing as the mystery guest on a game show. Or sitting on a panel beside Gordon Sinclair who's covering his face and shuddering. And then — it seemed a bit of a stretch, but a stretch that people loved — she'd be up there on a university's convocation platform, in the great gown and cap, accepting an honorary doctorate.

Throughout, she never stopped gathering news. One storekeeper remembers her style very clearly. She came into the store one day and wanted his opinion on a few of things. She suggested a chat by the fire. They went down to his house and sat down and she asked for some brandy to warm things up. She talked for an hour or two until she realized she was late for an appointment, thanked the man for his ideas, and left. And the storekeeper realized he had not said a word.

She finally sold the *Lillooet News*. The new owners gave her a weekly column on condition that she not interfere with the business. Unable to change, unable to stop, she kept on butting in and almost certainly scolding. There is television footage of her striding among the massive presses, and gesturing and saying something to the typesetters, who appear ill at ease. The new owners fired her. She was eighty-five. She said, "I've had a wonderful life, really, and every day of it has been fun. I told you I wouldn't want to live one day of it over, for fear I'd miss some of the good things. Mind you, it ain't all been beer and skittles. There's been lots of ups and downs." And indeed there had.

Ma Murray's death in 1982, at the age of ninety-four, was a national event. She probably would have liked the funeral. The coffin was hot pink. She had chosen powder blue for George, twenty-one years earlier. She was buried beside him in the Catholic cemetery at Fort St. John. The best picture to remember is a simple image from television: She is old, and she is moving down the sidewalk — fast. As she herself might well have put it, "She is dead and gone . . . and we haven't seen her since."

◆　◆　◆

The History Television documentary was written by Robert Duncan and directed by Annie O'Donaghue.

Part Nine

J.B. TYRRELL
DINOSAUR HUNTER

In the pictures taken in the 1940s and '50s he looks frail, posing in his suit or in shirt and suspenders, sometimes beside his aged wife. By then he was a figure very different from the lean, pale-eyed, buckskinned nineteenth-century explorer of the Canadian frontier who shows up in the earliest photographs. When Joseph Burr Tyrrell retired, the Canadian geologist, prospector, and surveyor of the Northwest Territories moved to a farm on the Rouge River, not far from the little town where he had grown up. His marriage, which had been buffeted by the prodigious professional obligations that had taken him away from home so much, was finally settling down; his wife Dolly kept a garden, Tyrrell looked after the orchard, and from time to time he told extraordinary tales about a very long and very adventurous life.

He was born in 1858, in Weston, which then was way out in the bush northwest of Toronto. In his childhood, there are some discernible conditions that may have influenced his life choices, given him the taste to spend weeks paddling the whole length of the Kazan and Athabaska Rivers, or to venture alone into some of the most forbidding places in Canada. Defects in his sight and hearing that had cursed his youth also gave him a kind of comfort with solitude, and a definite preference for the bush lands of the Humber rather than the streets of the city. By the time he was twelve the solitary, self-sufficient kid had become an indefatigable collector with a very unboyish fastidiousness about precisely annotating and cataloguing the detailed results of his scavenging through the countryside. He gathered every grasshopper and spider he could find in the Humber Valley where it ran through his parents' farm. Mud turtles and crayfish crawled across his bedroom floor. He had a strong sense of and fascination with the texture and heft of physical things. Although he was demonstrably bright, words were not his best medium. He never even completed the autobiography that the scientific community urged upon him in his later years. But back then, in Weston, his fascination with the life in that river valley, and in the river bed itself, were beginning to turn him towards a vocation.

As so often with unusually talented children, Tyrrells' parents had a hard time trying to understand him. They were gentry; they thought of science as something close to manual labour. The boy's fascination with what he found in the dirt was unseemly, and a life work informed by that kind of curiosity was certainly not something for a Tyrrell. At one point they invited John A. Macdonald to lunch to investigate the possibility of getting the boy into law school.

In 1867, the year of Confederation, Canada started to appear in atlases as an independent nation, strung out along the St. Lawrence and the Great Lakes and across the prairies and the mountains to the Pacific. Tyrrell was nine years old. He began staying late at school, fascinated by those areas in his atlas that were largely empty. He would "explore" them with his pencil, filling in guessed-at details of forestation, rivers and lakes, and geological features.

In Upper Canada College and later at the University of Toronto he compensated for the problems with his eyes and ears with a defensive assertiveness and aggression, and by living high and fast until exhaustion brought him down with tuberculosis. The doctors told him that if he wanted to live any length of time he should find something to do that kept him working outdoors. The photographs of this period do not look like a young man who was having problems with self-assurance. He looks serene, tall, fair-haired with budding side-whiskers, mustache, and spectacles. Once again his father contacted John A. Macdonald, now Prime Minister of the new nation, and within weeks the young Tyrrell had an indoor job with the Geological Survey of Canada, based in Ottawa. They started him off literally in the cellar, unpacking the crates of fossils sent back from the explorers out on the survey. It was familiar stuff, calling on that fastidious taxonomy that he had taught himself as a boy in the Humber Valley.

But the bureaucratic politics of the Survey establishment were very different from the comfortable solitude and silence of his basement crates and catalogues. It was hierarchical and competitive, and when the men gathered for a group photograph in their dark suits and severe expressions they looked like a collection of bankers about to foreclose on a mortgage. They were obsessed by credentials, and another young talent in the Survey, one George Dawson, told his chiefs that he thought Tyrrell's credentials were not very impressive. Perhaps aware that Tyrrell was a protégé of the Prime Minister, the Survey's white-bearded director Joseph Selwyn adroitly gave Dawson the task of smartening up the new boy by taking him out into the field. So the job did turn into an outdoor assignment after all, and would remain so for much of the next two decades.

It was not, however, an agreeable assignment at first, going into the field under a man who would have preferred to sack you, and who definitely resented having to not only drag you along but also to teach you the trade. The expedition of 1883 took them into genuinely unmapped territory. There is a picture of them taken at a place called Maple Creek (there must be fifty Maple Creeks in Canada; this one is in southwest Saskatchewan in the Cypress hills). A picture of the crew posing against their wagon shows most of the men in their frontier-fashionable (and contrived) battered upturned hats. Tyrrell is a bespectacled dandy in long-fringed buckskin and large, floppy-brimmed pale hat. Dawson is short, slightly hunchbacked, with a scruffy beard, flinty eyes, and a sly and amused expression. On his head is an ancient top hat that makes him look like a cross between the Artful Dodger and the Mad Hatter.

Tyrrell's granddaughter, Katherine Tyrrell Stewart, says that Dawson "seemed to make lots of friends, but he also seemed to make a few enemies." He was an old hand, having been in the survey that mapped our border with the United States. He did not suffer fools gladly, and neither did his apprentice, Tyrrell. At times they took one another for fools and the tension was palpable. Dawson put Tyrrell in a position where he would be the last to see anything, walking behind the team, measuring the distances they covered. At night it was Tyrrell who had to stay up and keep watch over the horses; Dawson was said to care more for animals than for his men.

But it was great to be out of doors. He was used to being alone, and content to see as little as he could of his chief. The long active days were toughening him. His lungs felt clear and his determination to make something out of himself in the Survey just got tougher and tougher. In spite of his poor eyesight, he became the best shot on the survey. The men found it entertaining, the diligence and precision with which he collected stuff. He even studied the fleas on the horses and wrote them up. Dawson did not find this as amusing as the other men did, but they were soon treating him with affection and calling him "J.B."

The 1883 expedition eventually took them west into the Rockies. Tyrrell's eye was caught by something that still puzzled him. The massive U-shaped valleys had been scraped out by glaciers, which he estimated to have been a half-mile in thickness; but the markings that must have been made by the ice were an enigma. Those markings would later bring Tyrrell an indisputable victory over his difficult survey boss.

Tyrrell spent the following winter back in Ottawa, writing up the summer's findings, relieved to be away from George Dawson. Arthur Selwyn recognized that Tyrrell had more than proven himself, decided to protect him if necessary from the carnivorous bureaucracy, and find opportunities to put in his way. He put Tyrrell in charge of a new expedition. This was the survey that would make his name in the summer of 1884. The area northeast of Calgary was vast, bleak, much of it steep and devoid of vegetation, a stark desert in the summer and a snow-covered moonscape in winter. Forty-five thousand square miles of what is now Alberta, and Tyrrell was to geologically map it, fix elevations, collect fossils, and record mineral deposits. He would be responsible for recruiting a team and purchasing the horses. "The Geological Cavalry," he called them. And he was in charge of the whole enterprise. He was twenty-five years old.

There were few maps of any practical value. David Thompson's two-hundred-year-old survey did not extend to the deep, impassable canyons of the Red Deer River. The pack horses soon looked nothing like cavalry chargers, often bogged down under their loads as they struggled across the swiftly flowing gorges. Photographs show the whole crew sometimes half submerged. The rivers were the only navigable highway, and Tyrrell began to think that slicing through the aeons of rock layers as they did, they were more revealing than any other single feature. He would get a canoe. Then he could really study what were essentially the earth's paleolithic graphics, mineral diagrams laid out before your eyes in the endlessly layered strata in the rock.

It is one of the world's most eerie landscapes. There are palisades bigger than anything conceived by man, curious pillars capped with huge flat boulders, and in the most colossal formations, melted and twisted by millions of years of fire, wind, and water into strangely beautiful forms. Local Native people told Tyrrell about the Serpent People, whose spirits still roamed in the creeks and coulees. They warned Tyrrell to go no further. But the party continued, and what they found was not ghosts but gold, black gold, not real gold, gold you could burn. With a geologist's hammer you could pick it out of the stratum before your eyes.

On the seventh and eighth of June he discovered, noted, and mapped part of what would turn out to be one of the largest coal deposits ever found. These huge coal deposits in the Red Deer Valley would be a political plum for his boss Selwyn to present to his minister, and their discovery would give Tyrrell another sudden career boost.

It was to be a productive week, a productive three days, in fact.

On the ninth of June he was high on the crumbling ridges, just about to get out of the noonday heat, when he saw a kind of fossil he had never seen before. At first it was just an odd, dark, pointed ovoid, no, a series of them in a line, protruding out of the pale flaked layer of shale like, well, like what? They looked like some kind of gigantic teeth. He took out his trowel and brush and began to clear away the flaked stone. The teeth were set in an immense jawbone. Mapping the location, he found other bones, vertebrae scattered down the hillside. Then another tooth, different this time, sharp-edged, serrated, the creature had eaten meat. Carefully he uncovered it. When he told his granddaughter about it years later he said, "Here was this great ugly face looking out of the cliff at me!"

It was wonderfully preserved, grinning below its

huge arched empty eyes, with a great snout, massive teeth, and black nostrils. Maybe this was where the Native people had got the idea about the serpent spirit, some ancestor lost, stumbling upon the apparition, racing away terrified, magnifying what he found, in his terror, investing it with life and menace.

J.B. Tyrrell could not know immediately that what he had uncovered was sixty-four million years old; or that it was the head of what would be the first complete carnivorous dinosaur skeleton in Canada: *Albertosaurus sacophagus*.

Eventually that bit of luck and skill would lead to the richest field of dinosaur remains in the world and the foundation nearby of the Royal Tyrrell Museum of Palaeontology. The jealously competitive George Dawson had ten years before he found the very first dinosaur bones to be discovered in Canada and there were bound to be repercussions when he learned that this . . . this *upstart* . . . upstaged him. It struck J.B. that in Canada's Geographical and Geological Survey good news often led to bad feelings.

In the spring of 1885, the peace of the prairie was broken by civil war: the Riel Rebellion had got under way and John A. Macdonald was sending regiments into the area to force the rebels into submission. The survey was suspended, and to Tyrrell's disappointment, so was his work in the dinosaur beds of the Red Deer River. As the war rattled on and J.B. waited for news in Calgary he had accepted the fact that the summer was a write-off, when one morning Ottawa telegraphed permission to explore as long as he avoided the war zone. Tyrrell went straight to a Native village on the edge of town, the Stoney Camp, and hired a guide. A snapshot shows the grave, powerful, nearly black profile of a Native man from the Prairies. He had adopted the name William to avoid the hostility that all First Nations people were feeling from whites angered over the war with Riel's Métis, and who were not much interested in the difference between the Métis and the full-bloods. William and Tyrrell headed west, moving slowly along the eastern slopes of the Rockies, living off the land as they went, and exploring the watersheds of the Clearwater and Saskatchewan Rivers.

It was now that Tyrrell made a very different kind of discovery, a discovery that in some ways would affect his life as much as his spectacular successes of the previous summer, perhaps even more so, for the young Stoney Indian seems to have put the young scientist and explorer in touch with his spiritual side. William talked of how the land, from its great canyons to its grains of sand, from the gigantic skeletons to the fleas on the horses, the leaves, the crickets, and birds were all possessed of spirits. Tyrrell sensed a kind of wisdom in the young man and found himself listening with a calmness that was new to him. He had not thought before about the idea that the land and its living burden were not simply resources to be exploited, but rather gifts towards which we have a custodial responsibility, an obligation to protect and pass on. To whatever extent such ideas had been approached in his Christian upbringing, they had meant little more than the pious mouthings of elders for whom he had little respect. As William talked, Tyrrell felt he had found a mentor he could trust. He had been brought up in a culture that spoke with contempt of the Native people; now his feelings for his young teacher led him to a new respect for them. The aggressiveness and swank that he had used to deal with his deafness had kept him away from close relationships; now he felt a new hunger for companionship, and even began to think what had been unthinkable: that he might meet a woman whom he could love and even marry. William died young, of tuberculosis, the same disease that Tyrrell had survived. The loss was grievous, but he felt that his soul had been tempered.

Back in Ottawa that winter of '85 to '86, some of the brashness came back again as he moved among the bureaucrats. He now sported a substantial blond walrus mustache. His colleagues probably still thought him too single-minded to pull away from the niceties of differentiating paleolithic strata in order to go to a party, but that was the old Tyrrell. The new man began to move out in society, a bit tentatively at first, the tentativeness soon mediated by his meeting with Edith Carey, nicknamed Dolly, a serious Baptist whose father was a local clergyman. Dolly was struck by the explorer's rugged physique and newly tender manner. Her father was very much impressed when Tyrrell expounded a geological discussion of the probable nature of the bones in the Old Testament story of Ezekiel. Dolly and Joseph came to love each other unreservedly, a love that would last for a very long time. "There was a kind of gentleness when they were together," Katherine Tyrrell Stewart said. They could not seriously contemplate marriage yet. Tyrrell's salary was only eight hundred dollars a year, and despite his successes many of his colleagues still thought him a lightweight. The Geological Survey was underfunded. He might lose his job.

However, they found him another assignment, he would be employed at least through the summer. Not a promising enough situation to give him the confidence to propose marriage but, better than nothing. The 1886 trip to Manitoba would not be nearly as dramatic as the Rockies and the Alberta Badlands had been, but he had hopes of turning up something exciting, of extending his earlier run of good luck. He bid Dolly farewell, and got on the train for Winnipeg.

He had a newfangled device with him on this expedition, a Kodak Hawkeye camera. He traced the shoreline of Lake Manitoba in his boat, the *Pterodactyl,* and photographed almost every mile. He learned about the old fur trade from what he could, detective-like, narrate out of the remains of the old fortified log trading posts. He thought about Dolly a lot. He worried away at the edges of David Thompson's two-hundred-year-old survey maps and just knew that he should be surveying the uncharted land beyond those edges. Maybe Arthur Selwyn would extend his employment with the Survey long enough to at least make a start. He wrote to Selwyn. Selwyn agreed. He was secure for a bit longer; time to stop dithering about Dolly. He proposed by mail. Dolly accepted, but he still had to carry out that survey before he could come back to Ottawa for the wedding. He began to assemble his team and resources.

The plan was to cross Lake Athabaska and then move

north by river to the watershed that divided the boreal forest from the tundra. His time with William had convinced him that wilderness exploration needed the instincts and experience of Native people, and he tried to enlist men from the Dene Nation. But the Dene told him that they believed the Inuit whom they would meet in the north were cannibals, and they wanted nothing to do with them. Tyrrell sent for a group of Mohawk paddlers from the Kahnawake reserve near Montreal, and hired his brother James as interpreter. In addition to the big canoes, they had a number of flat-bottomed freight barges with upturned prows to deal with the expected whitewater sections of the Athabaska River. In the photographs, their baggage train seems big enough for a small army. The paddle across Lake Athabaska was straightforward and exhilarating, but once over the watershed both the land and the river became more forbidding. The distances accomplished each day diminished steadily. The low riverbanks stretched out into melancholy fields of stones. It was so bleak that Tyrrell found it hard to imagine human habitation would be possible. But on July 25 the expedition came upon a small tent camp and a group of Inuit, who were apparently terrified by the aspect of the unwashed, sun-blackened explorers, and fled leaving their fires smoking and their few possessions in simple skin tents. Tyrrell left packets of steel needles and tobacco in the tents: tokens of friendship.

He thought of Dolly hourly. He had sent her one last letter before he reached the end of the known world. A blue flower was pressed into it, and Dolly told her granddaughter that the scent filled the room, dried and faded as it was. That letter would be the last for six months. The snows came early. The great dark river ran endlessly northward, taking them with it, their supplies of food and fuel shrinking day by day. Tyrrell had expected the river to turn east toward Hudson Bay where they would be able to return by boat rather than spend the winter in that murderous emptiness. But the river kept going north and soon a life or death decision faced them: should they retreat back south, upriver; or should they cross the divide into the tundra where they might find caribou, maybe a coastline with seals and fish, maybe even people whom they would be careful not to frighten this time, who might guide them, help them find food?

All the while, Tyrrell had to keep making observations; particularly about glaciation that was still little understood. The striations in the rock had suggested a massive concentration of glaciers in a single area. George Dawson had made something of a geological splash by demonstrating, conclusively as he thought, that the glaciation of this part of the continent had all flowed in from a single source. The Survey had instructed Tyrrell to look for that source.

He wrote a lot while they were on the river. It was sometimes so calm enough that he called it "my writing desk"; and sometimes turbulent enough that they all had to hold on for their lives as the barges were sent flying over rocks and then plunging into the whitewater and its bone-chilling clouds of spray.

They were moving against time and against the weather, trading off the delay that a stop for hunting would entail, and the subsequent risk of being overtaken by the snows before they could make it to the more congenial tundra they were sure they would find. They pressed on, sometimes close to starvation. And then the breezes in the morning began to bring in a new smell, of something alive. The endless fields of stone blended into sparse, stunted vegetation and then to grass.

One afternoon they suddenly felt the earth vibrating, drumming all around them. Tyrrell wrote in his journal, "When we came around this bend there was a grassy meadow right over there, and we saw these caribou and they leapt up and kept coming and coming. . . . It was a beautiful sight." The half-starved explorers leapt from the boats with their rifles. They feasted that afternoon, and in a few days they had a month's supply of dried meat.

The snows began in August. Sleet at first, and fast-dropping temperatures, but at least they were now heading east again, towards Hudson Bay. They reached it a month later than planned, and pitched their sad-looking vulnerable little tents along the brutal shore. The sextant, however, showed them not far from Fort Churchill. A day's rest, and then the walking began. They had been out of touch with Ottawa for months. Speculation there was gloomy. By October Dolly was sure he was dead and she abandoned.

But, in fact, the team had made it to Fort Churchill after all, having travelled 1400 miles. Tyrrell had lost fifty pounds. You can see him in a group picture taken in the snow, smoking a pipe as if nothing had happened, his skeletal frame hidden in a huge fur coat. They went by snowshoe from Churchill to Winnipeg, and warm beds and cooked food. Then, they took a train back to Ottawa and Dolly. He brought her the snowshoes as a memento.

The wedding was February 14, 1887. Afterwards they dined with Governor General Lord Aberdeen and his wife, and made an influential friend. Lord Aberdeen became a kind of patron. Tyrrell would soon need support.

To the government who had to pay the bills — some seven thousand dollars for those 1400 miles — it seemed as though the Athabaska expedition had not produced very much. There was a debate in the House of Commons, and one MP said derisively, "They even starved on that money! Imagine what it would have cost if they'd eaten well!" For a while it looked as though Tyrrell's exploring days were over. Then his new patron stepped in. Lord Aberdeen persuaded a wealthy fellow Scot, Munroe Ferguson, to fund another expedition. Dolly would have to be patient once again. It would not be the last time.

Just north of the point where the new territory of Nunavut meets the provinces of Manitoba and Saskatchewan, two connected lakes give rise to the Kazan River. The river then zigzags northeast through more lakes and finally flows into Baker Lake, which issues eastward into Chesterfield Inlet which in turn leads to Hudson Bay. Tyrrell's assignment was to navigate the Kazan from its source to Hudson Bay before the onset of winter. Giving themselves the better part of the year, the team set out in spring. The black flies were appalling. Ferguson had supplied the expedition with tar oil as an insect deterrent, but Tyrrell reported that the bugs seemed to love the stuff, and the men were better off without it. So they covered as much of their bodies as they could, and forged on sweating and slapping and still dripping with blood from the bites.

One day in the silent motionless wilderness, small boats in groups of two or three appeared from behind several points of land. The river had been empty, and then suddenly the boats were there. They were Inuit, who remembered an offering of needles and tobacco from a year before, and somehow made the connection. They gave the travellers food and firewood, and Tyrrell's Hawkeye recorded the poignant image of a line of kayaks with their generous paddlers, who had asked for nothing in return. It more than confirmed Tyrrell's affection and admiration for the First Nations people of the North.

For all of the hardship, and his yearning for home and Dolly, Tyrrell often felt a deep sense of peace in the North. Returning home to warmth and comfort and affection carried the price of going back to the Survey offices and Dawson and the rest of the bureaucracy. During the next few years his time in Ottawa was characterized by a growing, warm domestic scene. Their first son would be born in 1897. The trust and affection between the couple deepened year by year, but the atmosphere was somewhat clouded by financial anxiety and bureaucratic tensions. Dawson was still on his case, and may well have been the one who made sure that Tyrrell's salary never met his family's needs.

We know that Tyrrell had asked for an increase after Dawson succeeded Selwyn as director of the Survey, in 1895. The next year gold was discovered in the Yukon, and the collection of tents and huts from which the prospectors streamed out to the gold fields was named Dawson City, after the new Survey chief, who seems to have taken some credit for the discovery of the gold. Dawson refused Tyrrell's raise. Things between them were not helped when Tyrrell brought out his paper on the glaciation issue, which was published by the British Association for the Advancement of Science. It persuasively contradicted Dawson's theory of a single source, Tyrrell demonstrating that the ice that had once covered North America had radiated not from one but from several epicentres. Tyrrell's theory won the acceptance of the international community of geologists, and Dawson was furious.

In the spring of 1898, Dawson gave Tyrrell an assignment in the midst of what had become the anarchy of the gold-mad Yukon. Tyrrell was forty, and despite his prodigiously important discoveries, especially during those amazing three days in the Alberta badlands fifteen years earlier, he was no more secure than he had ever been. Landing in Skagway he got his first taste of the gold-driven madness that infested that dark town. The mere act of asking directions from some men in a bar nearly cost him the thousand dollars Dawson had given him to finance his project. He had escaped, he later found out, from a saloon known as "the slaughter house" while the town itself bragged of a murder rate of three per week. The day he arrived at the pass over the mountains twelve men were killed in an avalanche. That caused no break, he noted in his journal, in the continuous trail of humanity that moved upwards day and night in search of wealth. He pressed on past the skeletons of overburdened and beaten horses that lined the way. It may have been on the sailing barge loaded with hopeful prospectors that the idea came to him: with his finely tuned geological antennae he might just make one hell of a prospector himself.

When he landed at the city named after his detested boss, there were an estimated hundred thousand prospectors, gamblers, entrepreneurs, criminals, confidence men, and other parasites stumbling around the frozen slough. The town was in constant change, building, expanding, thriving, being corrupted, by the power of gold. Its cheery symbol was a picture of a woman raising her dress to show her underwear for money.

But when J.B. Tyrrell followed his keen geological nose that summer, and found himself at a place called Ben Low's Fraction, and said to himself that it might just be the richest little piece of ground in the world. He looked around and saw people sometimes finding the equivalent of his whole year's salary in a few minutes' panning in the creeks, and he knew what he was going to do next.

It took a few months, but he made a strike, finally, "below Hunter Creek, a valley over from Bonanza." He got a loan from the bank, told George Dawson to shove it, quit the Survey, and began to develop his find. It took six years. Dolly came to stay with him twice, but most of their intercourse was on paper for the next few years, until he finally had extracted everything he could from the Yukon, and it was, at last, really and truly time to come home.

George Dawson died in 1901 at the age of fifty-four. Tyrrell said he felt a little sad that their old battles were over, but it did not mean very much anymore. He and

Dolly had moved into a fine house in Toronto. He became the residential agent for a London-based investing syndicate, Anglo-French Explorations, and had his photograph taken in a pinstriped banker's suit with the syndicate's board of directors. Two more children arrived — three sons altogether. And when he was asked to take a look at the abandoned mines at Kirkland Lake, to see whether there was anything left to do with them, the boys were old enough to be left at home with paid help for the time it took J.B. and Dolly to get up there to the Northern Ontario town and take a look. It did not take him long. He quickly determined that the veins were far from exhausted. It did take long — almost ten years — to convince investors that the gold mine was a gold mine, but it was worth it in the end. He was comfortably busy in the meantime, and when Kirkland Lake reopened he became chairman of the board and a millionaire.

And the rest is serenity, with a little nostalgia thrown in, an elderly adventurer's fond memories of some times that were tough, at an age when you could handle tough. Katherine Tyrrell Stewart was there from time to time when he would hang a sheet at the end of the hall and get out his old black-and-white slides and project scenes of the North that he had crossed with such courage and determination, and tell some of the stories again. He settled into a routine of comfortable predictability, occasionally brightened by a family visit. "If dinner was at 6:30," remembers his granddaughter, "dinner was at 6:30, and you went into the dining room precisely at 6:30."

She also recalls venturing into her grandfather's

study, and discovering that there was something about the grand old gentleman that was still a little boy:

I would sneak into the sunroom . . . just so I could be there in the same room with him and hear him writing. Every so often he'd get up and he'd go and take a book out of his bookshelves and then later I'd go and sneak and see what the books were. They were all sorts of geological survey reports, journals of this and journals of that, and then mixed with them, there were a whole series of Tarzan books . . .

The first of the Tarzan stories was published in 1931, so the great geologist could not have read them before he was in his mid-fifties.

Having survived tuberculosis, the wilderness, near starvation, and corrosive years of professional rivalry, he survived Dolly, who died in 1945, and lived on twelve more years at the farm. He survived his sons. He watched colleagues and friends vanish from his horizons one by one. At the end he was alone, a grand, faded monument to the map of Canada, sparkling with blue rivers and lakes he had paddled, veined with minerals he had identified with such assurance, home to those mysterious bones he had stumbled upon, and gazed at with a wild surmise when he was twenty-five. In 1957, J.B. Tyrrell died, one year short of his century.

◆　◆　◆

The History Television documentary was written and directed by Tom Radford.

Part Ten

SIR ARTHUR CURRIE

AN EXTRAORDINARY ORDINARY GENERAL

In small towns all across Canada, there is almost always a public feature that is at once a little strange and a little reassuring. The town will have, usually near its main intersection, a stone, sometimes a large plaque, sometimes a four-sided pillar, with between four and twenty names inscribed on it. The names are of townspeople, usually young men, killed or missing in action in France and Belgium between 1914 and 1918. There will often be names from the '39 to '45 war too, but the list from the First War is longer.

How many Canadians pause to ask why those World War I numbers were so great? General Sir Arthur Currie, field commander of the Canadian Army, wrote to his brother: "We have never been called upon to perform a harder task. The obstacles to be overcome in the way of hostile defences, bad roads, bad communication, difficulties of assembling, were greater than any we had ever encountered."

Currie was a general and as such he listed the most immediate and practical problems. The summer of 1917, the fourth hideous summer of the war, was the wettest on record. There lay before him, in the area of Passchendaele, a sea of mud stretching to the horizon. It was inescapable. It was in your food, you slept in it, it seeped through your clothes, it rotted your feet. The wounded disappeared in it, the living lived in it, and even the able-bodied men moving forward on an assault could drown in it, or in the stinking, murky water that filled craters called shell holes.

By 1915 there were four million men living in trenches. There are millions of photographs. The camera was newly cheap and relatively portable, and hundreds of soldiers — those lucky ones who survived — brought home numbing pictures of unbelievable misery. They show the mud and the shell holes and shattered trees as a backdrop to the staring, pale, stunned faces of Canadian soldiers in the remains of trenches. In one famous shot there is a putteed leg and booted foot protruding from the mud wall of a blasted trench.

Sometimes on the horizon we can see a few shattered walls of the houses that once formed a village. The rest is a single black-brown mass. On this ground, throughout that hideous, cynically directed and spectacularly useless war, advancing troops, of either side, if they achieved anything at all would measure their day's success in yards, not miles, of ground.

Today on that piece of otherwise unremarkable Belgian countryside, there are three cemeteries containing the bodies of the thousands of Canadian men who died there eighty-five years ago in the Battle of Passchendaele. Many if not most are marked "unknown," a brief and neutralized reference to what was so often the indescribable condition of the remains that his comrades had to gather up for burial.

And behind all that wasted sacrifice, coolly ordering it to happen, day after blood-soaked day, was an arrogant, distant, glory-maddened, cowardly and spectacularly incompetent commander-in-chief of the British forces (to whom the Canadians were attached), Field Marshall Sir Douglas Haig.

Haig told his masters at Westminster that he could "gloriously" win this boggy, cruel, and motionless war simply by throwing thousands upon thousands of "gallant" men across the impassable land and into the shell and machine-gun fire. And in the old newsreel footage (some of it faked in Canada for propaganda purposes as we would find out decades later) you can seem them moving towards their deaths, not running, not charging or yelling, but great broken lines and knots of them walking slowly, tediously forward. It was almost as if death had become an acceptable routine, which, to Haig, it certainly was: not just acceptable, but glorious and gallant.

General Arthur Currie detested much of what Haig sent him to do. But he had eagerly sought this command, and, despite this hopeless supreme commander, despite the hopeless field, Currie actually won the mud-and-blood-bath of Passchendaele, April through November 1917, taking the strategic objective from the Kaiser's grey-coated army at the cost of sixteen thousand Canadian casualties.

Here, from its website, is the 28th Canadian Battalion's own historians' account of a November day close to the end of the Passchendaele campaign:

Clear skies, turning to cloudy but no rain. Pastor van Walleghem observed an enormous artillery barrage by several thousand cannons firing explosive and shrapnel shells with red and white rockets intermixed is opened up

on the German positions from Wytschaete to Vrijboch at
6:00 a.m. The Battalion moved forward as the barrage
began. They came under heavy machine-gun fire as the
men struggled in the deep mud of the Ravebeek valley. The
6th Brigade report records that the men "being knee deep,
and in places waist deep, in mud and water."

When the 28th entered Passchendaele, the buildings
had been smashed flat and mixed with the earth. Corporal
H.C. Baker recounted that shell exploded bodies from previous attacks were scattered everywhere so that you could
not avoid stepping on them and the German's fought a
tough rearguard battle that was murderous for both sides.
Men of the 28th were "falling like ninepins" but it was
worse for the Germans. If they stood to surrender, they
would be caught in the machine-gun fire from their rear
and killed, if they tried to move back, they were caught in
the Allied artillery barrage. The advancing men moved
from shell hole to shell hole and crouched in the cellars of
destroyed buildings. By 7:10 a.m., the Canadians were
streaming through the village, and bayoneting the
Germans in the rubble along the main street. When they
encountered pillboxes, especially at the north exit of the
village, the soldiers laid down covering fire with Lewis
guns and rifle grenades and then outflanked them. By
8:45 a.m., the village had been taken.

Corporal Baker's own note says:

I went up the trench and called out "Hi there." There was
no answer but I could make out blurred figures below, so
I slithered down in, thinking they were sleeping. I shall
never forget what I found. Down that stretch of trench the

boys were sitting in grotesque positions, and every one
was dead. The trench was only shell holes joined up, and
it was open to overhead shrapnel fire from both sides.

And Private Jacques Lapointe of the 22nd described
the scene he saw when he arrived in relief:

In a flooded trench, the bloated bodies of some German
soldiers are floating. Here and there, too, arms and legs of
dead men stick out from the mud, and awful faces appear,
blackened by days and weeks under the beating sun. I try
to turn from these dreadful sights, but everywhere I look
bodies emerge, shapelessly, from their shroud of mud.

General Haig who had seen nothing of this, spending
the day comfortably in the safety of his distant chateau,
wrote in his diary that that day was "a very important
success."

If Passchendaele had seemed impossible, Canal du
Nord was absurd. On the field, Currie had sixty thousand
Canadians and Haig wanted them hurled at the Germans
over territory not unlike Passchendaele, except that a canal
lay straight across it. What was more, the Germans were
dug in along a ridge and not a single one of their units was
without a full view of the twenty-foot-deep water-filled
ditch. If the Canadians moved over this field against the
heavily fortified German line, with their tanks and light
artillery far behind them blocked by the canal, they would
have been facing nothing less than a mass execution.

But that was the kind of attack Haig wanted. Currie
refused, rightly. Still, this was war, and the deadlock had to
be broken. Currie decided to attack at night, somehow
moving all of his sixty thousand men across the canal in

the dark to silently form a new line under cover of darkness, and then to surprise the Germans when the light came back into the sky.

Haig, to whom the regular suicidal, frontal attack seemed a matter of plain logic and gallant tradition said that he found Currie's subtle and plausible manoeuvre impossible, but agreed to send over General Julian Byng (later Governor General of Canada) to assess the plan. Byng said to Currie, "If you really think this is going to work, I'll recommend it to Haig. But if there's a disaster, then all that's going to happen is you're going to lose your job and your career." Practically before the man had finished, Currie said, "Okay, let's go."

Among the long catalogue of Haig's failures of comprehension was his ignorance of the engineering skills of Currie's Canadians, and of the importance of those skills. In his nineteenth-century mind you didn't fight battles with engineers, you sent men out to get killed. But Currie's men carried out seemingly impossible reconnaissance missions, and in the dark, the engineers got prefabricated bridges set up all along the canal, where they could be thrown across the water in minutes at first light. They did practice sessions at first, in the dark, got the construction time down to half an hour, and took the bridges down before morning so the Germans would see nothing. On a strategic road, they found and dug out three hundred anti-tank mines, again, with no light. Finally, when everything was ready, they set up those prefab bridges in the dark, threw them across the canal at first light, attacked moments later, surprised the Germans, and smashed their line.

There seems little doubt that Currie's manoeuvre at Canal du Nord was one of the actions that brought about the beginning of the end for Germany. In the last three months of the war, he and his Canadians ploughed through German defences in victory after victory. The British and the French had both tried for two years to dislodge the apparently impregnable German installations at Vimy Ridge. Currie's repeated successes now earned him a shot at it. He planned meticulously. Once again, night work was essential, and Currie is sometimes credited with inventing the stealthy patrols of two or three men, creeping silently to the edge of the enemy trenches sometimes only a few hundred feet away, slipping silently over the edge to capture a sleeping sentry and bring him back for interrogation. When his Vimy plan was ready, Currie calculated that he would hold the ridge by midday. They went over the top at first light on an April morning in 1917. By 1 p.m. as planned, they had secured the first of the key German positions, and by the afternoon of the third day, again as planned, they controlled the ridge. That battle convinced all the combatants that the Canadians were a force to contend with. It had an electrifying effect on Canada's self-confidence as a nation newly emerged from its colonial origins.

But as Currie neared that final triumph, there was another war brewing. This was a civilian contest at home, a contest that would prove, in a way, tougher than anything he had faced in Europe. A younger man named Garnet Hughes had asked Currie for a chance to command. Currie thought him not capable, and had refused, and in doing so put himself in very hot water with Hughes's father. That father, Sam Hughes, was the powerful, flamboyant, eccentric minister of the militia (whose story we told in Volume I of *The Canadians*). Sam Hughes already had some unfinished business with Currie, and Currie's refusal of his son wouldn't make things any better for the General when he returned. As the subsequent mess developed, for a lot of the men who had fought in that war and were fiercely proud of serving under Currie, like the father of one of the writers of this book, it seemed that there was no achievement so great, no military record so stellar, that vindictive rivals would not try to destroy it.

In late nineteenth-century Ontario, there were not many ways to escape the farm, but Arthur William Currie had found one. The third of seven children born in 1875 to Jane and William Currie of Napperton, Ontario, he completed normal school and then went to teach in nearby Strathroy. There was a lot of talk about opportunity in the fast-growing British Columbia, and around the turn of the century Currie got on the train, and then the boat, and found a job in a high school in Victoria, population 20,000. He tried his hand at insurance on the side, and that led to real estate, and before long he was a senior partner in a major Victoria real estate firm.

Currie was a complex man and displayed many contradictions. And one of those was the co-existence of a strong sense of his own honour with a discreet tendency to social climb. One way to climb was through the army. British Columbians thought of themselves as the defending bulwark of Canada's Pacific coast. The militia in the provincial capital was more or less a gentleman's club, and if you could get in there you were usually set for life. Currie joined a regiment called "The Dandy Fifth." Before long he had a commission and a fiancée, Lucy Sophia Chaworth-Masters, who lived in the same boarding house, a discreet and elegant place run by Currie's aunt. People found them a great match, her tireless high spirits providing some mediation of Currie's tendency to stuffy self-importance.

Whether through ambition or through a sense of duty, Currie was at the armoury 150 nights a year, when most militiamen were giving maybe two hours a week. He was desperate for action, but the type of action he got was probably not what he had in mind. A hard-fought strike by coalminers had resulted in six deaths. Currie and the Dandy Fifth were called in to bring order.

That was when Currie became friends with Garnet Hughes, the man he was to turn down some six years later, during the final offensive at Vimy, the man whose father Sam Hughes was to start a campaign against Currie. But in these early days they were friends and fellow officers, and the younger Hughes asked the elder, Sam Hughes, minister of the militia, to keep an eye out on behalf of his pal Arthur.

About then the first signs of trouble showed up. Most of Currie's money was in real estate, and the market went desperately flat. In his desperation — and this still seems strange set against what we know of the cool and confident commander at Passchendaele and Vimy — he did something much worse than foolhardy. He embezzled money that had been allotted to his new regiment, the Fiftieth Gordon Highlanders, to pay for uniforms made by Moore Taggart of Glasgow, regimental outfitters. In one photograph Currie himself is wearing such a uniform. The white fur sporran, the kilt, the plaid, the doublet, the ostrich feather bonnet, and a host of trimmings look embarrassingly costly. The allotment was ten thousand dollars. In those days before the war, working women made less than a dollar a day, men in menial jobs only a little more, the Prime Minister earned eight thousand a year, and if you take it against any other measure — the price of eggs or a train ticket or a new Bible — the comparison with today's dollar has got to be in the vicinity of twenty to one. Those ten thousand dollars Currie had been given for uniforms were worth not far off what a quarter of a million would buy today.

He quietly took the money for himself. Officially the crime would have been called "fraudulent conversion." It could have brought a convicted man three years in penitentiary. For Currie it could mean instant cashiering from the army and the loss of that precious social standing.

He was saved by the outbreak of war in August 1914. Before anyone noticed that a huge sum had gone missing, the officer in charge of the Gordon Highlanders had been tapped by his friend Garnet's father, given a brigade of nearly five thousand men, and was on his way to France.

His behaviour now became more and more curious. He left his family abruptly and only occasionally kept in touch in spite of longing and affectionate letters from his daughter. He did nothing about the money.

When Arthur Currie got to the front the French were already taking a beating. In April 1915, the Germans had surprised everyone with poison gas at the battle known as Second Ypres — 5700 canisters of chlorine gas, released through holes punched in the parapets just ahead of the German troops, and just ahead of a light wind from behind them. A *New York Times* correspondent wrote that the "vapor settled to the ground like a swamp mist and drifted toward the French trenches on a brisk wind. Its effect on the French was a violent nausea and a faintness, followed by utter collapse." The poet Wilfred Owen saw it through a gas mask, which gave the seer the aspect of an enormous insect, no less inhuman than what the seer saw:

"Dim, through the misty panes and thick green light/
As under a green sea, I saw him drowning."

It was early in the fighting at Second Ypres that Currie witnessed the weaknesses that would later lead him to refuse a command to his friend Garnet Hughes. In the St. Julien sector, a part of that battle when poison gas was used for the first time in history, Hughes's misunderstanding of an order had led Hughes's commander, General Richard Turner, to call for a disastrous retreat. Currie's brigade was left alone, against a much larger enemy force. Instead of responding traditionally, Currie outraged his British superiors by personally leaving his position, and his men dug in, and finding his way alone to another brigade whom he brought back as reinforcements. Had he followed orders or tradition, and stuck to his position unreinforced, he and his men would almost certainly have been wiped out. He was not a "chateau general," the type of commander who lived with his batman and his aides, receiving news and giving orders in the comfort of a fine chateau far from the front, untroubled by the fall of enemy shells or the rattle of machine guns, insulated from the muddy stench of his grimy troops; that was Haig's style, not Currie's. Even young Winston Churchill, still an MP when he arrived at the front with a command, would get himself flown back to Britain when he felt like it, to go to a debate in the House of Commons or spend a convivial evening with his beloved Clemmie. But Currie stayed with his men every night during that St. Julien episode, and that became his trademark as a commander, to expose himself to what the troops were getting hit with.

And yet they did not admire him much, and certainly they did not like him, those soldiers. After the war, after the victory at Vimy had been analyzed and shown to be the extraordinary tactical event that it was, even those who had disdained him in the field came around and admitted that the facts showed him to have been a great commander, but not a loved commander.

Pompous, distant, he was a man who, a private noted "didn't have the trick of rubbing fur the right way." Another reported angrily that Currie had with prodigious insensitivity tried to give his brigade's morale a shot in the arm by saying, "Soldiers, your mothers will not lament your death. You'll step into immortality." The men jeered him from the trenches. Even after the war and out of uniform he kept this air of self-importance, insisted on being called "Arthur," and admonished his family when they called him "Art."

The historian Desmond Morton argues that Currie's extraordinary successes prove him not to have been some kind of military genius, but in fact a man who benefited from ignorance of the rules and traditions. Unlike Haig and his wrong-headed, confident general staff, Currie was a civilian, an amateur soldier. He had not been to officers' training. He didn't know and didn't care how it had been done at Amritsar or anywhere else in the Empire where the great successes had built such blind confidence in, for example, the cavalry charge, that long after this new weapon the machine gun had demonstrated the complete ineffectiveness of men on horses, the old generals were still sending those mounted boys out to their certain (gallant) destruction.

Currie was just an Ontario farm kid, a practical guy, looking for advantage. That's what led him to those night patrols at Vimy, and some other innovations we'll come to shortly. He was totally unencumbered by the old rules, codes, routines, and dusty habits that were sending thousands of men to die under fire before the generals had taken their morning tea. Currie wanted to find ways around the rules, simple tricks and manoeuvres that did not come from staff college and in the end probably weren't much more complex than a plumbing problem, a blocked drain, a wet supply of firewood, a cow gone missing. Few of his British superiors, most of them from wealthy families, many who had bought their commissions, would have had the faintest idea what to do if confronted by blocked drains.

They did have dash and bearing, though, those high-born Brits, and hard as he may have tried to seem superior, dash and bearing were not part of the Currie personal armamentarium. He was tall, six-foot-four to be exact, but he had a soft, clean-shaven baby-face in contrast to the angular mustaches of many of the other allied commanders, the almost clichéd indicators that their wearers were men of authority. At over two hundred pounds, Arthur Currie was heavy around the lower middle and had a large posterior; he was so pear-shaped that his belt rode up over his stomach. Mounted, he looked as if he might break the back of his horse. They tagged him "The Old Man" and it was neither a respectful nor an affectionate epithet.

But the brain inside that mushy-looking head was a serious piece of work, and a close look at the photographs — perhaps only because we now know a lot of what was going on in there — seem to reveal a feral seriousness in the eyes; the seriousness, perhaps, of a man who — unlike so many of his British fellow officers — knew that his social class was not going to save him if he made a mistake.

Currie had no confidence in the virtues of endurance and attrition that guided the tactics of the generals on both sides. He was interested in winning, not in mere survival. He nagged his junior officers and drove them to hone their own skills and the skills of their men. He was constantly thinking about communications and never distracted by The Way To Do It. If the phones broke down or the lines were cut, if it took too long to reel them out again on the old bicycle wheels they used, Currie knew that the safest way to move messages around a dark, messy battlefield was to entrust them to the hands of courageous running men.

When he found that the maps young British officers were making on makeshift tables in the field were often wrong — and the archives show some with mistaken names, and even one with the compass rose reversed — he made sure his men understood, as at Vimy, that under this bleak field, as it began to dissolve into an unfigured, monochromatic quagmire, there were actually the remains of roads, there were villages, there was a theatre of combat with features you could find if you looked more carefully. You could find them and frame them, and build a plan on them. But you had to know where they were. He wanted this understood at the molecular level so that his men would know where they were over every foot of the ground. He wanted them to know where they were going and precisely what and where the objective was. He wanted them to understand that, even amidst the chaos described in those reports above at Passchendaele, or in what the young Lieutenant H.L. Scott of the Canadian Engineers wrote home about: "The whole earth in the air. Hundreds blinded, arms and legs blown off. One man without any arms and legs still living."

In the midst of this horror, Currie didn't merely hope for the best or trust in God, or in the valour of his men. He made objective plans designed to ensure that he would win, and without which he would not give the order to advance, however much Haig would babble about gallant lads. At Vimy when he found his properly mapped terrain to be, in the end, impossible to advance across, he ordered the men to dig a network of tunnels. He went into those tunnels and spent serious time there, watching how his men reacted to the dim confusion of the half-lit warren. He made sure the tunnels were tall enough to move through, rapidly and upright with your heavy kit of weapons, ammunition, rations, and a groundsheet. The walls were damp chalk and it was freezing down there, but the tunnels got them closer to the enemy. When they told him there was no way men could carry enough water through those tunnels, for themselves or for the fifty thousand horses they would have to bring up, he built a pipeline.

In that winter of 1917–18 Currie came up with another innovation that he believed would help him deal with the massed German troops that faced his men. Between the two armies lay not only a plain of half-frozen mud, but also an endless channel of barbed wire a hundred yards deep. On the German side of that wire, thousands of machine guns and artillery pieces awaited anyone who might try to cross. Currie had no desire to continue Haig's policy of sending unprotected soldiers out against those guns. He invented his own form of "creeping barrage," a moving wall of artillery shells, coming from cannon whose trajectory started so low that the first line of shells fell just far enough ahead of his advancing men that they themselves would not be hit. But nobody could see them coming through the clouded chaos of that line of exploding shells. Then, as the troops moved forward, the gunners raised their sights, and the line of exploding shells moved forward at the measured rate of the advancing infantrymen, masking them, shielding them, taking out those great coils of barbed wire, vaporizing them, showering the German machine-gun positions with their deadly fragments of shrapnel, as the Canadians came invisibly onward behind the creeping barrage.

Currie and his men took Vimy Ridge in a few hours. The men to whom he gave this and other victories respected him. But they could still not love him. And yet, he achieved something that no other Canadian commander — or politician for that matter — had ever done. By leading regiments from Halifax and Toronto and Montreal and Dryden, from St. Boniface, Moose Jaw, Red Deer, and Penticton up the smoking ridge, shoulder to shoulder, he made them aware that they were Canadians in a way that no Canadian had ever felt before. Their signatures are still there on Vimy Ridge. Their presence is still vivid today in the Vimy tunnels, now preserved as a museum. It looks like an endless horizontal mineshaft buttressed with timbers. All the detritus, the rusted metal and equipment, the great rot of war, has been left where it lay. The cold tedium and the heroism that came from it remain in the intricate graffiti, here a heart, there the tracing of a gun, here the name and date carved by a soldier into the chalk wall of a passage.

Arthur Currie was taken back to London to be knighted by King George the Fifth, and this winner of unwinnable battles was promoted corps commander.

But there was other business that he had neglected. He now had a respectable income. He could with little difficulty have acknowledged his "mistake" about the uniform allotment. He could have arranged to pay it back. He did nothing. In the same year of his knighthood, 1917, Moore Taggart, Glasgow outfitters, sent the letter that had to come sooner or later.

The Prime Minister of Canada swallowed hard, decided that the country should not have to bear the disgrace of a war hero, and persuaded two well-heeled political cronies to come up with the ten thousand dollars; he would deal with the general later. When Currie was briefed, he quickly said no, he would look after it himself and found two well-off younger officers to advance the money. Now he was clear at last. The money was not, as it turned out, in the clear. The then colonel of the Gordon Highlanders seems to have gotten his hands on it and vanished. What has famously come to be known as "the clothing file" has remained open. The regiment is still short of that ten thousand dollars.

But Currie's war continued, undisturbed by scandal. There were the victories of Passchendaele and Canal du Nord. And then came the fateful time when Currie refused to let Garnet Hughes command, remembering his incompetence at St. Julien.

Here and there, in the fall of 1918, the last hundred days of the war, the German line began to dissolve. In November, Currie advanced on Mons, Belgium, not sixty kilometres east of Vimy Ridge. His troops arrived, as you see them in the photographs, ghosts of men, their aged battle dress caked with mud. The Germans put up a solid, skillful resistance. The fighting was brisk right to the end. At the very moment that Currie took the city of Mons, two things happened: at 10:58 a.m. a certain Private George Price of Nova Scotia became the last Canadian to die in the war, killed by the last bullet of a German sniper. In Mons today a plaque to George Price serves as a goalpost for kids playing football in the street. Two minutes after Price fell dead, at the stroke of eleven, the armistice came into effect. The hostilities were over. It was November 11th. As Currie put his troops on parade before a grateful crowd of Belgians, in the vast, cobbled square and main thoroughfare of Mons, he could not have guessed that this simple, final victory would almost be transformed into his greatest defeat.

It took ten years. It happened in 1928. By then Currie would, on ceremonial occasions, pin on his chestful of medals for an appearance at McGill University, in Montreal, where he was now Principal. Old-school academics had protested this appointment of an unlettered mere soldier to an academic post. Even his friend the economist and humorist Stephen Leacock had said it wasn't right, but that did not bother the general. There was, indeed, not much from day to day that did. Until that afternoon when Sir Sam Hughes, father of the slighted Garnet Hughes, declared in the House of Commons under parliamentary privilege that "You cannot find one Canadian soldier returning from France who will not curse the name of the officer who ordered the attack on Mons. . . . Gallant fellows butchered!"

Not long after, an Ontario newspaper, the *Port Hope Evening Guide* expanded on the story that Sam Hughes had been the first to broach. The paper's story said this:

It was the last hour and almost the last minute when, to glorify the Canadian headquarters staff the Commander-in-Chief conceived the mad idea that it would be a fine thing to say that the Canadians had fired the last shot in the Great War.

Thirteen million soldiers had been killed in that war, and thirteen million civilians. Even the Americans, who had not come in until 1917, lost 320,000. On a per capita basis, Canada's 232,000 casualties, including our 59,544 dead, all those names on all those village memorials, were huge. It was an allegation of the very gravest consequence to charge that a Canadian general had, for his own glory, led men needlessly to their deaths. The story dominated the front pages. Even Babe Ruth was shoved to the back of the paper.

Principal Currie sued the *Evening Guide* and its editor, William Preston, for libel. Stephen Leacock tried to persuade him to withdraw, but Currie said no, it was untrue, his honour was at stake, he was claiming damages of fifty thousand dollars. The trial would be sensational.

The courthouse in Cobourg has been meticulously preserved, the fly-in-amber metaphor appropriate for its colours at least, its beautiful mid-nineteenth-century interior just as it was. The painted coat of arms in meticulous detail sits enormous over the judge's bench. In 1928, this was a terrain to which Currie was unaccustomed, a field that may as well have been as covered in fog as the battlefields on which he'd made his name.

A telegram came from the father of that last man killed at Mons. The contents were astonishing, but reassuring:

> As the father of George Lawrence Price, the only Canadian killed on Armistice Day, I wish to convey to you, Sir, my humble hope you will succeed in bringing to justice those responsible for bringing this case before the public,

*because all this simply renews old wounds that are better
forgotten.*

But some people very much wanted to open those
wounds. The *Evening Guide*'s editor Preston engaged as his
defense counsel a man named Frank Regan who set out to
save his client by ruining Currie. He brought into the
courtroom a gruesome imaginary painting showing the
streets of Mons littered with dead Canadians. He claimed
he had a hundred witnesses — simple infantrymen who
had survived. He brought in respected officers who actually had served with him and had documented the whole
campaign. When he stood face-to-face with Regan, the
counsel for the defence declared flatly that since the war
had been virtually over, the general could have spared the
lives of his men. Currie said simply that two days before
victory was not victory, but that in any case there had been
no Canadian casualties at Mons, except poor Price. He
should have waited to see if the war was ending Regan
scolded, and Currie replied that that would be treason, he
had sworn to obey orders and he was obeying orders.

Regan, in his summary, said, "I therefore impeach
Arthur Currie before this bar on behalf of the widows who
lost their husbands and mothers who lost their sons for a
needless, heedless, frightful loss of human life in this useless attack on Mons."

It took three and a half hours for the jury to file in with
its verdict, and it seems that most of that time was arguing
over the size of the settlement. They found *The Port Hope
Evening Guide* guilty of libel, but reduced the damages
from $50,000 to five hundred dollars. When Arthur Currie

got back to McGill the students gathered by the hundreds and yelled, "Arthur C . . . Arthur C . . . Don't take guff from anyone."

It seems likely that Currie's defence of his honour had damaged his health. The emotional strain had been prodigious: the libel had been uttered by the father of a friend, once a very close friend. Currie was a man who, for all his carelessness about money and his arrogance and his stuffiness, had striven to do everything he could to protect the lives of his soldiers, but for weeks his fellow citizens had been told that he had thrown their lives away for glory. It was a shameful calumny; winning the case could not heal the wounds.

For all that, he still had his soldiers' welfare at heart, even though they found him distant and offensive. He launched a campaign to lobby the government for better pensions for the veterans. He was at that work in 1933, on Armistice Day, November 11th, an appropriate day for a soldier to die, when the strain hit him with one last blow. His heart gave out, and he collapsed. It was fifteen years to the day since he had captured Mons. He was fifty-eight years old.

Sir Arthur Currie's honours included Knight Commander of the Bath, the *Légion d'Honneur*, Knight Commander of the Order of St. Michael and St. George, *Le Croix de Guerre*, and the US Distinguished Service Medal. Heroic in military matters, he remained, even after his death, puzzling about matters involving money. In his will he had provided his wife with a pittance, only eight hundred dollars a year. It was the government who saved her from humiliation and penury, with a capital fund of fifty thousand dollars, an endowment in the order of a million dollars in today's money. And the official statement from Parliament said, "The day will come when veterans of the grand army of Canada will be proud to say to their children, 'I served with Currie.'"

◆　◆　◆

The History Television documentary was written and directed by Roxana Spicer.

Part Eleven

GEORGES PHILIAS VANIER
Soldier, Statesman — Saint?

Canadians like to speak of their country as a mosaic, not a melting pot, meaning that while another country might work hard to assimilate its immigrants into the dominant culture, we have established laws, institutions, and traditions that honour and nourish the cultural riches that the newcomers bring with them. We hold as central to our values at least the toleration of difference and at best a rejoicing in diversity.

It was not always so. The first European settlers brought with them much of the religious and political division that had troubled their homelands, divisions that had often, especially in the later centuries, been the propelling force that led them to choose the New World. These ancient essentially tribal attitudes would lead in some cases at their worst to the genocide of many of our aboriginal people, and there are more than traces of that racism active today. The anti-Semitism and other strains of xenophobia that were common in Canada as late as the mid-twentieth century are shameful to recall. Young people today will find it hard to believe that only sixty years ago a Canadian judge would send a young white woman to jail as an "incorrigible" because she had been found in bed with a Chinese-Canadian man, and that her pregnancy, which she revealed in order to beg the mercy of the courts, was instead taken as proof of her criminal behaviour.

The French and English streams of our national culture have had their periods of violence and injustice too. In comparison with nationalist struggles in other parts of the world, that rough seam in the fabric of our civilization seems pretty tame most of the time. Neither in terms of violence nor duration can it be compared with other tales of countries divided. But these two hearts are beating in *our* breast, not in some distant latitude, and those old metaphors of Two Nations and Two Solitudes do not seem likely to disappear soon from the cultural landscape.

A soldier and statesman named Georges Philias Vanier, very much driven by his deep religious convictions, is one who is honoured to the point of reverence for his lifetime insistence that those two cultures would be stronger together than apart, had much to give each other, and in harmonious co-existence could give Canada a significant role in international affairs far greater than she could achieve were they divided.

Contributing to the History Television biography of General Vanier, military historian Jack Granatstein said simply, "Was he the exemplar of a kind of Canadian that we should venerate? Well, yes." If veneration seems an unusual word in the context of national development and French-English relations, another contributor's observation goes even further and explains the reason for the provocative title of this chapter. The Jesuit historian Fr. Jacques Monet said,

There was a dimension to him that really was remarkable and that was the spiritual dimension and that deserved

recognition. And I think for Catholics that would mean that he should become a saint.

Georges Vanier was born in Montreal on the 23rd of April, 1888. His mother, Margaret Maloney, was Irish. His father Philias's French forebears came to Canada in the seventeenth century. Raised in Montreal, he grew up in a home where the usual language was English; Margaret was more comfortable with it than with French, and Philias found it useful for business.

Georges and his brothers were sent to the Jesuit-run Loyola College where Georges became president of the literary and debating society. Fluently and elegantly bilingual, he was a serious boy, studious and romantic. He enjoyed writing and, while still a high school student, was able to get some essays published in local newspapers. There was a religious society at Loyola called The Savality of Our Lady. The Virgin Mary's day is Saturday, and the members of the Savality — "The Savalities" they called themselves — would start that day with an early mass and then go out into the community to work with the poor and the sick, "A concern," Fr. Monet says, that was also "a devotion, a practical one but also a prayerful one."

While his home had tended to favour the English-Canadian side of Quebec's cultural life, at Loyola Vanier seems to have made a conscious decision to embrace his French-Canadian identity. He had not yet thought about the military career that would become an important stage for the playing out of his nationalism. After Loyola he took his bar exams — law, medicine, and the Church were effectively the only professions open to French Canadians. He was practising law in Montreal when war broke out in August 1914.

He was twenty-six. Posters began to appear urging young men to sign up "For King and Country." But most of Vanier's young friends were hostile or at best indifferent to Canada's involvement in a meaningless foreign war that was being played out by ancient empires on the other side of the world. Before the war was over Ottawa would enact conscription legislation, and the province would be riven with riots whose scars are not completely healed. Jack Granatstein said,

For a French-speaking Canadian to decide to go to war was an act of will in a very real sense. For English Canadians it was the thing to do and it took an act of will not to go. For French-speaking Canadians, it required a conscious decision of duty, service and a willingness to fight.

Fr. Monet said that Vanier's decision was motivated by his religious conviction. He saw the German attack on Belgium and the atrocities against women and children that British propaganda gruesomely (and falsely) reported, not only as inhuman but also as hideously un-Christian. As in almost all the major decisions of his life he explicitly explained this one in terms of his faith, and off he went to war. Because he was a university man he was automatically a candidate for an officers' commission. Professor Desmond Morton of McGill University describes what Vanier found as his training began:

The expeditionary force is formed up at Val Cartier outside Quebec City and there are French Canadians repre-

sented there. What is missing in this organization is a
French Canadian battalion. So noticing this, the relative-
ly few military minded Quebeckers said we better do
something. The Vandoos, the 22nd, is authorized and
formed.[1] And Georges Vanier was one of the young offi-
cers, totally inexperienced and untrained, who joined and
who proceeded to try to learn the business. Easier for him
because his English was pretty good, but having to learn
it with English language textbooks and manuals, from
English-speaking instructors for the most part in an
English-speaking kind of military organization.

In fact, some 50,000 francophones served in that war, and
while that figure is less than one-tenth of the 650,000-
strong Canadian army, from a community who had for
almost two centuries been systematically told by their
anglophone rulers that they, the French Canadians, were
not welcome to the full fruits of the increasingly prosperous young nation, that 50,000 is a very substantial figure.

Many of those men were poor and this was at least a
job. The same was true for tens of thousands of anglo-
phone recruits. Many, like their English-Canadian counterparts, were just looking for adventure. In both communities Georges Vanier was a standout "right from the start,"
historian Jack Granatstein says, "because of his pan-
Canadian, his imperial sense of duty and service." He
enlisted with the rank of lieutenant and soon became
actively involved in recruiting for the Royal 22nd
Regiment. In March 1915 they set off for Nova Scotia for
more training. At times this simply meant marching twen-

1. "Vandoos" is the colloquial anglicization of *vingt-deux*.

ty miles in the snow "to toughen them up." Later that summer the Vandoos were shipped off to France with Vanier as their machine-gun officer. He wrote:

Never in my wildest flights of imagination could I have foretold that one day I would march through the country I loved so much in order to fight in its defence. Perhaps I should not say "in its defence" because it is really in defence of human rights, not solely of French rights.

Vanier's letters from the front at first downplayed the drudgery, despair, and horrors of the battlefield. He wrote home to his mother,

At night the effect is faerie-like, fireworks illuminating the German lines, shells exploding in a burst of light which is fantastic and picturesque. One gets so quickly accustomed to the most abnormal sort of life. The trenches are relatively safe. If a chap keeps his head well down, he's not likely to be hit. This of course applies to rifle and machine gun fire. Shell fire is harder to avoid. And whether you're hit or not is largely a matter of chance. The game is worth the candle. I would not exchange the marvellous experiences I have gone through for five years of life. The weather has been very favourable and the trenches have been very dry. But as soon as the wet weather sets in, we shall probably be ankle deep in mud.

He wrote almost daily. His words demonstrate that his sense of family was a sustaining force for the ordeal that soon became very different from what he had described in his cheerful letter about the relative safety of the trenches. As he had forecast, the November rains changed things drastically; the tone of his letters home changed too.

A dismal morning, low clouds. Everything is heavy. You feel oppressed and stifled. You paddle in a foot of mud and water. These are appropriate conditions for the month of the dead.

He had found the challenges and the comradeship of the army stimulating and rewarding, and trench life in those first weeks an adventure. It was an adventure that soon became filthy and depressing, but he had enlisted for the long term, not for a good time, and he stuck with it. In June 1916, Vanier, already decorated for bravery, was knocked out when a German shell exploded close by. He said it was only the fact that the ground had been softened by all that rain that saved his life. The injuries were serious enough to land him in the hospital and then in a convalescent centre back in England. Jack Granatstein told us that Vanier was badly shell-shocked, the name given to the prodigious damage to the nervous system that is committed by a combination of the explosion itself and the pervasive fear that a conscious act of courage can keep at bay. But after an immense explosion has blasted you into unconsciousness and you awake covered in your own blood, shell shock can invade the spirit and destroy the will to live.

Shell shock [usually] finished people. Or if they came back after a bad period in the trenches, they weren't much good afterwards. People probably have only so much courage and after a time the well runs dry. Well, Vanier clearly was able to pump up the level again and to continue to serve and to sound optimistic to his parents, to persuade his troops that they were doing something important and to persuade himself that what he was doing was important.

After his time in the convalescence centre, he volunteered to go back to the battlefield but was offered a support post well back from the frontlines. He refused. "I feel it's my duty to see this sacred war through," he wrote.

I don't mean that I revel in the noise of bursting steel. There's the tremendous consolation of being in the thick of it, of the biggest fight that has ever taken place for the triumph of liberty. That sometime or other, we have all wished that we had lived in Napoleonic days. But the present days are fuller of romance, of high deeds and of noble sacrifices.

The elevated language is characteristic. His biographer Deborah Cowley said, in the documentary, that he was

passionate about poetry and he carried a little copy of Shelley's poems in his breast pocket throughout most of the war, together with a picture of his mother and his favourite sister, Frances. So he's sort of Georges Vanier the romantic, as well.

It was not uncommon for soldiers in that war to carry poems into battle; many of those men were university students or graduates. A pocket book popular among the British university lads, who had all studied the classics, was *The Odes of Horace*. Stories circulated about how books of poetry or of prayer carried in a breast pocket had stopped a bullet and saved a life. But poetry and prayer, while they comforted the men in the trenches, did not mediate the life and death decisions of every day nor stay the hand of even the devout and gentle Georges Vanier when it came to exercising the traditional authority of a wartime commander. Jack Granatstein told us about one aspect of the maintenance of discipline that now seems sufficiently extreme to have, in 2001, led a group of parliamentarians in Ottawa to publicly apologize to the families concerned.

> *There was a sense on the part of the officers and certainly on the part of the men as well that it would be disastrous if [The Royal 22nd] should be seen as anything other than the equal or the superior of any of the English-speaking battalions and discipline therefore was a matter of French-Canadian pride. Discipline was a matter of showing the English that we could do it just as well as they could. And there were something like twenty-five Canadians executed by firing squads in the First World War for cowardice or desertion or other military crimes. Vanier himself presided at at least one execution of a deserter. This was extraordinary, except that it was deemed necessary by the commander of the unit, Colonel Tremblay, because he believed, as Vanier did, that we had to demonstrate that we were the best disciplined, the best battalion, the one that would do anything to achieve the objective. And if it meant shooting your own men who broke down or deserted, well then so be it.*

The 22nd fought effectively at some of the most decisive battles of World War I, including the blood bath at Ypres, which the soldiers called "Wipers." Then, at 5:30 a.m. in the morning on the 9th of April, 1917, the attack on Vimy Ridge began.[2] The French and the English had already failed to take the ridge, and Canada had inherited

2. For an account of the Vimy campaign, see Part Ten.

this seemingly impossible task. It would be a turning point for our armies' reputation in Europe, and for the country's sense of self-esteem and independence.

Vanier wrote home about how the infantry leapt out of the shell holes and trenches and emerged from secret tunnels right up against the enemy lines in a hail of bullets and a bitter northwest wind. The leading battalions gained their objectives quickly and the 22nd followed through, capturing machine guns, trench mortars, and hundreds of prisoners. The troops' morale was high and Georges wrote about the wonderful consolation to be driving the *Boches* out of France. But there was another battle that ended Georges Vanier's war, and came within a hair's breadth of taking his life.

It was a German offensive at a place called Cherisy. The machine-gun fire was ferocious, and in the first few minutes two bullets ripped into Vanier, one of them smashing some ribs. His wounds were serious but not life-threatening, but as the medics were dressing them a shell exploded right beside them. He wrote restrainedly that "this final explosion caused rather unpleasant shrapnel wounds to my right and left legs." In fact the right knee was shattered, and the leg was amputated the next day. Many of the 22nd's officers were killed at Cherisy, and not a single one survived unwounded. Once again Vanier would draw on his faith. Deborah Cowley said,

Even though when he'd had his leg amputated, he rarely said anything that gave any indication of the pain, the suffering. The only word of complaint I ever read in his letters was "Oh, God, how the nights are long!"

And Jack Granatstein added,

The extraordinary thing is that he decides he wants to stay in the army. There he is, with one leg, a wooden leg in effect, and he is convinced that he can continue to serve. And Arthur Currie, the commander of the Canadian Corps during the war, says to him, it's impossible.[3] You can't serve, you've only got one leg. And Vanier says, do you want people with brains or do you want people with legs? It's a good line.

Among the many changes that World War I wrought in Canada was that now the French Canadians had their own regular force regiment, the Vandoos, the Royal 22nd, a regiment of the highest distinction after Vimy. Vimy had brought Georges Vanier the *Légion d'Honneur*, pinned on him personally by France's minister of war; he had also been awarded the Military Cross and Bar, and the Distinguished Service Order. And now the Vandoos were home, based at the Citadel in Quebec City, and Vanier was the regiment's second-in-command.

One day in 1919 his old friend and sometime commanding officer, Tommy Tremblay, took a striking young woman for lunch to Montreal's Ritz Hotel. Vanier was at a nearby table. Tremblay pointed him out to the woman, saying, "That's the man for you."

Pauline Archer was the only child of Quebec Superior Court Judge Charles Archer and his wife Thérèse. Pauline had grown up in a large house on Sherbrooke Street where she had an entire floor to herself. When she met Georges Vanier she was twenty-two. A few months later, he pro-

3. The story of Sir Arthur Currie is the subject of Part Ten.

posed. On September 29, 1921, they were married at Montreal's Basilica. His brother came along on the honeymoon as the chauffeur, Georges being uneasy about driving with his artificial leg. But it wasn't long before Georges slipped his brother five dollars and told him to get lost. Professor Morton said,

It was a very good marriage. She was very intelligent, very able . . . a very supportive kind of person. I mean not exactly in the modern style of equal partner, because I think she had great strengths that he didn't have, particularly her awareness of the realities of culture and what was current and interested in music and so on, probably much more than he was, I think. But she has her strengths, he has his and they worked together.

The postwar governor general of Canada, Lord Byng, had been the British Commander of the Canadian Corps in Europe, and in the optimistic atmosphere of the early 1920s Byng and Vanier cemented a friendship that had begun in the trenches. Byng had "no side, as the British would say," according to Professor Morton.

He wasn't an arrogant guy in any way. He was very friendly, a bit scruffy-looking, didn't go in for spit and polish. Perhaps that was pretty good for the Canadians because they didn't either. And he kind of got to know and like the Canadians and they kind of got to know and like him. And after the war, he becomes the governor general. And for the first time, instead of bringing out a British officer to help guide his affairs in Canada, he invites his old friend and admirer, junior friend, Georges Vanier, to come to Government House [as Aide de Camp].

There are odd bits of gossip that emerge from the story, some seemingly inconsistent with the image of propriety that attaches to vice-regality, though certainly not to the rich sense of humour that the Vaniers shared. Pauline was said to have remarked to a visiting British aristocrat that he should not hesitate to take advantage of a Rideau Hall chambermaid, but perhaps the story says more about the colour of the inner circle they moved in than it does about the real person. The Byngs and the Vaniers became close. Byng arranged for Vanier to spend some time at the British Staff College at Camberley, near London, and it was there in 1923 that their first child, Thérèse Marie Cherisy, was born. In 1924 he was promoted Lieutenant Colonel. Back in Canada, probably with a word from the governor general to open the door, Vanier was invited by External Affairs to be the Canadian military representative at the League of Nations in Geneva, working on the Disarmament Convention. When their fourth child and third son Jean was born in 1928, Lord Byng sent a note saying that perhaps Pauline was thinking of starting a league of nations of her own.

It is worth pausing at this point to note that while it seems natural enough today that a distinguished and much-decorated soldier should become a highly placed diplomat, such a sequence of events was not at all natural in the 1920s if the soldier in question happened to be a French Canadian. Jack Granatstein told us that this was

a time when a French-speaking officer in the Department of External Affairs writes a memorandum in French to the Prime Minister and the Prime Minister says, this man has gone mad. Literally says that he's crazy because he sent this memorandum in French. Vanier would know not to send a memorandum in French. But he's a French Canadian who understands that at this point in Canada the anglophones rule and French Canadians have to go along to get along.

Lord Byng died in 1935, and within a few years a number of old friends and relatives were also gone. Vanier began to reflect on death in a way that was different from those dramatic years in Flanders. He became more diligent than ever in his religious observance, going to mass almost every day, and taking half an hour for private prayer. Busyness was never an excuse for overlooking his acts of devotion. Professor Morton said that "for him the Catholic faith was a living entity."

It guided his life. He believed profoundly, but not super-stitiously. He was a remarkable Christian because his brain never got in the way of his faith. He could reconcile them, which is not a common or universal achievement. And he made people feel, certainly I did in his presence, that this was something I too should explore.

In December 1938 Vanier was posted to the embassy in Paris. The events that would build the launch pad for World War II were in rapid motion. In July, Germany and Russia signed a Non-Aggression Pact, and in September the uneasy peace that northern Europe had known for scarcely two decades ended with the Nazi invasion of Poland. By May of 1940 it was clear that France could not hold out. Georges sent the family to London. A month later, among the last foreign diplomats to do so, he made his way to the coast where a Canadian destroyer, HMCS *Fraser*, brought him to England and the family.

When Hitler conquered France he found some powerful officials willing to collaborate, including, ironically, a distinguished World War I soldier, Marshall Pétain, who set up a puppet government in Vichy. The resistance movement, and the "Free French" in exile, looked to General Georges de Gaulle for leadership. "De Gaulle saw himself as the embodiment of Free France," Desmond Morton said, and

> *Vanier saw de Gaulle in much the same way. [He] was dismayed to find his country, Canada, had continued to keep diplomatic relations with the Vichy regime. Why did Canada do that? For two reasons. One was that Quebec thought that the Vichy regime was just about the right government for France. The [Vichy] slogan of "travail, famille, patrie" would have been a good slogan for Quebec society. A Catholic presence in the government — [which] Pétain insisted on — looked pretty good to Quebeckers. What was wrong with all of this?*

So the Ottawa government did that for Quebec reasons and also for Allied reasons. Somebody should stay in touch with France. Maybe Vichy would be a good listening post, at least that was the polite explanation given to English Canada. "Our Allies want this from us." Well! Vanier wasn't buying either line.

He wrote a letter to Prime Minister Mackenzie King asking to be relieved of his duties. The letter was ignored. He was instructed to take command of the military district of Quebec, a tough job in a province that had not forgotten the conscription riots of World War I. He persuaded the High Command to bring more Quebeckers into command and strategic planning, and was moderately successful in increasing the numbers of volunteers from Quebec over what had been expected.

Their fifth and last child, Michel Paul, was born in July 1941. That same year, their thirteen-year-old son Jean announced that he was joining the navy. Pauline and Georges recognized that Jean was serious. Volunteers that young were much a part of British naval tradition, and here was a bright young Quebecker bucking the tide that was holding back so many of his friends. They signed the consent forms, and he went on to become the youngest executive officer on any warship in the history of Britain or Canada.

In 1942 the Canadian government withdrew its recognition of Vichy, Vanier was in favour again, and was promoted major general. A year later he was appointed ambassador to the Free French. De Gaulle set up the exiled capital in Algiers, and Vanier got on a military flight to North Africa. Jack Granatstein told us that the British and Americans found de Gaulle a very difficult ally.

You know Churchill's story that he had many crosses to bear during the war but the cross of Lorraine [the double cross-barred emblem of Free France] was the heaviest cross of all. De Gaulle acts as if he's the leader of a great power and demands that his concerns, his status, his role, his nation's role be respected in everything.

This drove Churchill crazy. It certainly upset Franklin Roosevelt. And the Canadian government —

which is a minor player in this, to be fair — isn't going to take the initiative, isn't going to step out in front and urge the British and the Americans to recognize de Gaulle. But there's no doubt that such support as de Gaulle has in Canada is led by Vanier and de Gaulle knows it. . . . [And yet] de Gaulle will eventually betray them.

Pauline wrote that it was impossible to describe the atmosphere in Algiers, a mixture of heroism and decadence that would make the film *Casablanca* seem a masterpiece of understatement. A long line of guests came and went from their new home. Among the regulars were ambassadors, resistance fighters, and of course, de Gaulle and his entourage, who wanted recognition by the Americans and knew that Vanier was his first advocate. It would be difficult, maybe impossible, to evaluate the extent of Vanier's influence in Washington, but in 1944, President Roosevelt did beat the other allies to the punch and declared American recognition of de Gaulle as the leader of the government of liberated France.

Meanwhile the Royal 22nd Regiment distinguished itself brilliantly again, in the Italian campaign, and as its former commander in chief, Vanier was invited to the Vatican to meet Pope Pius XII. Vanier had been outraged at the Vatican's refusal to allow priests in Vichy France to administer the sacraments to resistance fighters, and according to Fr. Monet, he took the opportunity to speak out.

Georges Vanier was increasingly shocked at how many of the Catholics and the Catholic hierarchy in France were much more sympathetic to Vichy and to the Pétainists than they were to the Free French and said to the Pope that this was going to be a great scandal for the church. A few weeks after that, the French bishops started allowing the French priests to be chaplains to the Underground.

With the German surrender of Paris on August 26th, 1944, the Vaniers prepared to return to their old posting there. But France was still far from safe, and Georges was advised to return without Pauline. He said, "You try to stop her. I can't." Someone suggested that she might be safer in uniform. She borrowed one from a Red Cross worker on leave, and entered Paris with Georges on the 8th of September as the Canadian Red Cross Representative to France.

With the liberation, minor collaborators faced humiliations and the court of public opinion, but more serious offenders were in danger of prison or worse. Vanier's loyalty to the church may have skewed his judgment at this point. Historian Jack Granatstein says that some of these dubious characters were actually helped into Canada by the Vaniers — at the request of the church.

He becomes a conduit to get into Canada a number of French fascists who were fleeing de Gaulle's regime. Quite extraordinary that this gallant soldier who understood the horrors of fascism would still nonetheless be prepared to turn his gaze away from someone's undoubtedly monstrous record. It's a blind spot in him. It suggests to me that a recommendation from a priest was worth more than the good judgment of his own common sense.

As ambassador to France he accompanied de Gaulle on the French President's visit to Ottawa in 1945. It would be years before Vanier had any reason to doubt de Gaulle's friendship. Hadn't the general written to him that "from the very first day you were the faithful friend of the Free French and the evident defender of their cause. Every fresh proof that France gives of her vitality is homage to your clear-sightedness."

When Colonel Tremblay died in 1950, Georges was named honorary colonel of the Royal 22nd. In April the Vaniers sailed to Canada for the ceremony and to see their son Byngsy enter the priesthood. The country was approaching another step in the long weaning away from its past as a British colony: we were now ready, for the first time, to advise the Queen that the next governor general, HM's official representative and the titular head of state, should actually be a Canadian not another Brit. Vanier's name came up, but since Canada already had a French-Canadian head of government, Prime Minister Louis St. Laurent, it was thought impossible to appoint a French-Canadian head of state. Vanier went into retirement, and began to spend time at the old family retreat at Lake Memphremagog. Perhaps he had even put any future pub-lic service out of mind, but he had, in fact, not been forgot-ten in Ottawa. It was in 1959, "perhaps to his surprise," according to Professor Granatstein, that

John Diefenbaker, as Prime Minister, approaches him and asks him to be governor general. His surprise I say, because he is a Liberal. But Diefenbaker decided it would be a good thing to have a francophone as governor gener-al and shore up some support in Quebec. And so Vanier is asked, and being a man of duty he says yes.

The appointment was decided officially at a special cabinet meeting in Halifax, over which the Queen herself formally presided. His installation speech began, "My first words are a prayer that God will give me the strength to carry on this responsibility. I am very weak and it is only out of my weakness that I can get God's strength." They moved into Rideau Hall and began remaking both the building and the role of governor general. Biographer Deborah Cowley said in our film,

The first thing he and his wife did when they entered Rideau Hall was to transform one of the upstairs bed-rooms into a chapel and he visited the chapel briefly every morning of his life in Rideau Hall. And if he was travel-ling, he made clear that he had that time for prayer. They inspired people. They brought an inspiration to Canadians that I don't think has been matched since. They travelled to little villages, to large cities non-stop, even though they were both in their seventies, late sixties by that point, sharing their passionate belief in both parts of Canada, French and English. And since they both were completely bilingual and bicultural they could do this so beautifully.

Some of our French-Canadian statesmen and women, among them Louis St. Laurent and Jeanne Sauvé, have had a patrician presence seldom if ever seen among their anglo-phone counterparts. In this regard Georges Vanier was striking. Tall, his bearing was always stately despite the limp. The full-swept white mustaches flowed out from beneath a pair of sharp eyes that always seemed to have a humorous twinkle at their corners. Even when he was dressed in the plainest of civilian clothes you could almost see the gold braid on his cuffs and the gleaming row of medals across his chest. The Queen appointed him to the Imperial Privy Council in 1963.

Every Sunday they went to mass in a different local church, to meet citizens on their own ground. Only Pauline knew how difficult it was becoming for Georges to be a public person, but on April 8th, 1963, when he suffered a mild heart attack, it was time to stop. He would stay in harness long enough to say an official farewell to John Diefenbaker, the man who had appointed him governor general, and to swear in Lester Pearson as Prime Minister. He was surprised when despite his heart attack Pearson asked him if he'd stay on beyond September 1964, when his term as governor general would end. Georges agreed so long as his health and the Lord allowed him to. In the spring he attended the annual press gallery dinner, a traditionally rowdy affair whose principal speakers vie with each other in rough language and outrageous jokes, and the hottest ticket in town to which non-members of the gallery, if invited, are made to feel that they have been accorded one of the great privileges of life. On that occasion, which this writer attended, it felt like such a privilege: General Vanier's speech as guest of honour so far outstripped the others in both laughter and wisdom that everyone felt agreeably humbled. His theme was the occupational options open to an unemployed governor general.

It was a period in our history when those old wounds and divisions that began this chapter began to grow very nasty once more. The generally relative calm of Quebec's

Quiet Revolution were punctuated by a couple of bombs. "The temperature is getting hotter," Jack Granatstein said, *and Vanier probably is seen by many in Quebec as a sell-out, a* vendu, *not a* Vandoo . . . *but a* vendu, *a sell-out. And he I'm sure must have found this excruciating. Here he was, someone who believed in Canada, believed in a pan-Canadian vision of the country, being damned in his own province by his own people.*

During the St-Jean Baptiste Day Parade in 1964, both Vanier and members of the Royal 22nd were booed while a small plane cruised overhead dropping separatist pamphlets. The majority of the crowd shouted down the separatists, but Vanier was furious. Later he would laugh about it, saying, "What would you like separatists to do? To give you an ovation?"

A few months later, despite the Quebec situation, the Queen herself paid a visit to Canada. Hers was soon followed by one from an old friend of the Vaniers. Professor Granatstein said,

De Gaulle seems to, by the 1960s, seems to be supporting what Vanier sees as the destructive elements in Quebec, supporting the separatists. Thinking of Canada as an anglo country only, thinking of Canada as part of the United States almost and therefore a nation that is not really able to play a part in the world. To Vanier this is a betrayal by a man that he had revered, a betrayal of the country that he believed in and it's shattering to him.

Georges Vanier died two months before that betrayal culminated with de Gaulle idiotically shouting a separatist rallying-cry from the balcony of Montreal City Hall. But "I don't think it was a surprise to Madam Vanier," Deborah Cowley said,

what he did in Montreal . . . shouting "Vive le Quebec libre." She knew ahead of time, and she had a devastating meeting with him and his wife in Paris at which General de Gaulle indicated that this was his feeling about Quebec. And all she said was: "I am so glad my husband is not alive to hear this."

On Saturday night, March 4th, 1967, he had watched his hockey team, the *Canadiens*, beat Detroit, and the next morning he was dead. "The outpouring of affection . . . was absolutely incredible," Deborah Cowley said.

Messages that came in by the thousands, poured into Government House and it was very heart-warming. And even more so was the funeral that I remember very well on a wintry March day in Ottawa. First of all he lay in state in the Senate chamber for quite a long time as people thronged to pay tribute to him. Heads of state from all over the world came to pay tribute. Then after that, the casket was put on a train and travelled to Montreal and on to Quebec City and he was buried in a chapel on the grounds of the Citadel.

That chapel, where our documentary of George Vanier's life comes to an end, was constructed under his order when he had lived at the Citadel, the home of his beloved Royal 22nd. Pauline would live another twenty-four years, be appointed to the Privy Council, and serve as Chancellor of the University of Ottawa. She spent her last days in France at *L'Arche*, the community for handicapped adults that her son Jean had founded. In 1991 at the age of ninety-two, she died and was buried next to her husband in the chapel at the Citadel.

Of the many honours and acts of recognition that came to them both, the last is the most striking testimony to the central role of their Christian faith in those two extraordinary lives: their nomination by the Vatican for beatification, which could pave the way, as Fr. Monet thinks it should, to sainthood.

◆   ◆   ◆

Deborah Cowley is the author of *Georges Vanier: Soldier*. The History Television documentary was written and directed by Daniel Zuckerbrot.

Part Twelve

VLADIMIR VALENTA
OF TRUTH AND COMEDY

When he first came to Canada, we didn't see clearly enough what he had to offer; he was struggling to learn English, and had a hard time getting his ideas across. But I came to see that he had the greatest integrity of anyone I ever met. He lived by his principles. He could not bend his principles.
  – Patricia Phillips, Producer

CBC Edmonton television host and interviewer Colin MacLean remembers his feeling of astonishment: "The phone rang and someone said, 'There's this Academy Award winner washing cars down here at this car wash.' I said, 'No, give me a break.' He said, 'No, no, it's true; I think his name is Valenta.' And I said 'Uh, Vladimir Valenta?' Well I was thunderstruck. I took our cameras down there and then we sat down and talked about why he was here, why he had come to Canada, why he was in Edmonton."

Vladimir Valenta had played a major role in the Czechoslovakian movie *Closely Watched Trains* that won the Academy Award for Best Foreign Film in 1967, and at that point in his life he was famous in the acting and movie community, but he was broke. But that was only the surface of a story that went much further underground, and in an important part of it, quite literally so.

Valenta, who came to Canada from Czechoslovakia in

1968, had done time in Shebram Prison, a brutal holding pen for the slave labourers who were sent down to work the uranium mines there. At forty-two stories beneath the surface it was said to be the deepest mine in the world. Valenta had indeed earned his living as an actor, and a comic actor at that. But both his comedy and his life were driven by a profound commitment to human rights, not a popular motif in the Communist-ruled Czechoslovakia of the postwar period. And while some of his friends afterwards said that Vlad did not like to talk about his time as a political prisoner, in 1990 not long after the Berlin Wall came down he went back there with a group of his fellow former prisoners for a kind of reunion at Shebram.

It was not a sentimental reunion: Vladimir Valenta was on a quest for justice, a constant motif in this plump comic actor's dramatic life. He and his fellow prisoners had been tortured, some of them to the point of death. They had been starved, tormented, often driven mad by their Communist captors who were trying to get confessions out of them and break their wills in order to put them back into the community as penitents, loyal to the great Soviet Cause after all. Valenta was furious when he discovered that in the new Czechoslovakia, among the thousands of former officials who had run the old oppressive regime and sent hundreds of thousands into forced labour camps, torture, and death, only nine had been sentenced for their crimes.

Vladimir Valenta and the other veteran prisoners were filmed by the CBC[1] visiting the abandoned Shebram gulag,

1. This was for a CBC Edmonton project entitled "Closely Watched Freedom."

where they found the underground cell where he had been kept in solitary for three weeks because he insisted on singing the Czech national anthem on the traditional National Day. With the cameras rolling he went down the crumbling weed-grown steps, bent, crept into the tiny square concrete box, looked back at the camera and said,

[I told them] "It's a pig house, but you cannot make me a pig too. I will not eat here." So every day they brought, you know, food, and put it here, hoping that I will touch it, I will give up. I drank only water, I had to leave coffee and the food untouched."

As he looks around the squalor of this low-ceilinged memorial of a nightmare, you can hear a voice off-camera saying, "Watch your head," and Valenta snaps back, "You forget that I was a miner, you idiot."

This was the abrasive man who had returned to post-war Czechoslovakia, to a delicate situation where freedom fighters and the collaborators they detested were trying to work out some kind of co-existence. Valenta was impatient with process, with trying to work things out. He always wanted action now, results now. He didn't mind if his candour and his insistence embarrassed anybody, or made them nervous; that kind of consequence he shrugged off; the consequences he was after were much bigger: to punish the bastards.

When he arrived in Canada in 1968, a big man with a huge belly, a broad, bald head, wide grim face and heavy, black-rimmed glasses, his role in *Closely Watched Trains* brought him small roles in a number of television projects and a few larger films. One who cast him in those early days, the pioneer Canadian director Allan King, describes him as "stern, imposing, authoritative." Voices of people who had known him float through the soundtrack of our documentary. "He had one of those kinds of amazing faces that would look sad even if it was joyful" and "It's hard to imagine . . . Vladimir as a romantic guy because he wasn't. He was grumpy and gruff and that's what he appeared but I mean, he was a romantic at heart."

Nelu Ghiran, another director and believe it or not admirer, said, "He was a prick . . . he didn't care if he hurt your feelings. He didn't mean to."

It was speaking out without regard for the consequences that had put him behind bars in the first place. They threw him into the Pankratz Prison in Prague in 1949 and sentenced him to twelve years for treason against the state. With its nineteenth-century walls and rows of windows it looked like a traditional insane asylum, but inside there were so many highly educated men that they were able to turn the jail into a sort of institution of higher learning, and share their minds with their fellow prisoners. Part of the captor's strategy was to give the prisoner the impression that release was only a month or two away and then just stretch it out, move you to another prison and then another prison and another and so on. This transient incarceration was intended to prevent any effective conspiracies among the prisoners, and bit by bit to morally break them down with one disappointment after another.

One cruel punishment you discovered only after your release. Wives were commonly told that their imprisoned husbands were enemies of the state, imperialist agents, and that they would never see their men again anyway and should divorce them. A man would race home, free at last, to find that he had no home.

One of Valenta's companions, Lumir Salivar, said about the prisons in winter:

You came here to die. It was very cold. The average temperature at that time was around twenty, minus twenty degrees Celsius. We were hungry. It was not enough food. Some people, they committed suicides or some people were killed. The walls were not insulated. The water from the air condensated on the walls. So they were licking the walls just to [get something to drink].

The teaching sessions were permitted as long as they did not get expressly political. Valenta's "higher education" group — perhaps courting a certain amount of emotional danger — tried to keep themselves going by meeting every afternoon to describe to one another the best meal they had ever eaten. If it drove them crazy, they said afterwards, it still gave them marvellous dreams of liberty. Oddly, they were given a film to watch from time to time. Once, Valenta was astonished to see a title come up in the darkness: *Svirdomi (Conscience)*, and then the credit, *A Film by Vladimir Valenta*. And there he was, "In a bloody concentration camp for God's sake!" watching one of his own films, a film about personal responsibility and justice.

The mine at Shebram sent raw uranium to Russia for nuclear weapons and the electrical power generators. Before dawn the prisoners were packed into a small elevator and sent down the forty-two-floor shaft to the chosen working level. They had no protective clothing, just a work jacket, shirt, trousers, and a soft-brimmed hat. Day after day, by hand, they dragged wagonloads of uranium sludge along a gloomily lit tunnel with a single endless track. At twelve hours a day, seven days a week, one prisoner logged his time in the mines at 3658 days.

Valenta's anger and resolve were apparently never eroded. He had enormous mental discipline, and a reverence for the power of words. Another fellow ex-inmate said, "You will discover what a word means and how many times a single word can save you, not your life but your soul." After Valenta's release, another prisoner found dozens of poems he had left behind, scribbled on toilet paper, about life in the camp and the spiritual struggle to retain your sanity and will. His irrepressible anger at injustice and total inability to keep his mouth tactically shut drove him to take terrible risks by provoking his guards with challenges to their humanity, their sense of fairness, their intelligence. The day he went too far was October 28, Independence Day for the old republic of Czechoslovakia, traditionally a day of marching and singing and banners and drinking. But under the Communists the day was silent, the churches closed, public gatherings forbidden, and the national anthem itself outlawed.

One of Valenta's fellow prisoners remembers: "During roll call, (Vladimir) stepped forward. He began to sing the National Anthem. Twenty-five-hundred inmates stood at attention and began to sing with him." Another remembers, "The guards did not dare do anything. We finished the anthem. Vladimir suffered the consequences . . ." A third adds: "They put him into the bunker. There was nothing inside, no washroom, no bed, no chair, absolutely nothing." That was the cell he was filmed revisiting, at the Shebram reunion, a windowless eight-by-eight underground concrete room, with a rusty pair of handcuffs lying in wreckage outside it.

When Valenta began his hunger strike in that cell, soon the whole camp knew that he was living on water and nothing else. After twenty-three days, perhaps fearing that his death would trigger an uncontrollable uprising, the authorities allowed him back into the general prison population. Not, however, without exacting their own petty revenge: they told him his wife had deserted him to marry a Communist party official. He grew very dispirited. He was down to half his weight. He was beginning to think that he would be a prisoner for the rest of this life, when, without any discussion with officials, a letter came announcing his release in 1956. There had been a retrial and he had been found innocent of the charges against him. It had been seven years.

Vladimir Valenta was born in Prague in 1923, four years after Czechoslovakia had become an independent republic. In the national legend, centuries of struggle by artists, farmers, townspeople, and their leaders against foreign occupation had finally led to triumph. He told a friend once that wherever it came from, his commitment to the idea of truth made it hard for him to tell lies even as a kid when a few white lies here and there could have smoothed the way with a difficult parent or teacher. A snapshot shows him on a rocking horse, a little boy with a man's face, a dark earnestness. Much of his childhood was spent in the Stromofka Park, where he would later take his daughter Eva to learn to ride a bicycle, secretly removing the training wheels, after she had climbed aboard. She remembers him saying, "Don't worry, I'll hold you," pushing her into the independence that for him was so primary a value he was prepared to risk her hurting herself. She stayed upright, and was pleased in the end, and perhaps he had in fact been right there, sure she could make it but ready to catch her.

In 1938 Hitler's armies invaded Czechoslovakia announcing the start of World War II. The fantastic misted city of Prague, a many-spired movie set of medieval buildings, beckoning galleries, and lanes, resounded with the sound of jackboots. The new government cancelled the freedoms to which the Czechs had become accustomed. A survivor said, "We did hate the Nazis because they behaved like slave drivers, they behaved like you are nothing and we are everything, we are the supermen of the world."

The Gestapo arrested people for listening to the BBC, their only source of reliable information. There is a photo of Vlad and his younger brother Jiri, both looking profoundly grave. They trusted each other well enough to join the resistance together when Vladimir was seventeen. Once, when he and a friend were delivering a message, they were stopped by a German soldier. As the man approached, Vladimir whispered to his friend to step to the curb and take a pee. When he did, the guard turned away and the boys ran to safety.

When their father was jailed for listening to foreign broadcasts, he found on the walls of the holding cell the signatures of hundreds of Czechs who over the years had also been jailed for defying authority. "It was like the side of a monument," he told the family later. And among all those names he found his own father's signature.

But they survived that most terrible war in their history, and at first the liberation of 1945 was full of hope. The citizens of Prague tossed bouquets to the soldiers clustered like flies on the Soviet tanks rolling in triumph through the beautiful old city, the heroes, the liberators. But within two years any hopes for the return of democracy had been shattered. A venal Czech variant on the Soviet oppressive ideology had replaced the Nazi tyranny. The liberators became an army of occupation. There was a substantial Czech Communist Party, dating back decades, and Stalin's men had no difficulty setting up a puppet government of officials who would do Moscow's bidding disguised as a legitimate government of Czechoslovakia. The formal date of the new occupation had been marked with a veritable ocean of humanity massed around the statue of one of Czechoslovakia's oldest heroes, Jan Hus. To understand the determination of Vladimir Valenta, who lived five and a half centuries later, it is useful to take a brief look at the Hus story, and at the Hus legacy.

Jan Hus (1371–1415) became rector of Charles University in Prague in 1402, and as the various claimants to the Vatican throne (there were three at one point) were snarling at each other over who should be the next Pope, Hus began to attack what he saw as a whole catalogue of serious abuses of clerical authority. His sermons had a distinctly democratic flavour to them. He argued for the right of all communicants, not just the celebrating priest, to drink the sacramental wine, and most importantly for the patriots who over the following centuries rallied around his name (and later his statue) he called for the scriptures to be translated into and the mass to be celebrated in the Czech language. When one of the papal claimants proposed selling indulgences (the forgiveness of sins for money) in order to finance a war, he raged against it, and probably sealed his own fate by declaring that there was no holy ordinance establishing the papacy in the first place.

He was charged with heresy, really just to control his insubordination. He would not recant as demanded, and was burned alive on July 6, 1415. For Czech patriots Jan Hus became the personal symbol of their national aspirations. His story strongly affected Vladimir Valenta, who saw himself as carrying forward the national hero's commitment to the people and to the culture. He decided to deploy the most modern of media and went into film.

His first film, *Conscience*, has been acclaimed as one of the best of Czechoslovakia's postwar period. It is the story of a man who accidentally runs his car over a baby carriage, killing the baby, and driving off without looking back. But while Valenta's aim was a hard-edged moral lesson about the nature of personal responsibility, it was characteristic of the man that he never let it all sink into a swamp of polemical seriousness; he would never abandon his sense of humour and his sensuality. In one scene in

Conscience he has a bureaucrat sensually remove a young woman's underwear in order to apply an official stamp to her buttocks, while she closes her eyes and smiles. All of this in the face of Communist Puritanism and correctness.

Eventually life under the Stalinists got difficult not just for artists and rebels, but also for everyone. Now you had to watch what you said, even in ordinary conversation. People discovered that they could not trust friends or workmates. People began to disappear for speaking out, and, what was worse, sometimes for speaking privately. Many were killed; most went to the camps. Valenta, perhaps foolhardy, just never shut up. With a group of kindred spirits at the studio, he wrote for and helped put out a magazine of reviews and features, ostensibly on film and theatre, but carrying enough thorny comment about the regime to get them all into trouble, It was a piece of Valenta's, in that magazine, that got him charged, convicted, and jailed for treason.

Those seven unspeakable years in the prisons and uranium mines did not break him; they intensified his loathing of the regime and his determination to do something about it. After he was released, abandoned by his first wife, he married a pharmacist named Eva Francova. They moved into Vladimir's father's apartment, and for a while it was a good time to be on the stage and screen. A long-time Communist, Alexander Dubcek, was rising in the ranks of the party and encouraging his colleagues to allow a little more artistic freedom. The anti-Nazi film *Closely Watched Trains* went into production early in 1966, with Valenta superbly cast in the subtly comic role of the stationmaster, and as we have noted it won the Academy Award for Best Foreign Film the following year. The Canadian writer and film director David Cherniak says of it,

That was a marvellous film and the first film, the first Czech film that I'd ever seen and probably one of the, one of the dominant influences which made me want to go study film then. There are some images in that film that stick with you and one of them is Vladimir with the pigeons on his shoulders, talking to them like they're his children. It's a very powerful image.

At that time Valenta was not an experienced actor. The director of *Trains*, Jiri Menzel, said that he had trouble with his lines, but that the face and the natural charisma made it impossible not to watch him with fascination and delight. The film is about resistance to dictatorial authority, its hero a young railway employee who smuggles bombs aboard German munitions trains during the Nazi occupation. Although both the citizens and their Communist rulers detested the Nazis, the Czech-Canadian novelist Josef Skvorecky said, in our documentary, that *Trains* was, all the same, a very courageous movie to make under Communist rule. Although its story was set in the time of the Nazi occupation, it was in fact an indictment of the very kind of brutal authority with which the Communists themselves ruled the country.

We encountered a parallel in Bucharest, filming there for *The Struggle for Democracy*, in the early spring of 1992 just after the fall of the Ceausescu tyranny. The minister of culture in the interim government was Ion Caramitru, a classical actor and theatrical director. When we filmed an interview with him he told us about directing an uncut version of *Hamlet*, in Romanian, during the Ceausescu years, when the theatres were on short rations of heating gas, and people came to the production wearing heavy winter coats and hats and mittens. He told us that after the production the audience would meet the actors at the stage door to talk about their interpretation of the play, and the issues it raises about conscience and personal responsibility that Prince Hamlet faced under the tyranny of his patricidal uncle, and that only the thought-police failed to understand that what they were really discussing was life under the Ceausescus.

In *Closely Watched Trains* a group of citizens in a small Czech town sets about dynamiting German munitions trains. The movie would go on to inspire filmmakers in the free world, probably more for its comedy and its characters than for its politics. Certain sequences became emblematic: there was Valenta as the stationmaster, feeding and talking to pigeons; and then a woman conductor at the railing of the last car in the train bending and kissing her soldier lover as the kiss is slowly broken by the train pulling away.

In the early months of 1968 Dubcek came to power. Dubcek had joined the Communist Party in 1938 when it was illegal, had opposed the Nazis both as a guerilla fighter and organizer of the national resistance movement, and had been appointed a member of the powerful Central Committee soon after the formation of the postwar Communist government. In 1967, encouraged by what seemed like widespread public unrest, he had begun to move against the arbitrary and unpopular party chief, Novotny. Moscow, under Brezhnev, was preoccupied with its own problems and did not support Novotny. The Party made Dubcek first secretary, whereupon he announced that he was sweeping away the old instruments of repression, that Czechoslovakia's Communism would become what he called "socialism with a human face," a true people's government. Freedom of speech, open discussion, and even dissent would be not tolerated but encouraged. Czechs could travel; a new wind was blowing. The world called it the Prague Spring; Valenta was doubtful. Prison, the camps, and all the worst aspects of Communism had taught him that liberties handed down from above are not real liberties. And he was right. At eleven o'clock on the night of August 19, 1968, Soviet tanks rolled across the Czech border. August 21 became Czechoslovakia's day of infamy as Soviet armour filled the streets of Prague.

This time the people were not protesting local Communist rulers. It was the Soviets they were talking to now, the Soviet commanders and soldiers in the streets. Under the statue of Jan Hus — whom they had blindfolded as if to save him the sight of another occupation of his country — the Czechs, many of whom spoke workable Russian, asked the soldiers why they were there: "We are your friends. What are you doing here?" The soldiers said, Well, they didn't know exactly. Some of them weren't even sure where they were. Some said they thought they were putting down a German uprising.

For a while a group of citizens held the radio station and tried to keep the people informed about what was happening. A permanent watch was set up around the statue of Jan Hus. Crowds coalesced around the tanks in the streets, as if their sheer moral courage could stop those tons of armoured force; they could not. Many were killed, crushed under the grinding tracks. All the while, at the dreary, dirty steel-and-glass Communist-era broadcast centre, the Prague station played *"Ma Vlast," (My Homeland)*. When the Russians forced their way into the studio, the Czechs fought them with bare hands until the studio floor was awash in blood.

Vladimir Valenta was abroad in London to promote *Closely Watched Trains* when the news of this new Soviet occupation broke. A difficult decision lay before him. He and Eva had children now, and for Valenta to go back and fight the Soviets would be to put his family in danger. He decided to emigrate. As a boy he had read Jack London. For him, as for so many Europeans, Canada had a romantic appeal. A friend said he closed his eyes and put his finger on a map. Within a week they were on their way to Edmonton.

If a lot of Canadians think of Edmonton as just another prairie capital on a cold, endless flat plain with nothing but cattle, wheat, and oil, for Vladimir Valenta it was an adventure in a snow-covered movie set where you could do and say and write whatever you wanted: wide-open spaces, wilderness, freedom, independence, privacy. He told people that he was going to be a lumberjack.

The Czechoslovakian lumberjack living with his family in a remote cabin in the bush, howling like a wolf (like a character he would later play in a Canadian made-for-TV movie) didn't quite materialize. At the beginning he bore the immigrant's cross with dignity. In Colin MacLean's footage you can see him, bald, with his great stomach and heavy dark glasses washing a car at the Edmonton car wash with the vigour of a man half his age, or strolling with his stiff rolling walk among the pines on the outskirts of town, his eyes roving happily over the snowy landscape.

Producers cast him in clichéd fat-man heavy-accent immigrant semicomic parts, never a principal, never a hero. He wanted to play something meaningful, dignified, mature, but they often made him a clown.

His blunt, uncompromising discourse did not help; he was restless with, perhaps even contemptuous of, Canadian tact and concern for image. He felt that he was being taken for granted as the available guy with a funny accent. After thirty or so television shows and a couple of tax-shelter unwatchable films he had had enough. He approached both the University of Alberta and the National Film Board to see if his film and stage experience could be put to use in teaching. They both gave him contracts. Valenta was an uncompromising idealist; for him the theatre was a temple and film an instrument of social awareness. But the mainstream of Canadian film and television had long since abandoned such ideas, vigorous as they had been in the early days of CBC Television. As the pioneer Canadian director Allan King said, "We have an industrial manufacturing approach to making films, even more so for television, which is simply a vehicle for advertising." Valenta found that disgusting. Students found him blunt to the point of rudeness. He was always correcting them. But many said later that while he was more charismatic than comprehensible, there was a power in his polemic and in his person, and they found themselves using what he had taught them, imitating his style, and reproducing his passion.

Eva found a good job as a pharmacist at the University of Alberta hospital, and Valenta could easily have retired. He gave up teaching, and for five years he financed, edited, and published *The Telegram*, a newspaper monitoring Communist regimes around the world, largely written by freelance expatriate Czechs. There was even a children's page. *The Telegram*'s voice joined others like Josef Skvorecky and the poet and playwright Vaclav Havel, crying out for freedom and justice in Czechoslovakia. He was warned that he had better not try to visit Czechoslovakia, as he would be thrown in jail for treason once again. And yet his sense of the rightness, even the nobility, of his cause was marred by a reaction from the homeland that hurt him deeply: some of the very people in Czechoslovakia whose treatment he had protested and exposed now shunned him. They felt that by emigrating he had avoided the real battle at home.

Then, in 1989, the old Communist regime began to crumble in Russia and its protectorates, along with the Berlin Wall. During that almost completely unexpected change in the axis of the world, that winter of '89 to '90, Valenta was online on the Internet, and as these spectacular events came over the newswires and airwaves of the Western World, he was sending out messages just as fast as he was able to type, brimming with the latest news. Censorship kept most of the Western press out of the Soviet-ruled countries at first, but Valenta's computer gave him access to all the newspapers he had time to read, and he was able to provide his Czech friends on both sides of the Atlantic with an international summary of everything that was happening.

In Czechoslovakia Vaclav Havel became the leader of a bloodless transformation they called the Velvet Revolution, and his people asked him to take over as president of the republic: the Czechs made a poet and playwright their head of government. Next they would bring Dubcek back from exile to cheers in the streets and to a National Assembly that would unanimously vote him their chairman.[2]

It may seem a little odd that out of this journalistic initiative in newly hopeful change in the greater world, Valenta would emerge with a new and irrepressible enthusiasm: he would star in a cooking show on TV. The goofy premise was that he was the long-lost relative of the female co-host, and he had just arrived in Canada with a suitcase full of sausages. Valenta was massive and had a sort of sad comedy about him, while that co-host was a sprightly, small, funny, and provocative Irish woman. It got a little wild and confused for a cooking show. There were frequent arguments between the two cooks. Valenta and the director would get into shouting matches after thirteen takes, in each of which he drove the crew nuts because he did something they weren't ready for.

2. Alexander Dubcek died in 1992 of injuries sustained in a car crash.

Perhaps it was a brilliant idea that failed, or even a show before its time, given the proliferation of oddball cooking shows in the new universe of specialized cable and satellite channels that was in place within the decade.

That Irish woman, the co-host, was Patricia Phillips, an actor and writer and later the executive producer of *The Canadians*. Phillips had first met Valenta in about 1987 when she was invited to Edmonton as a script editor to help producer Tom Radford and this Czech immigrant named Valenta polish up an earlier proposal for a television series on the early days of Alberta. She says that she found

this big huge bear of a guy who had a Tandy 100 laptop computer and his one hand completely covered the keyboard. He was totally intimidating. I said, "What have I gotten myself into?" He had the most extreme views on everything. On the first day we worked together it just all fell apart towards the end of the afternoon. We had a huge fight, and I went back to the hotel saying, "That's it. It's all over." But next day he turns up with a big cardboard box, and he brings out all this food, sausages, containers of soup, and he says, "Now we eat." We started to eat and talk over the stuff from the previous afternoon, and it was a great day. And at the end of the day I loved him.

They developed the cooking show *Too Many Cooks* around 1992, after Phillips had moved to Edmonton to start a production company with her husband Andy Thomson. It was probably a good thing that it did not last, because that was when the idea bloomed of going back to Czechoslovakia to try bringing to justice the officials who had put him and his colleagues through such misery and pain.

The film of that visit shows him shambling gloomily across one of Prague's many bridges, then with a group of fellow ex-inmates pushing open the rusted, barred gate of the Shebram mines; and with the same companions in the cruel low-ceilinged bunker where he had lived in solitary confinement without eating. And finally in the countryside where he had been raised, outside the Church of the Dissident Brethren, we see twin cypress trees that once stood as a secret sign of the outlawed faith, from the time when Rome was killing its heretics. Inside, in the gentle gloom Valenta looks in total absorption at the words of Hus's sermons inscribed into the walls by Jan Hus himself.

There was even a reunion for the people who made *Closely Watched Trains*, held in the train station where it had been shot. Cast and crew welcomed home the big, gruff man who thirty-three years before had played the station-master, who had fed and talked to pigeons. The villagers who were served by the station turned out as well, and let the filmmakers know that they, the local citizens, considered that the movie really belonged to them.

So there were some warm and rewarding aspects to that journey, but it was not, he felt, really a journey home, nor was he any more inclined to forget and forgive than he had been when he set out. This was a man who was almost brutally obsessed with what he took to be the meaningful truths, the truths that mattered—a man whose candour punished his enemies but also often embarrassed his friends. Everywhere he saw the transforming greed and corruption of power. He saw Nazis who had become Communists and now those same Communists holding power as capitalists. He had no intention of staying: "No," he had said to a friend who asked, before he left Canada, if he would renounce his new citizenship and return to live in Prague, "I will go and get my business done. I will go and visit my friends, I am Canadian." Not surprisingly, he did not succeed in finding the justice he had hoped for. He visited his friends, and he went home.

During his last years he was blessed with a grand-daughter, Dashenka. In a snapshot he lies holding her in his large round arms: one of those rare moments that filled his face with innocence and made him smile. "It's unfortunate that he wasn't around for more of her life," his daughter Eva said,

> they were really starting to understand each other, and you know, it clicked between them. I remember at one point there was even a children's page [in The Telegram]. He wanted to make sure that the children would, you know . . . he wanted somehow to keep the Czech spirit alive even though, you know, people went to Canada or Australia or, you know, Western Europe.

He died on May 13, 2001. Five months later, Czechoslovakia celebrated its Independence Day, and the trim ranks of her very own briskly marching soldiers in dress uniform centred the celebration not on the statue of Jan Hus but on that of a modern dissident and founder of the republic, Thomas Masaryk, the statue newly restored and remounted after having been found in a Communist-era warehouse. There were among the celebrants many more than he would perhaps have guessed who knew about and valued Vladimir Valenta's commitment to justice and liberty. Happily, before he died they had awarded him the Masaryk Medal for service to his country.

In some ways he was an unlikely hero, but those rough edges, the rudeness and impatience with compromise, unquestionably contributed to the big man's credibility, and to the love he engendered among those able to overlook the prickly parts. A friend said, "He's like some big shabby cathedral . . . you know, that had this huge history behind it; that had a kind of beauty and grace about it and this shabby kind of human skin." A living monument of a man who always insisted: "Go back to your heart, go back to your soul . . . go back to your kitchen to find the truth."

Vladimir Valenta, 1923–1991.

◆ ◆ ◆

The History Television documentary was written and directed by Tom Radford.

Part Thirteen

MOSES COADY
BEYOND THE MOUNTAIN

The world calls loudly for a real democratic formula to bring life to all its people. It is not going to be done by guns, making armies or bombs, but by a program in which the people themselves will participate. This is democracy not only in the political sense but it is participation by the people in economic, social, and educational forces which condition their lives.
– Michael Moses Coady

As risky as it is to propose any part of this country as the possessor of landscape that is uniquely memorable, few who have spent time on Nova Scotia's Cape Breton Island would begrudge that blest territory some such encomium. Almost no matter which way the wind comes from, it carries the scent of the sea, and that briny freshness blows across green fields and hills of an Irish intensity, and up the slopes of ancient mountains that the millennia have rounded off but left looming and majestic. Like the Great Lakes, the Prairies, the Tundra, and the Rockies, Cape Breton often gives people who were born and grew up there an inclination to attribute the best parts of their character to the inspiring beauty of the Island that nourished them. Moses Coady was one of those. Coady was a Cape Breton boy who walked out of the Margaree Valley and into the pages of history, and when people asked him whence came the poetic spirit, the insistent creativity and the irresistible confidence, he would point to the hills. Ellen Arsenault who worked for him in his later years said, "He thought there was no place like [the] Margaree. He loved where he was born and brought up, and it was beautiful, there's no question." And Father MacDonnell, a former president of St. Francis Xavier University, told us,

> *Oh, he had the soul of poet. Going down, driving along the shore road to Halifax, one day he came into some marvellous rock faces. And oh, he took off. "How Mother Earth must have shuddered when she delivered these marvellous things unto us," he says. He loved this country. There's no question about it.*

This poetic spirit was not attached to the person of a dreamy and idealistic preacher, although he did his share of preaching, and both dreams and idealism were very much part of the man. Moses Coady was a hands-on, down-to-earth activist. His ideas and energy — and above all his *presence* — stimulated thousands of men and women to free themselves from economic feudalism. His practical approach to community self-help was an alternative to both the insidious deviousness of communism and the cowboy capitalism of America, but he was not a politician, an economist, or an industrialist. He was a Roman Catholic priest.

Moses Michael Coady was born on January 3, 1882, high up on the mountain overlooking the Margaree Valley. Throughout his life he came back to the Margaree when he needed to straighten things out, recharge his batteries, or stiffen his resolve.

Moses was the second of eleven children born to

Michael J. Coady, known as "Whistling Mick," and Sarah J. Coady, who was born a Tompkins. He was baptized Moses after the progenitor of a founding Margaree family, the Doyles. His grandfather had fought England for Irish economic independence. It is likely that young Moses's Irish heritage contributed to his poetic sensibility. The Tompkins and the Coady families lived together in a frame house you can still see up on the mountainside, and as the babies kept on coming and the few small rooms kept shrinking, Michael Coady found some farmland down near Margaree Forks and began building a house. There are still Coadys living in the house today.

Most Margaree families worked the land, raised livestock, fished, and cut timber. The children would be out in the fields as soon as they could handle a rake or a hoe. Young Moses would often look up from the soil he was working, and wonder what might lie beyond those beautiful hills, and whether whatever it was might hold something for him. His older cousin Jimmy Tompkins (a "double cousin" — two Tompkins married two Coadys) had already left the valley to become a teacher. Moses found that intriguing, what it might be like to go and live among other people, and teach them. The teaching he himself received as a child was often interrupted by the endless demands of the land and seasons. It was not until he was fifteen and the farm more settled and prosperous, that Mick Coady realized he had to give the boy a bit of room, a bit of time to see what that ravenous young mind might do for itself if it had a chance. Moses started attending the Margaree Forks School full-time.

That was 1897, the year that Moses's cousin Jimmy went to Rome to study for the priesthood. He wrote to Moses frequently, sending pamphlets, an old rosary, a pocket Bible, and a great variety of other books. Moses's imagination was fired up by the idea of the great and legendary city whence all these kindnesses had come. Historian Jim Lotz said that this correspondence opened things up for the teenaged boy:

It showed Coady there was a world beyond this small rural community in which he lived. I mean it was accustomed rounds in these communities. It was a healthy life. It was a good life. You were surrounded by your family and friends and your kin. But Coady was always dreaming beyond the mountain. He was always seeing beyond. And then these packages and these parcels and these letters coming from Rome, and this feeling, Hey, there's a bigger world out there. And I want to go out there and I want to see it.

At the turn of the century, Moses Coady received his high school graduation certificate. Cousin Jimmy was his model. He would go into teaching now, he said, and set out for the normal school in Truro. He did all right — intellectually, spiritually, and physically (he was now tall, massive, commanding of presence) — and was a great deal better than "fair." What did they know down at Truro? City folks. So when Moses Coady came back to Margaree for the summer, a small delegation came around to the house to chat about the normal school experience and ended up doing what they had planned to do in the first place, namely, ask him to take over the Principalship of the Margaree

Forks School he had graduated from only a year before.

He accepted and began his teaching career in August 1901. Jimmy Tompkins came home from Rome the next year an ordained priest with a professorship of Greek and algebra at St. Francis Xavier University (St. Francis Xavier College at that time) in Antigonish, about halfway between Sydney and Halifax and twenty-five miles west of the Canso Straight that separates Cape Breton Island from the mainland.

Father Jimmy was twelve years Coady's senior, but throughout their lives there was a strong bond between them. Tompkins told Moses that normal school and a rural high school were very nice but that he, Moses, was ready for more challenging stuff now, and kept on badgering and encouraging the young teacher to go for a university degree. No doubt he made sure that St. F.X. would make room for him when he inevitably applied for admission.

When Moses applied for admission to St. F.X in 1903, Father Jimmy's confidence proved well founded. It only took the young student two years to finish a bachelor's degree, complete with medals in Greek, philosophy, and history. He came out of college with a nickname too, Mighty Moses of Margaree, which had more to do with his athletic achievements than his academics. He had been a star on the football team and a champion at the hammer throw. That was okay with Father Jimmy, who liked an all-round guy. But he had been quietly nursing his ultimate ambition for the kid he was mentoring, and came down to Margaree to talk things over with him during the summer evenings when Moses would come into the house all bronzed after a day of pitching hay and still wondering what might be out there for him on the other side of the mountains. Jimmy Tompkins knew what it was, and seeded the idea quite explicitly at last. Moses would later say that it was waking up to the sound of a distant church bell, which seemed like some sort of message, that finally decided the issue. He would become a priest.

In those days in Nova Scotia the Church was one of the few ways in which a person from a relatively poor family could find a solid career. Teaching was not bad but the priesthood was really something. The diocese of Antigonish would be sending a couple of students to Rome that year, and Father Jimmy Tompkins was not at all reluctant to let them know who one of those students should be.

Rome! He had already formed a picture; he had the smells, the sounds, the music of the place in his head before he even got off the boat. The Bishop of Antigonish encouraged him to do a Ph.D. in philosophy and theology, and that was fine with Moses. But what he wrote home about, and talked about when he finally came back, was the city, the streets, the people, the smells, the food, the opera, the language (in which he had become fluent). He was in Rome for five years. His family began to wonder whether they would see him again, the letters about life in Rome were so rhapsodic. What could possibly bring him back to Margaree?

But he was a Margaree boy. He missed those hills. And he was a teacher, after all. He missed his people, and he wanted to share what he had feasted on, and lift their spirits, of his people back home, and give them a taste for a larger world of the spirit and the intellect. Father Jimmy got him a post at St. F.X., teaching Latin and mathematics. He was a natural teacher, a spellbinder. Physically imposing, with massive shoulders and head, coal-black eyes, and a striking demeanour, he had a rhetorical style that was homey and poetic all at once. He drew them in whether they were registered for his courses or not. He was a star. He didn't mind the crowds. They would sit on the floors and the windowsills. "It was a question of what the windowsills would hold," said Father MacDonnell.

After five years he felt the need for more study, and spent a year at the Catholic University of America, in Washington, DC. He worked on his rhetoric, on speaking to crowds, which he had begun to enjoy a lot. When he came back to Antigonish in 1916 the bishop made him Principal of the St. F.X. High School. The war was on now. It had transformed the port of Halifax, a major departure point for troops and supplies and munitions. Moses was thirty-four, beyond the call-up age. He and Father Jimmy began to spend evenings together talking about what they ought to do next. Father Jimmy had already begun to promote the idea of adult education as a way of helping Nova Scotians out of their almost feudalistic lives. The fishermen then were virtually the indentured servants of the packing industry, and the farmers not much better off. He had been "nagging the hell out of the university," Jim Lotz told us, saying

> "Take the noise to the people. Go to the pitheads. Go down
> in the mines. Go to the wharf, etcetera. Go to the places
> where people are. Take the knowledge to the people. Don't

expect the best and the brightest to come to the university."

He called his plan the Antigonish Forward Movement, but it was not moving forward very rapidly. As he would sit there by the fire listening to Moses talk about where he'd been and what he hoped for, Father Jimmy was aware that the very impressive man had acquired a new sort of glow. Father Jimmy was, Jim Lotz said, "the size of a pile of dimes," and Moses was almost a giant. Jimmy had a squeaky little voice and not much presence in a crowd. He was very persuasive with one or two people, speaking quietly but urgently in a farm or fisherman's kitchen about how they had to get some learning so that they could take charge of their lives more effectively. But he couldn't work the crowds. The message had to get to crowds, and this towering charismatic cousin of his, he realized, was the guy who could do it. Jim Lotz said of Father Jimmy that

> *he wouldn't put the cat out for you. He'd spend the whole night sitting up with you, nagging you to put the cat out. Now, Coady was the guy who would have put the cat out. So that's it. Let's get on with the next thing. It's the impressive physical presence and the way in which he put these simple words forward with passion. . . . Once you heard him speak, you could never be the same again.*

When Father Coady got involved, the Antigonish Movement would ultimately become the foundation of a genuine new social order in Nova Scotia. But in the meantime the war had drained able young men from the already faltering primary production-based economy of eastern Canada. The priorities and preoccupations of the war made it difficult, for the time being, to get anyone's attention for proposals about adult education, or the Antigonish Movement. So for now Moses Coady kept on running the high school and planning with Father Jimmy what they would do when the world came back to something like normal after the war.

Father Jimmy also began to promote the idea of merging all the small educational institutions in the province into one big University of Nova Scotia. The many Nova Scotia universities and colleges were too small for big ideas, said Father Jimmy; their resources should be combined to form a united secular university in Halifax, following the American model. What happened next was a very complex episode in Church politics. It involved — indirectly — the Carnegie Foundation, which Father Jimmy had been pretty successful in interesting in some of his proposals, and a number of other clerics on both sides of the amalgamation debate. St. F.X. had been a pioneer institution in bringing working men in for adult classes and had established a "People's School" in 1921, something that Father Jimmy was very enthusiastic about. But Father Jimmy was a man who often pushed too hard and did not know when his agitation was counterproductive. Tompkins just kept pushing Bishop Morrison until he could not listen to him anymore. Those senior clerics who opposed the amalgamation scheme held the upper hand, and both Father Jimmy (who had never worked as a parish priest) and a Father Boyle, who was supporting him in the amalgamation issue, were in effect exiled to small rural parishes.

Both Father Jimmy and Father Moses Coady were

stunned by this, but that negative response of the ecclesi-astical authorities had at least alerted them to the need for a more adroitly political approach to getting the Antigonish Movement to move. Coady himself had already made one move in a secular direction that the Church authorities could not openly object to: he had become head of the Nova Scotia Teacher's Union. When he spoke in public now it was to stress the importance of education in the future prosperity of the province, a message that seemed innocuous enough before the authorities realized what he really meant. He was also teaching part-time on campus, and still running the high school as well as leading the teachers' union. Imagine a Principal leading a teachers' union anywhere in Canada today.

Now he got an idea for a new enterprise, and found the time to go over to Margaree to help build a school there — literally and physically, digging and hammering, as someone said, "down in the trenches." He enlisted the Sisters of Saint Martha, an order he admired very much, which had been established at St. F.X. in the late 1890s. They would teach in the Margaree School, and he would help them start a convent there. He would later help them establish their independence from St. F.X., and they still express their gratitude for that. "If I had fifty Marthas I could save the world," he once said.

The postwar world of rural Nova Scotia was certainly in need of saving. In June 1925, the Glace Bay miners struck the oppressive British Empire Steel and Coal Company. The company broke the strike with scab work-ers from as far away as Scandinavia. And then, calling the strikers Communists, they simply cut off the striking miners and their families, forcing some of them literally into starvation.

The fishing industry was also in a lamentable state. Beginning in the late 1800s, large fish companies had moved into the coastal areas. They bought fish and sold the fishermen the hardware and groceries and other goods the fishermen needed, setting the price for both. It was a time of poverty and despair in fishing communities throughout eastern Canada. Canso, where they had sent Father Jimmy for his sins, was as badly hit as any. Father Jimmy saw it all, and became newly energized about the movement. Jim Lotz said that he was telling the fishermen to "raise hell and get the government to do something about it." Father MacDonnell said,

He was obsessed with doing something for the fishermen, the poor fishermen, who were being done in by entrepreneurs from away. And he finally managed to get government people, schoolteachers, the clergy, together for a meeting. And he harangued them. Told them they simply had to do something about this situation.

But it was not just a blind lashing out this time. With Moses Coady's help, Father Jimmy's haranguing had begun to take on political shape and energy. They got to the press, and the editors loved the story. The movement, now usually referred to as the Antigonish Movement, began showing up on the front pages, and now there was real public debate. The federal government saw an opportunity and convoked a commission of enquiry, which called 823 witnesses. Not surprisingly, one of the most impressive was a priest named Moses Coady. Coady outlined for them a simple, cost-free way to improve the lives of the fishermen: they should be encouraged to form, and protected in the doing of it, producer and consumer cooperatives. The commission agreed, and decided that the very man to go about the province helping to spread the idea and enlist the fishermen was the big charismatic guy from Margaree. The government could easily pay the salary of one man. It was time to give up the teaching job and go on the road.

And so over the next ten months, Moses Coady travelled a thousand miles around the province, sometimes exhilarated, sometimes exhausted, but day after day, without let-up, preaching to and teaching the fishermen and their families how they could throw off the lethargy and desperation of near slavery by uniting as a single voice. In June 1930, 208 delegates met to found the United Maritime Fishermen. The world was changing, and the fish companies could not stop it because the government of Canada had given its blessing, and the press were watching closely.

Of course in the long run, the whole province would become more prosperous, but it would take the bosses a while to realize this.

Father Moses Coady now had a profile in the province. Now he seemed the ideal man to help realize a project that many had been agitating about for a long time. The alumni, the Scottish Catholic Society, and the industrial conferences had been urging the governors to start an extension department. Once again there was a complex political situation here, among those for and those against, but in the end the governors invited Coady to set up an extension department and to head it. At that time he was totally taken up with his organizing of the fishermen and could not begin work on the extension department right away, but he knew that extension would be another powerful instrument to help realize the dreams that he and Father Jimmy had for helping people get the good and abundant life. In 1930 he set to work.

He went back on the road to tell the fishermen that they should not just settle for their co-ops; they needed more education. He knew where they could get it, and he was ready to persuade the university to help bring it to their doors. Canon Russell Elliot, an Anglican friend, told us,

His technique was to get people to talk. People had very little education in most cases. But that didn't mean they weren't wise or that they didn't have good minds. And so as they sat around in little groups looking at things together, he could toss in a little bit, ask a question or two. Inevitably they came from the meeting having learned something.

And Dougald MacDougall, who got to know Moses well through the co-ops, added,

He used to say, "I'd like to take the nut out of your head and pour in some knowledge. Because with knowledge will come hope. And with hope will come a better life. And people will become masters of their own destiny." Those are the things that I learned from him.

That was the way he talked. He used language as a

tool. He would tell them, "You can get the good life. You're poor enough to want it and smart enough to get it." His voice was being heard across the Maritimes. Ironically today, the sound of that voice exists in just a handful of archived sound clips. On one hissing old tape you can hear him saying,

> *You start work. Get the people interested where they are. Find their interests. Lead them up. And when they see that thinking pays, they'll put in some, they'll put in some . . . The most exciting and thrilling of all things . . . in this world, is creative thinking, you see. To know life is ahead of you. And life is there. And if you're smart enough to find the techniques by which you can siphon it down to yourself. That's, that's our philosophy. Our formula for social progress is the complete mobilization of the adults of this country. The workers, the farmers, fishermen, lumbermen. To get the knowledge and the social techniques that will give them the good and abundant life. That's the story. That's what the Antigonish Movement is.*

Sometimes the philosophy became a bit unrealistic, but it always sounded as though it were grounded. Father MacDonnell told us about driving down with him once to the community of Judique, a hundred and twenty miles or so southwest of Sydney, on the west coast of Cape Breton.

> *On his way down there one evening, he happened to notice these vast stretches of wonderful land, all the way down to the ocean as he came in. And nothing in particular going on. So he started out by picturing an incredible development of a cabbage industry in the community of Judique. And the cabbage would be so wonderful and so plentiful*

*that no one with any sense of palate at all would dream of
having any other cabbage but what came from Judique.
They knew perfectly well that they weren't going to do
this. But they were enthused. And then in would come
people like A.B. Macdonald and other good workers who
would do a lot of the organizational work.*

With Coady goading them into working together, the
Judique community pooled its resources to not a cabbage
industry but a lobster-canning factory. Another group
formed a marketing co-operative to sell the product. These
were among the first producer and marketing co-ops in the
country. The idea took hold. Within three years, Maritime
fishermen could look around them and see and touch the
new prosperity that had come from their elimination of the
middlemen and the cod lords. Soon, with the guidance of
Coady and his workers, the idea spread to farming communities. Sheep farmers started butchering, processing,
and selling their own animals. Then the people of Cole
Harbour and Port Felix opened co-op stores to sell the
increasing number of co-op produced products. By 1935,
this network of producer, marketing, and consumer co-ops
was threatening the established business community and
returning substantial profits to co-op members. And then
along came a new co-op idea, the credit union, which had
been invented by the Quebec Hansard Reporter Alphonse
Desjardins at the turn of the century, and now made its
way up into Nova Scotia from Massachusetts and Maine.
The fishermen said at first that they had enough difficulty
making a few pennies, let alone putting anything aside,
but Coady kept at them, and before long taking your sav-

ings to the co-op, however small they were, became something everyone did. Dougal MacDougall told us,

[When] I was a youngster going to school . . . we had those, I don't know if many of you remember, those big black pennies. They were big ones. Twice as big as a little penny. And we used to save those and put them in the credit union in Antigonish. And [Father Coady] always believed that people could do much, much more than what they were doing. If they could work together, gain knowledge, because with knowledge came hope. And with hope came a better way of life. That people could walk with their heads held high and dream a bit. And look into the hearts of their fellow brothers and sisters. And to be able to share in a good and abundant life which is throughout the world for all to have.

The Nova Scotia newspapers began to refer to Antigonish as "The New Jerusalem" and to Coady as "The New Moses," as if it was going backwards to a simpler time. Indeed his vision always took him back to Margaree. "It was his Shangri-La," Jim Lotz said. And he unquestionably found the virtues of the simple rural life to be way ahead of that grubby oppressed wharfside life the fishermen had lived before the co-ops. But he saw all this as a road to Rome, in a way; not Rome meaning the Vatican and his theological studies, which now seemed so far away, but Rome meaning the full life of the intellect and the senses, music, language. "We're going to bring them to Shakespeare," he used to say, with a big laugh, "open up their minds, their imaginations. That's what it's for, finally."

Moses Coady was not just a solo act. His brilliant rhetoric made him look like a star, but it was always in the service of getting people working together, and much of the time that meant working with him. He was a team leader and always tried to find people smarter than he was. Father MacDonnell said,

He surrounded himself with a group of very good people, and I think particularly of the women who worked for him. Creative people. Being on the Coady team was an exhilarating experience for people.

And Jim Lotz again,

Hey, it must have been fun to be around these people, because you never knew what was going to happen. You never knew when his book was going to be thrust at you, and he'd say, "Read this by tomorrow." Or you know, when Coady would say, "Let's go up to the Margaree and pick strawberries." So it was a wonderful time. I mean this is the great thing about talking to the people involved in the movement. It was a wonderful time in their lives. They didn't feel they were doing good works among the poor. They didn't even think, I think they were doing development. They were just learning, having fun, and working with like-minded people to alleviate some of the prevalent miseries of the time.

Ellen Arsenault was living in Prince Edward Island when Coady advertised for a secretary. She said,

Dr. Coady himself told me that he had about fifteen or twenty applications for this job of secretary. But they were all teachers. And I had been a teacher, but I had also worked in a bank. He told me later, anybody that can work in a bank can do anything. That's how I got the job.

One of her tasks was to help publish *The Maritime Co-operator*, a monthly newsletter about the movement, which had built a growing readership. Another woman who got involved was Irene Doyle, a Cape Breton girl who came to Coady to see if she could drive over to Antigonish with him one day.

And he says, "You're going to join the Marthas?" And I said, "Yes." And he said to me, he said, "Did you ever drive sixty miles an hour?" I said, "No." "Well," he said, "you're going to do it this afternoon." So on those twisty roads, you know, we got here in very short time. But I mean that was what, the impression you got about him was energy.

He loved to drive fast and hard. He spent thousands of hours in the car, tearing around the province from one project to another, lining up other drivers to give him a break when he could. He used everyone as a helper, a referee, a testing ground. Every colleague, employee, or friend. Father MacDonnell told us that Coady turned to his staff — most of them women — not just to do his bidding, but to help guide his hand, as a staff is supposed to do.

He could toss an idea at them and they could come up with an essay or a letter very quickly. He'd want to try out his speeches on them. And he knew he had a marvellous speech. And he'd come down with great enthusiasm and he'd gather the circle around. And he'd deliver the speech, only to find that quite occasionally heads would start shaking. No, you haven't got the right emphasis here. That idea should be downplayed. You should emphasize this more. And for a few moments he'd look like a spanked boy

in the classroom. But then the battle would be on as they
debated. But he'd take their counsel. He listened to them.
He never heard of the term feminism. *But he certainly*
appreciated the talent of women.

Sister Irene Doyle was often there, one of two Marthas who came to work in the extension department.

[We] were having a little meeting. And I said, "What's
'Little Mosey' think of this?" "Oh," he said, "she's calling
me 'Little Mosey.'" Now he liked that. He would like that
far better than for somebody to cower in front of him. He
wouldn't mind arguing with them. So I think that in that
way he was a big man, he was.

Resolute and confident in his faith, he was, however, in no way a complacent servant of the institution. In a way it was the reverse. Coady "stood on the Church," Canon Elliot told us,

[in order] to be able to jump into society and help it out.
So it was not really a Church movement in one sense. But
it was using *the Church, motivated by the Church to do*
things for the community at large. So it was not a Roman
Catholic movement in itself at all.

One day in a conference someone said to Father Jimmy, "Well, you know, you Catholics are doing very well," and Father Jimmy's acerbic rejoinder was, "there's no Catholic or Protestant way of catching fish." But critics among the businesspeople who felt they had been hurt by the Antigonish Movement — and elsewhere — could not shake the idea that there was some kind of sectarian thrust to the movement. Canon Elliot said,

People who were in the financial world didn't like what

was going on. . . . [N]ot being a Roman Catholic, they would say oh, you're just falling in the hands of the Roman Catholic Church, you see. That was their way of doing it. Roman Catholics who were in business or whatever and didn't like the co-operative movement would use another way of criticizing.

This meant, according to Father MacDonnell, himself a senior Catholic cleric, that

In some quarters he was considered a Communist. Certainly a Red-eyed socialist. He was not welcome in some dioceses in Canada at all. Because these were the days when we saw a Communist Red behind every bush. It's hard for people to understand today how apprehensive people were about this menace. Coady's work was regarded by a lot of people as not being very suitable church work.

Here is Coady's own voice:

Now we, we admit to the accusation of materialism. We want to explain right away that that's not our ultimate objective. Our aim is Shakespeare and grand opera. And we think that's the road to it. And they say, how long are you going to be in this messy materialism? And I don't know. But I think it'll be several decades. It'll be my lifetime. But I hope there will be enough idealism implanted simultaneously with this thing, that the boys who succeed us will carry on to the higher place we have in our mind.

But the hierarchy of the Church had seen the blessings embedded in this good man's work, despite the secular criticism, despite his "standing on the Church," as Canon Elliot put it, using the institution as a base from which to pursue his social programs, the authorities recognized that the priest was doing what they saw as God's work. When they elevated Coady to monsignor, Coady claimed to be displeased. Jim Lotz quotes him as saying, "The sons of bitches, they can't do that to me." Lotz says that the priest believed deeply that he was

"primus inter pares," first among equals. I think that's how he saw himself. [And] I think internally there was an awful lot of struggle in this, in this man's mind about whether he was really sort of bringing his people forward, or taking them back into an imagined past.

Father Jimmy Tompkins suffered no such conflict. They had exiled him but they hadn't stopped him. When the Reserve Mines of Cape Breton co-operatively built a settlement of seventeen modern homes they called it Tompkinsville. By now, the Antigonish Movement was widely hailed as a plausible educational co-operative process for achieving a new economic and social order. Antigonish had become an international centre for social reformers. They had enlisted A.B. Macdonald to take over the management side of things, and this allowed Coady more time to travel and spread the word. In 1936, the Carnegie Foundation sponsored him on an international tour. Ellen Arsenault told us that the staff began to worry about his stamina,

He spoke in so many different places. But somehow we always missed him when he was gone, you know. You'd always know when, it seemed to me that everybody perked up when Dr. Coady would come back from a trip. Because they could hear his voice and that would, I don't know,

*there was something about his voice that brought us all to
the alert, you know, and realize he was back home again,
thank God, you know.*

In 1937, the Rockefeller Foundation invited Moses
Coady to use their retreat centre in South Carolina to write
a book about the Antigonish Forward Movement. He
accepted the invitation, but even as he boarded the train to
head south he complained that he was not feeling well.
The staff at the Extension Department were used to hearing him complain; he was a noisy hypochondriac. But by
now, knowing the incredible demands he was making on
himself, they were probably beginning to worry. As they
should have. Arriving at the Rockefeller Retreat Center he
started on the book, but before long he was so run down
and racked with chest pain that they sent him up to Boston
for tests. After a month in hospital there, he went back to
Antigonish, where the St. F.X. extension staff worked
through Christmas to help him complete the writing. He
felt well enough to take the finished manuscript down to
New York for discussions with the publishers, but once
more had to be hospitalized.

The book about the movement, *Masters of Their Own
Destiny,* was published in the fall of 1939. A few weeks later
he had a severe heart attack, and when he came home from
the hospital this time it was with firm and unequivocal
instructions to rest for at least a year. In fact it was two
years before he felt strong enough to begin again. He had
been terribly restless during his down time, thinking about
all the ways in which he could have been helping the
movement to profit from its new respectability, bring more

people into it, spread the word further and further. He had the sense to know he had to give up the cigars and the fast driving, but he was determined to get back on the road. "He was very fussy who drove him," Dougald MacDougall said. "He would not sit in the back seat . . . and he would check you out about a week before you were going somewhere with him."

Canon Elliot was one of the drivers who passed the checkout, just in time for a trip to Halifax.

It sort of just happened to be my privilege, I guess, to be the driver for Dr. Coady. We started down this grade late at night, pitch dark. And my car lights went out. As I did on many other occasions, I aimed for the centre of the road as much as I could in the dark. And with the other hand I reached under the dash to find and fumble with the fuse for the lights. And sometimes by wiggling that, the lights would come on. And they did. And we were still in the centre of the road. And I turned apologetically to Dr. Coady sitting beside me. And he was fanning his face with his felt hat. And he was saying, "My God, and me with a heart condition."

By the time World War II broke out in September 1939, Moses Coady and the Antigonish Movement were known to social reformers all over the Western World. But while the war demanded more time from his volunteer workers and drained the financial resources of government, it also eliminated unemployment and put a lot more money in the pockets of workers and fishermen and their families. Some were beginning to think more conventionally about their financial affairs, and to be nervous about their mates

in the credit unions knowing much about what they had
and what they were doing with it. They began to turn to
the established banks. After a few years Coady began to
think about a Canada-wide co-op movement. But in
February 1952 he had another heart attack, came to terms
with the fact that at sixty-nine he really had to slow down
drastically, and asked the bishop to let him retire. " I think
he was kind of disappointed that the bishop did accept his
resignation," Ellen Arsenault told us.

*I think he'd like to have carried on. The bishop said that he
could keep his office, but he would retire from, you know,
actual working. And he would be named as director emer-
itus of the Extension Department.*

In an interview with Ken Homer at the new CBC
Television station in Halifax, he said,

*I retired five years ago, but I still stay here in my quarters
at St. F.X., which has been my home for forty-seven years.
I take a hand in some phases of the extension. I make the
odd speech. I teach sometimes in the short courses. I do
some writing.*

He kept his room at the university and ate his meals
with the other priests in the dining room. Father
MacDonnell was one of them. He told us how they particularly enjoyed

*the evening get-together around nine o'clock. . . . Coady
would appear on the scene, and we were a captive audience. And we were to be enlightened. He enjoyed company. And we enjoyed him. And he could be very, very
encouraging to anyone who did something worthwhile.
Time and again he'd single out some of the priests who had*

given a good talk somewhere or done something that he rather had fancied.

There was a continuing stream of American and overseas visitors coming to study the movement and to meet the founder. Careful to husband his time and his strength, he found these encounters good for his morale and he gave them as much time as he could.

From the time his retirement was announced, accolades poured in to the university. The old priest wrote to his niece Mary Coady, "a fellow never knows how popular he is until he is about to die," adding, "This year the extension has come to the point where there is not much possibility of it ever failing."

When A.B. Macdonald died of cancer in 1953, of the three pillars of the Antigonish Movement, there remained only Coady and his cousin, Father Jimmy Tompkins. Father Jimmy's physical and mental decline had hospitalized him at St. Martha's Hospital in Antigonish. Coady went to see him, and when he came back to St. F.X. he told Ellen Arsenault, "I never want to see him again like that. I don't want to remember him like that." Father Jimmy died in St. Martha's, in May 1953. One of the men who carried him to his grave in the Tompkinsville Cemetery said to a reporter, "By heavens, there was one hell of a man."

Against advice, Coady still accepted a few speaking engagements, and collapsed during one of them, in Madison, Wisconsin, in 1958. Father MacDonnell visited him in the Halifax infirmary.

He was great, even on his deathbed. He, oh he assured me that the world was just beginning to be interesting. And

*he would have enjoyed . . . all the technology development
and that sort of thing. He had the imagination to see what
effect it could have. He wanted to get people free time to
develop themselves culturally, into music, into arts, into
the finer things of life.*

On Tuesday July 28, Monsignor Moses Michael Coady
quietly passed away. The following Friday morning, a
steelworker, a miner, two farmers, and two fishermen carried him to his simple grave in the cemetery across the
road from St. F.X. Obituary writers had a field day with
metaphors about his broad shoulders fitted for carrying
the little people through adversity. Canon Elliot said, "His
heart condition, as far as I'm concerned, is only because his
heart was in people. And he gave his heart for everybody."

A year later, and within sight of his grave, the university began to build the Coady International Institute to
house and train community development workers from
less developed countries. The Institute, now directed by
Mary Coyle, is the big man's big footprint on the surface of
the planet. It has become a centre for extension work
around the world. Dougald MacDougall told us that the
Institute

*used to borrow me for seminars, out-of-country seminars.
There were a group who graduated from the Coady from
West Africa, and they went home to their own native
places in order to work the programs. And [The Institute]
felt that now was the time to get them together so they
could share and help [The Institute] improve their courses. I spent six weeks over there. And we had people from
six different countries of West Africa represented there.*

Each and every one of them were graduates. . . . Now,
that's twenty-five years ago. And the Coady program has
been improving every year since. They've graduated thou-
sands of students now working throughout the world. To
make the world a little better and more human for people.

"I think that's still a good philosophy," is what Moses
Coady would say. That was one of his favourite phrases:
"That's a good philosophy."

◆ ◆ ◆

The History Television documentary was written and directed by Whitman Trecartin and directed by Whitman Trecartin
and Matthew Trecartin.

Part Fourteen

SIR SANDFORD FLEMING
MAKING THE WORLD RUN ON TIME

He was the greatest man who ever concerned himself with engineering. . . . His hands were clean, his eye was single, his heart was pure.
– Sir Andrew Macphail, a man of letters at McGill University, speaking of Sir Sandford Fleming

The man who (more than any other individual) is responsible for the massive engineering project that knit this country together with a ribbon of steel rails was born in Kirkcaldy, a small town just above Edinburgh on the Firth of Forth, in 1827. His name was Sandford Fleming. One of the six children of Andrew Fleming, a cabinetmaker, Sandford spent much of his childhood helping out in his father's Glaswyn Road workshop where tidiness was a prime virtue and simplicity of motion in the achievement of ends was the mark of competence. Nothing out of place, moving parts and cutting edges oiled, messes cleared away as they were formed.

Sandford's clever mother, Elizabeth, kept the accounts. Historian Alan Wilson said,

Andrew could not have persisted being the pater *familias without a very strong lieutenant. And indeed, in many ways she also ruled the roost. Andrew had a very good reputation in the Kirkcaldy district. He was a first-class cabinetmaker and a respected man in many ways. And he was ambitious for his son. He was apprenticed, therefore, as*

*early as fourteen to John Sang [whose] reputation went
well beyond Kirkcaldy. He was acknowledged as an outstanding civil engineer. Also a surveyor. But as a civil
engineer, and as an experimental one.*

John Sang thought of his profession not just in terms
of its mechanical products, but as a way of also contributing to the public good, to the larger community. So the
boy's apprenticeship would give him a deep love of the
transformation that good design and math, and metals and
wood and stone, can creatively wreak upon the underpin-
nings of a nation. From his father, young Sandford had
inherited order and system, and a thirst for adventure from
his mother; her brothers worked overseas and wrote home
intriguing letters about the opportunities that lay in the
new world.

The boy had a big head of sandy hair, confidence to
match, tall, feisty, inexhaustible supplies of energy, and to
go with all that, big ideas. He would find a new country,
make influential friends there, and his name would
become a household word in his lifetime. A wit once said
that Canada was a railroad in search of a country, but when
Sandford Fleming arrived here there was not much of a
country and no railroads at all. By the time he left us, the
country was vast, railroads criss-crossed its length and
breadth, and Fleming had played a role in the development of most of them.

His mother was not the only one with overseas contacts. His father, Andrew, corresponded regularly with a
cousin, Dr. John Hutchison, who had settled in the town of
Peterborough, in what they then called Upper Canada.

That part of Ontario is increasingly urbanized today, but in the middle of the nineteenth century it was covered with huge stands of ancient white pine, some trunks more than a metre in diameter. Peterborough was still being carved out of that forest but it was developing quickly, and Dr. Hutchison urged the Flemings to come and share the promise of all this marvellous white pine. The lumber and the other natural resources of the area were already being exploited by a group of entrepreneurial Scots who ruled from Scotstown across the river.

When Andrew wrote back to his cousin expressing anxiety about the weather and the perils of the ocean voyage, Dr. Hutchison replied that "if it were not for the nights, I have seen far colder weather at home in June." But the boys had to wait two years for their father's permission to make the feared crossing. As they discussed that Upper Canadian opportunity, the idea began to form that they would all go, together. The boys would be the family's advance scouting party. On April 24, 1845, David, twenty, Sandford, eighteen, and Cousin Henry, twenty-five, stood excitedly at the stern of the ship, *Brilliant*. Andrew gave them three uneasy cheers from the quay, but the boys could see that their mother was weeping.

The voyage was stormy and the dreadful stories they had heard about cholera in the St. Lawrence ports loomed over them throughout the voyage, but they debarked safely and in good health. Ascending the Ottawa River to Bytown,[1] they travelled down the Rideau Canal to Lake Ontario, took ship for Cobourg, and fifty-five days after

---

1. Bytown is the original name of what is now our capital city.

leaving Scotland they arrived at Dr. Hutchison's door. The boys knew that they would find relatives in Peterborough, but they had not been prepared for the town itself. Peterborough today seems flat when you drive through it, but it was all peaks and valleys when the Fleming boys arrived, and the main intersection, George and Hunter Streets, was a swamp. Sandford wrote home about his surprise at finding not a real town but a poor little place with stumps still in the muddy streets, a wooden house here and there, and a few villas on some of the better surrounding farms. The Hutchisons' stone house was an exception, as was Sheriff Hall's brick house.

Cousin Henry set out for Toronto almost immediately, and David, who wanted to study wood carving, was not far behind. Sandford — it was one of the few times in his life that he demonstrated uncertainty — was not sure what he should do. For a while he stayed on with the Hutchisons, working at surveys and collecting the doctor's accounts. But when he learned that David had found a steady job with a Scots furnituremaker, and digs that they could share, he went to Toronto to join his brother. He had an introduction to another outstanding engineer, Sir Casimir Gzowski, the great-great-grandfather of broadcaster Peter Gzowski. Fleming perhaps hoped that Sir Casimir would be a kind of Canadian John Strang, but he was disappointed. Gzowski, he wrote to his father, said, "Why don't you go back to Scotland? There's no future for you here."[2]

2. I am sometimes corrected when I refer to Toronto in the early nineteenth century, by people who say, "Ah, but it was called York then, wasn't it?" In fact, the name first appears officially as Fort Toronto in 1720, shortened to Toronto twenty or thirty years later, and then changed to York in 1790, because Governor John Graves Simcoe disliked aboriginal names and wanted to honour the Duke of York. Council did not wait long after Simcoe was out of the way and re-established the original name in 1834.

He went back to Peterborough instead; at least he was getting a reputation there as a surveyor, and he loved the outdoor life. He was a very good draughtsman, and he began to get commissions for lithographs of outstanding buildings and to draw up plans for the expansion of Peterborough and the development of new towns in the region. By the time he was commissioned to design a spire for Peterborough's Catholic Church, Fleming had developed a considerable estimate of his own worth, and he and the commissioning priest, Father Butler, fell out over his fee. When it got acrimonious he went to law, and Fleming was eventually able to write to his father, "with Dr. Hutchison's advice, I sued him and gained. He had to pay the costs and all. Think of Sand Fleming having a lawsuit with a Catholic priest. It's not everyone has the honours."

Meantime, David was doing very well in Toronto. He wrote to his father describing Canadian mass production techniques and praising the quality of the factory-made furniture. "Not like our clumsy old-fashioneds," he wrote. "A Scottish cabinetmaker has to come here to learn, not to teach. And whether we farm or go into business, we're quite a colony by ourselves, capable of everything."

The historian Alan Wilson said,

David foresees a vertically integrated operation that starts in the forests and ends in the shops, for the whole family. But it is amusing that Sandford finds other reasons for the family succeeding if they come out. "My name is middling well known about this part of the country. You will excuse my flattering myself a little." He's twenty years old, and

*he's already caught that confidence in the country and in
himself.*

And he was now a big man, six-foot-two of hearty
spirits and self-importance. He wanted to challenge people, he said, and set them an outdoors manly model. Soon
his confidence and his skills made him feel ready to invite
the family to join him. For all the ego, family was always
his rock, his anchor, and the most important mirror for his
self-esteem. On April 16, 1847, their father, Andrew, wrote
to David: "I write you, and most probably for the last time
from this side of the Atlantic." Still fearing the St. Lawrence
plague ports, Andrew and Elizabeth boarded the ship
Mary in Glasgow, bound for Montreal. They had a much
easier trip than did the boys; they did not get sick, and
were thankful for a safe landing and a quick escort to
Canada West, as the Toronto area was then called.

Sandford recognized from the start that railways
would play an enormous role in Canada's development,
and he wanted to be part of that. He had moved to Weston,
northwest of Toronto, to study under a well-known surveyor named Stoughton Dennis. Surveying was heavy
work then. There was no such thing as a transit from which
you could take sights across long distances; you had to
walk every foot of the territory and measure your distances with a chain. To measure one mile, that chain had to
be spread nearly twenty-seven times. Surveyors would be
lugging those cumbersome hundred-link chains from the
Atlantic to the Pacific before long, and Sandford's surveying certificate would be his way of getting into railway
engineering.

When the parents arrived David met them at the boat and brought them out to a farmstead near Weston that Sandford had surveyed before buying it for the family. For seven years they all worked that land, young and old alike. They ploughed and sowed and harvested, built barns, raised some livestock, managed woodlots, leased a sawmill on the Humber, and cut and sold thousands of board feet of gleaming white pine. Andrew Fleming resumed cabinet-making and became a consultant to the firm that David had joined, Jacques and Hay, the colony's leading furniture manufacturer. David Fleming became one of their most respected carvers.

There was more and more talk about the need for railroads. Sanford looked for every possible commission that might build him the reputation he wanted to establish when the money started to flow. He was not, however, doggedly single-minded. He sketched buildings and designs for bridges, and designed and had constructed a pair of in-line roller skates, a century and a half before they would become the commonplace they now are.

He was also very good at what people now call "networking," constantly expanding his contacts, particularly in the world of engineering, finance, and building. One good friend was a temperamental and ambitious engineer named Collingwood Schreiber, who landed a commission to design Toronto's Palace of Industry and brought the young Fleming in as his partner on the project. Schreiber admired the younger man's breadth of vision and his promotional ingenuity. Not all the promotions were successful; he had campaigned for a railway down Southern

Ontario's spine, with Peterborough as its hub, but no one bought into it. Nonetheless that campaign did, as he might have said, help his name to become middling well known in railway circles across Canada West. In 1849, he was the leading spirit in founding the Canadian Institute, a professional association for surveyors, engineers, and architects. More contacts, at least that was the hope. At first they met irregularly, and it took Sandford some time to get the Institute going. One Saturday night there were just two of them at the meeting. But Fleming persevered, and out of a slow beginning there grew the Royal Canadian Institute, which still meets on Saturday nights. He also started the Institute's *Canadian Journal*, which would become an invaluable medium for scientific and technical information. His draughtsman's hand kept busy too, and in 1851, he won a contest by designing the first Canadian postage stamp, the three-penny Beaver. Today one of those stamps in good condition will fetch several hundred dollars in the collectors' market — more than ten thousand times its face value.

When the *Toronto Globe* announced that there was to be a rail link between Toronto and Lake Huron in anticipation of a further bold leap along the Great Lakes to the northwest, Sandford Fleming sensed that his time had come. He applied successfully to Chief Engineer Frederic Cumberland to be his assistant. "He got up there," Alan Wilson told us,

> and started building the railway up to Collingwood, and discovered that Cumberland, the man he was to work with, had so many irons in other fires that he, Sandford, was left doing most of the day-to-day stuff.

But he characteristically took it all on his own shoulders and stuck with it, and won the admiration of the communities through which the line passed. The people at Saugeen were particularly pleased with his decision to put a stop at their tiny community, and, he wrote in his diary, they "decided to found a library, to be called the Fleming Library, a great mark of respect to me." Adding, in good Scots Presbyterian style, "Must not be too vain, too sanguine, an evil day may come. An important week to me. How will it end?"

While he was using the project to teach himself the skills of the railway builder, and being none too modest about it, Cumberland's jealousy was aroused and he fired Fleming. Fleming shot back, telling the board of directors pointedly about Cumberland's absences and delinquencies. The board responded by naming him the Northern Railway's chief engineer. Meanwhile, he began to look for a permanent family homestead, something a bit grander than the Weston farm, and settled on a property just beyond the railway's terminus at Collingwood on Georgian Bay. It reminded him of Scotland. He named it Craigleith, and the family moved again. They all worked on the building of the house, David carving elaborate clusters of grapes around the eaves and constructing an ornate circular staircase. Now beginning to imagine a railway plan of considerably greater dimensions than the Northern's, Fleming declared that from Craigleith he could almost see the prairies.

In the meantime, always alert to opportunity, he bought more forest land, a huge acreage this time, which he gave to

his father who had become Jacques and Hay's chief suppli-
er. His brother David developed a lumber business, and
would go on to build some of the finest homes in the growing town of Collingwood. Not long after they settled in at
Craigleith, the Flemings announced plans for a new village.

*For sale. Valuable town and villa lots, beautifully situated
at the foot of the Blue Mountains with frontage on the
Georgian Bay. A quarry of the finest building stone, and
an excellent place for a fishery. From its salubrity and picturesque beauty, it must become a favourite summering
resort and watering place. A healthful summer retreat for
capitalists, merchants, and mechanics.*

They developed the waterfront for shipping, and,
with an abundance of wood, limestone and water power,
they opened a mill and a quarry, and then a general store,
and gave the community both land and materials for a
school and railway station.

In his diary on New Year's Eve, 1853, Sandford
Fleming wrote,

*An intimacy has grown up with Miss Hall of
Peterborough. How it may terminate, I do not know. An
amiable well-bred woman with her peculiarities.*

Jeannie was several years his junior, graceful, viva-
cious, as headstrong as Sandford and with a touch of the
tomboy that he admired. He sent her a love poem illustrated with his own watercolour painting of a bluebird.
Peterborough historian Jean Cole told us,

*They were somewhere near Lindsay and driving a little cut-
ter,[3] I think it was. At any rate, it crashed and he was flung*

3. A cutter is a horse-drawn sleigh.

out and injured. Well, when he came to, there was Jeannie hanging over him all anxious and whatnot. And she got a neighbouring farmer to take them in. Sandford was a number of days recuperating at this . . . stranger's house. And then when he got back to Toronto, he wrote to her and asked her if she would marry him. The very next mail came back with the answer, yes she would. One feels that that little episode outside of Lindsay pushed it on a bit there.

On New Year's Day, 1855, Sandford wrote in his diary, *At Cobourg on the way to marry Jeannie Hall, woke up at the Globe Hotel, a great big Canadianized Scotsman with rather an ungainly figure, large head, red or sand coloured beard and mustache. Such is my house of clay.*

It was a happy and bountiful marriage: five sons and four daughters, though three would die in infancy. Sandford encouraged in his own home all of the team energy of his birth family.

In 1862, a vengeful Frederic Cumberland talked his way back into favour with the Northern Railway's board, was named general manager, and immediately fired Fleming for the second time. It really did not matter. His marriage to Jeannie had opened a new door for him in the east. Jeannie's mother came from Halifax's establishment, and on his visits to Halifax, Sandford worked the busy port's social scene with his now well-practised charm. He became friends with Samuel Cunard,[4] and with the great democrat and then premier of Nova Scotia, Joseph Howe. Fleming knew that Howe had once brought a Halifax audience to its feet by declaring,

4. See Part Six.

I believe that many in this room will live to hear the whistle of the steam engine in the passes of the Rockies, and to take the journey from Halifax to the Pacific in five to six days.

Howe liked this confident cocky Sandford Fleming, and he was genuinely convinced about railways. He named Fleming chief engineer of railways for Nova Scotia. Samuel Cunard, who in addition to his shipping interests had an effective monopoly on coal in Nova Scotia, ordered a locomotive and began to promote the development of a line from Truro to Pictou. Sandford and Jeannie moved the family to Halifax and bought a fine house on fashionable Brunswick Street near the Cunards. His closest friend in Halifax, however, was not a business contact or a Nova Scotia blueblood, but a clergyman. Alan Wilson said,

Being a devout man, he would go to the appropriate church, which was St. Matthew's. Here's this young twenty-five year old livewire, George Grant, in the pulpit there at one of the churches of the town. And so he's caught up in the life of Halifax very quickly.

St. Matthew's was originally the Christian Dissenters' Church, but more and more Presbyterians had joined, and had ultimately taken over, with some Dissenters staying on and others leaving angrily. By the time Fleming got to Halifax, it was where the Halifax establishment worshipped and went to see and to be seen. The friendship with Grant was solid and it would be lasting.

With Fleming's advice as chief engineer, Joseph Howe let out contracts for Samuel Cunard's rail line between Truro and Pictou. But when Charles Tupper's Tories beat

out Howe's Liberals in the next election, Tupper discovered that there were serious delays and cost overruns on
the Pictou line. Sensing the political change, Sandford had
already shrewdly courted Tupper, who asked him what
they should do about the railway's problems. At that,
Sandford made his boldest proposal yet. It was outrageous. When they found out about it, the press screamed
patronage and collusion, and called Tupper and Fleming
the "Sinister Siamese Twins."

What Tupper did was to accept Fleming's brazen proposal to cancel all the existing contracts, and turn the
project over to him, Sandford Fleming, the former chief
railway engineer of Nova Scotia. Alan Wilson said,

Well, he did come in on time and under budget. We don't
know how far under budget. But I think an awful lot. For
example, when he ballasted, he voluntarily put 25 percent
more ballast[5] into that line than the contract called for.
You don't do that unless you anticipate a pretty comfort-
able profit.

All Halifax was gossiping and guessing about those
profits, particularly when Fleming acquired a substantial
acreage on Halifax's fashionable Northwest Arm, not far
from Tupper. But there was no denying the fact that the
Pictou line was a success. He had learned a tremendous
amount, and had made some innovations that were hailed
by American, Canadian, and British railway engineers.
Many of these would become standard railway procedures. He used steel rails, not iron. He had learned about

5. Ballast is broken stone or gravel of a consistent size that beds down firmly, drains well
to avoid heaving with frost, and thus provides a firm and unshifting base on which to
lay the rails.

embankments and stone bridge approaches from John Sang. He used iron not wood for bridges and laid track with the finished ballast. He did all the work that would lead to his being the natural choice as the guiding genius of the great transcontinental railways of Canada.

The 1867 Act of Confederation promised that the new federal government at Ottawa would build a railway between Eastern and Central Canada. One of the men competing with Fleming for the railway job was Charles Bridges of the Grand Trunk company. Bridges advocated building railroads quickly and cheaply, and then repairing and upgrading from operating revenues, sure that this would appeal to the new cash-poor federal government. But Sandford knew that along the Intercolonial's underpopulated and underdeveloped route any profit would be a long time in coming, perhaps generations away. Better to do it right in the first place. He stuck to his guns and won the commission. Then he fought to get iron bridges instead of wooden bridges, so trains of the day wouldn't set them on fire, and he won that battle only after the line was started and a couple of the wooden bridges did what he had predicted they would do and burned down.

The government had created a railway board to oversee the project and had appointed Charles Bridges to sit on it. There were frequent disputes between Bridges and Fleming, but when his old Siamese twin Charles Tupper became minister of railways and canals, Fleming seldom lost an appeal. When we made a *Heritage Minute* about him in 1992, I had the Fleming character climb flamboyantly onto a handcar, calling out to the board members who could scarcely keep up with him, "We're not just building a railroad, gentlemen, we are building a country." Alan Wilson said that for the most part Fleming

> *was revered on the line. But the trouble was in some cases, and he came under heavy fire from Bridges and others later on, for the fact that he let his people get away with too much. [But in fact] he did, and no one else had ever done it this carefully. He created a form wherein the engineers had to report on a very, very frequent basis. So he rode herd on them. But on the other hand, that other warm side of him often drew him close to people.*

But while he readily won friends and admirers, that strong and decisive personality also attracted critics and sometimes dedicated enemies. The work was difficult; he met strong criticism. But he was getting track laid. And then he was shaken by a message from Ottawa. Alan Wilson again:

> *He was asked to take on yet another responsibility. To bring British Columbia into Confederation, MacDonald had offered to build a transcontinental line. Fleming was asked to be its chief construction engineer, too. Now that's a huge burden, and he hesitated.*

George Grant may have helped him decide, Alan Wilson says, by proposing that they go west together to see exactly what the territory would demand.

> *A Pacific railway would be a vital link in an imperial global chain. And since Sandford had dreams of developing a cable link to New Zealand and Australia, surely this was part of a grand design. And remember, they're both Presbyterians. The whole idea of predestinarianism is very*

amusing. And in the summer of 1872, with his son Frank, and with Grant and a couple of others, he set out on the first of two exploratory journeys across the Prairies to the Rockies and beyond. And this was a pretty daring venture. Because Sandford, although he's only, he's still only forty-five, and Grant's only thirty-seven, they loved the outdoor life. But it was a demanding trip. And yet Sandford sat and sketched and did watercolours in the evening while Grant wrote notes for a book that would become a Canadian classic, Ocean to Ocean. *And that was matched by a serialized version lavishly illustrated, sold in chapter lengths, and priced for a popular audience.*

And so Fleming took it on. Grant said, "It's manly work, moving mountains." Fleming liked that, but the job's demands, the political wrangling, and then the death of his beloved father, were hard on his health; the next decade was a tough one. With Charles Bridges still harassing in Ottawa, he seemed to dither about the right route through the Rockies. This time his insistence on getting it right the first time was not well received. Parliament was impatient, and Tupper's loyalty to Fleming was splitting the Tory party. Tupper needed a decision, and Sandford seemed lost in the passes of the Rockies. He'd become a political liability. In May 1880, Tupper abruptly dismissed his old Siamese twin.

The settlement of thirty thousand dollars and the promise of a Pacific cable contract eased their separation, but at fifty-three, Sandford Fleming was out. For the first time in his life he seemed face-to-face with an uncertain future. When they had commissioned him to take on that first railway job, from Eastern to Central Canada, Fleming had moved the family to Ottawa and built an imposing mansion called Winter Home, whose tropical arboretum became his hobby. It was now a retreat and a solace. And his old pal from St. Matthew's in Halifax came up with a proposal that would, he hoped, be of some comfort.

In 1879, George Grant had been named Principal of Queen's University in Kingston, Ontario. Now he persuaded the governors to install his old friend Sandford Fleming as Chancellor. Fleming had confessed to Grant a certain diffidence about his lack of a formal, classical education; but Grant knew, rightly, that his friend would be a superb figurehead and advocate for the university. Fleming's inaugural address was a hymn to scientific learning. He worked his contacts to champion Queen's in its rivalry with McGill. He stayed on as Chancellor for thirty-five productive years.

He invested heavily in Hudson's Bay Company stock, and became a close friend of the company's largest shareholder, Donald Smith. Smith and Fleming knew that the Hudson's Bay Company held huge tracts of land in the West, land that might be of interest to the transcontinental railway. Smith got Fleming into the Montreal syndicate that had taken over the development of the transcontinental railway — the Canadian Pacific Railway Company under William Van Horne. Fleming liked this bluff engineering giant, who once told a doubting investor, "Go sell your boots, man, and buy CPR stock." Fleming did not have to sell *his* boots, obviously, but he did buy a lot of CPR stock, and in the famous photograph in which Van Horne drives the Last Spike, the tall figure at Van Horne's shoulder is that of Sandford Fleming.

His energy and his confidence had flooded back as they finished the railway. Now he turned to the submarine telegraph cable that would link Canada to the South Pacific colonies in the west and Britain to the east. He thought he had a promise from Tupper about this, but if he did, Tupper broke it. Fleming set out to raise the money on his own. He knocked on doors in England, New Zealand, and Australia. Eager as he was to see the project financed, he refused the offer from a group of British monopolists whom he felt had nothing but profit in mind. If the railway had been a way to build a country, the cable would be the way to build an empire. When it finally became a reality, it was New Zealand and Australia who showered the Canadian with the greatest praise for this modern link to the ancient world.

Then a not very uncommon incident in Ireland prompted him to take up what was certainly the most world-changing cause in his whole career. Missing a train in Ireland because of a confusion in schedules, he also missed his boat to England. He began to reflect on chaos in transportation that was caused by cities and towns setting their municipal clocks by the sun, more or less. And with the scores of different departure and arrival times for the railways across the continent, there was a prodigious safety problem: What time do you expect this train to be on this section of track? If two trains travelling in opposite directions are using different clocks, and the engineers driving them are not aware of those differences, something a lot more serious than missing the next boat is bound to happen, and to happen with mortal frequency.

Rail travel had made the industrialized world aware that the time issue was urgent. The American Society of Engineers liked Sandford Fleming's approach, and appointed him chairman of their official Committee on Time. What he proposed was a series of equal-width time zones, twenty-four of them around the world. In our *Heritage Minute*, we dramatize his invention through a conversation with a younger engineer in a construction shack during the building of the CPR.

FLEMING:

> *Between Halifax and Toronto, there are five different time zones. It's ridiculous. After the railway and the electric telegraph, what the world really needs is a system of standard time zones.*

ENGINEER:

> *But sir, cities set their own time by the sun. They'd never agree.*

FLEMING:

> *Well, we'll have to make them agree. Even if it takes years.*

It did take years. He published his first papers on the issue, in the journal of the Institute, in 1878. The idea caught on in North America first, and by 1883 every railroad in North America had built its schedules on the time zones that we still use on this continent. Fleming had to work on all the political establishments, of course, among other things dealing with national rivalries over who would be home to the prime meridian, the line of Zero Longitude from which the whole world's time system would start. He won it, in the end. In 1884 he was able to convene the international Prime Meridian Conference in Washington, DC, and by 1885 it was all done. His mark was now on the whole globe.

He had persuaded all those competing national interests to shake hands and establish Greenwich, just outside London, as the marker for the prime meridian. There is a plaque there marking the zero point with astronomic precision. But Fleming's name is not on that plaque and sadly nowhere in Greenwich can you find any mention of Sandford Fleming.

But under a Canadian maple tree in the town where he was born, in the front garden of the Kirkcaldy Museum, there's a small plaque commemorating Sandford Fleming, and a few metres away local and international travellers board trains that connect with services around the world — and all those services run on Sandford Fleming's Standard Time.

The pain of his father's death had receded by the time he had thus changed the world. But within a brutally short space of time his brother David, then his wife, and then his mother all died. The family, that old anchor, that rock, that mirror — and in a sense the legitimation of all his invention and accomplishment — was suddenly fractured, crumbling, sliding away from him. Alan Wilson says that he "went haywire" for several years, keeping up some work by mail and telegram, seldom leaving home, even his business correspondence tinged with grief.

He spent a good deal of time developing the property in Halifax, Alan Wilson told us.

He built a chapel. And he built a cottage. And he built stone walls across the front. He gave ninety-three acres of it to the city of Halifax to be used as a park. The whole property was known as The Dingle. He determined to rally as much support as he could (of course, he had friends worldwide) to build a commemorative tower in that public park.

What Sandford Fleming set out to do he usually finished. The support was found and the tower built. It celebrates the 150th anniversary of the establishment of representative government in Nova Scotia, the earliest such achievement in the British empire. Opened by the duke and duchess of Kent with great ceremony in 1912, its walls are embedded with plaques and carvings contributed by commonwealth members, universities, societies, and governments. The park is called Fleming Park.

Although that name is most importantly attached to the prophetic work of the 1870s and 1880s that culminated in Standard Time, just to list his other accomplishments is to wonder how one person could do so much. Sandford Fleming had surveyed new towns, designed buildings (and a prophetic set of roller skates), set standards for and steered the building of thousands of miles of railway, and guided and inspired a fine institution of higher learning. He had loved and encouraged, and gathered around him, a great extended family. He helped found the Northwest Mounted Police and the Royal Military College. He set professional standards for the new Engineering Society of

Canada, and helped found the Royal Society with a Science Division, reminiscent of his old Canadian Institute. He was an apostle of Canadian nationalism and science, and a staunch imperialist. He had honorary degrees from Canadian, American, and Scottish universities. In 1897 he became, by Royal Decree, Sir Sandford Fleming.

Through personal and professional adversity he had piled success upon success, and he was really not in any hurry to leave the world in which he'd played such a dramatic role. Jeannie was no longer there to be the gracious hostess that she had been for so many years, but he regularly welcomed his children, grandchildren, nieces, and nephews to Winter Home, where he held a number of modest galas. As the guests bundled up for their carriages at the end of these afternoons or evenings, he would take each by the hand and look at them with affection, saying a philosophical word or two.

It was, one said, a kind of extended leave-taking. He wrote once,

How grateful I am for my birth into this marvellous world, and how anxious I have been to justify it. It has been my great fortune to have my lot cast in this goodly land, and to have been associated with its educational and material prosperity. To strive for the advancement of Canada.

He died in Halifax, on July 22, 1915, aged eighty-eight.

◆ ◆ ◆

The History Television documentary was written by Whitman Trecartin and Alan Wilson, and directed by Whitman and Matthew Trecartin.

◆ Part Fifteen ◆

MARION ORR
A LIFE IN THE SKY

In Montreal in the winter of 1995 we produced a *Heritage Minute* about a pioneer Canadian aviator named Marion Orr. It was shot in the studio, though it very convincingly looks like the outdoor scene it represents, at an English RAF airfield during World War II. It shows the RAF controllers at a country fighter base, dense fog swirling around, and the unlikely sound of an aircraft engine in the distance, in weather that no sensible pilot would venture out in. We see the Spitfire flash by the control tower, half-veiled in mist, and when it lands and the pilot climbs stiffly out of the cramped cockpit, to be greeted by the ground crew, the young sergeant calls up, "Great landing, Sir!" and then has to amend his greeting with, "I mean, Ma'am," as Marion takes off her helmet and a cascade of dark and very feminine hair falls out.

I had been writing the script the previous spring, and when I had a draft ready I had a preliminary telephone conversation with the pioneer pilot, in which we agreed to meet and go over the story together when she got back from her upcoming Florida vacation. A few months later I saw an item in the newspaper one morning: "Pioneer Woman Pilot Dies." Sadly it was Marion Orr. She had become confused at a traffic intersection, driven ahead when she should have stopped, and been hit by another car.

Marion Orr was born Marion Powell, in Toronto, on

June 25, probably in 1916, although this was sometimes put into question because Marion late in life occasionally said that she had come into the world just when the Great War was going out, in 1918. And on some documents related to flying she has given the date as 1920. She was distressed at aging, not for the usual reasons but because she was afraid that a day would come when "they" wouldn't let her fly any more. Since she saw her first airplane when she was just a little girl she had told everyone that this was what she was going to do in life, fly airplanes. Before she was finally grounded she would have put in more than twenty thousand hours, many of them as an instructor and many as a wartime ferry pilot in Britain. She had flown nearly seventy different kinds of aircraft, including helicopters.

She was the youngest of four girls in the Powell family. Her father died when Marion was two, and her mother tried unsuccessfully to support the family by running a store, then took in boarders and got the children to help her as much as they could with the boarding house, cooking, making beds, cleaning house, doing laundry. Her friends from that time said that Marion was a pretty rebellious kid. Lillian Powell married again when Marion was an adolescent, and sent the girls out looking for jobs before they finished school.

Marion used to go up on the roof to watch for planes flying over. When she moved out of the house with her sister Marge, they shared digs and got jobs together in a perfume factory or a bakery. Marge said that on their days off Marion would often walk all the way up to Barker Field, at Dufferin and Lawrence, to watch the planes take off and land. Dufferin and Lawrence was raw countryside then. The farms started before you got to Eglinton.

Violet Milstead was a major contributor to the biographical documentary in the History Television series. She is a flying instructor who years later would teach the famous Canadian journalist June Callwood to fly, and she was an early professional colleague of Marion's. Milstead is another woman for whom a life in the air was an early dream and a continuing need, like food or breathing, and even she speaks of Marion's desire as something more intense and more profound than anyone's.

Aviation was and remains primarily the domain of males. In those early days they were mostly wealthy males and virtually all white. But Amelia Earhart would become a symbol and a beacon for women like Violet Milstead and Marion Orr: if Earhart could fly solo across the Atlantic, there was certainly no reason why they couldn't get into the air.

After one of those six-mile walks to watch the planes at Barker Field — more than an hour from her downtown shared rooms — Marion got up the nerve to approach Pat Patterson, the owner of Fliers Limited, and ask him about lessons. It was six dollars an hour then; Marion was earning ten dollars a week. She said later that she would go without lunches and makeup and do anything she could to get even twenty minutes of instruction. That walk, from Queen Street, was about six miles. When the twelve-mile round trip wore holes through the soles of her shoes, she put cardboard in them. She did go without lunches, and her weight dropped to ninety-five pounds. But she kept at it.

It was not by any means all six-mile walks with cardboard in your shoes and partial flying lessons and going
without lunch. The sisters had a lively sense of a good
time, too. Eileen Hobbs, Marge's daughter, said,

*Marion and my mom, they dated a lot and loved dancing.
Of course, the two of them were in the high kickers, dancing at the Royal York and Maple Leaf Gardens. So they
loved just going to the pier, the Palais Royale. Always had
lots of dates and sometimes someone would come to the
door and they were expecting another person to go out
with. At that point in time they looked very similar and if
my mom didn't want to go out with him, then she would
get Marion to take him out. But he didn't know that it
wasn't my mom, that it was Marion. And my mother
would be dashing out the back door. They used to do crazy
things like that. But they had a great time together. They
were like one.*

Violet Milstead was training at Fliers Limited at the
same time. The training planes were the earliest Piper
Cubs, two-seaters with forty- or fifty-horsepower engines.
The instructor sat in the back and the student pilot in front.
They took off at about forty miles an hour, climbed at fifty-
something, and cruised not much over seventy-five. But
they were real airplanes, a delight to handle. Marion was
ready for her flying test in 1939. "Taking flying tests was a
little different than it is today," Violet Milstead said.

*The inspector sat in his car facing the runway, and one
had to do X number of landings and you had to roll to a
stop within so many yards of the car. And then you had to
go up and do spins and from the spin you had to come and*

land and do the same thing — land in front of the car.

On Marion's test flight her engine quit. She had been taught procedures for dealing with this, which usually meant keeping on straight ahead to the nearest available flat patch of land — you could land a cub in a little more than a hundred feet of grass — but Marion was not about to abort her test if she could help it, and with extraordinary aplomb she turned back just at the right time to be able to make a dead-stick landing within a few feet of the inspector's car. He was very much impressed by both the skill and the cool-headedness, and of course she got her private licence. "And then after you have X number of hours, you're allowed to take passengers," Violet Milstead said.

Well, that was the best revenue you've ever had, you know, under the table, or under the, you know. Because you could take your brother or your sister or something and they all knew that you needed a little bit of money to continue flying. So you didn't refuse. And I think likely she did the same thing. I assume that we all did. I know I did.

Marion took the risk of being caught at this illegal commerce because she was now determined to get her commercial licence. The assigned instructor for this next phase was Deke Orr, a good-looking, rather domineering guy. Perhaps Marion's judgment was a bit bent by spending so much time in a small airplane with him. She accepted his proposal of marriage. "Not my particular type," Violet Milstead said.

Marion and I had been asked by Pat to go down to Windsor in a Cub to pick up a Stinson. So we set out, but you know, December gets to be a fairly short day. So any-how, we got down to Windsor and picked up the airplane. Quickly turned around and it was getting dark and we thought, "Well, should we or shouldn't we?" At least I did, and I'm sure she did. But I thought, "Oh, hang," and we made it. It was dark when we got around in the circuit. But the local custom is if an airplane is out after dark and you think they're coming in, why the boys get their cars out on the runway and do their thing the best they can to tell you which runway to use and it worked just fine. And Marion came in behind me, not too far behind. So every-body rushed up . . . and said, "We'll get you along and so on." And all I can remember is Deke sort of coming along to Marion and just sort of saying, "Get out of that air-plane," and just really upset. So, I don't know. Men! — that's all I have to say.

The marriage was soon over. World War II had begun, and fuel was getting short. Private and small commercial aviation was restricted. Marion was taken on as a con-troller in the tower at the Goderich RCAF base. In the meantime, Violet found out that the British Overseas Airways Corporation was contributing to the war effort by setting up an Air Transport Auxiliary, the ATA, and was hiring women to relieve combat pilots from the task of fer-rying aircraft from the factories to the bases. She went off to Montreal to check it out, came back with a contract in her pocket and a booking for England, told Marion to check it out as well, and within a couple of weeks she too was told to come down for her test flight. Historian Shirley Render said,

The check-out plane was a Harvard. So to go from say a Piper Cub, sixty horsepower into a Harvard which was a six hundred horsepower, retractable gear, and to be able to fly this big plane. And a person saying, "Hey, you can handle that plane, and if you can handle the Harvard . . . we can train you to fly Spitfires and Hurricanes and Typhoons and Beaufighters and all of these others." So right there, the adrenalin starts flying. The whole idea of women being able to fly military aircraft must have been so exciting for Marion.

The test went well, she got the job, and booked passage on the same boat as Violet. Marion's estranged husband Deke found out and was furious. He was actually in the Air Force, and here they were keeping him at home to train young idiots and his uppity wife was going off to the war. And off she did go, and before long she was, indeed, flying Spitfires and Hurricanes.

The training took place at a BOAC facility at Waltham. It was expected that six flights would suffice to familiarize the trainees with a new type of aircraft. Many of the women were much shorter than the male pilots for whom the fighters had been designed, and had to stuff an overnight bag under the parachute they normally sat on, in order to see over the forward cowling, and then had to pull the seat all the way forward to reach the rudder pedals, or stuff another bag or a folded towel behind them if the seat would not come forward as far as they needed.

When their basic training was completed Marion and Vi were assigned together to an all-female ferry pool at Cosford. They were expected to fly any machines in the same category as their training craft. Each type had its *Blue Book*, a detailed operating manual written in English perhaps slightly more comprehensible than today's software manuals. The ferry pilots would turn up at a factory — at Coventry, say, to fly a new type or an updated model of an older machine up to a fighter base in Scotland or Essex — and the first thing was always to pore over the *Blue Book* to make sure they knew what the take-off speed was, and that they would be able to find the undercarriage lever and the fuel-tank selectors.

Some of the aircraft were very eccentric. The *Supermarine Spitfire*, the most famous fighter of that war and some would say of all time, used a shotgun shell to start the engine. You had to prime the massive Rolls-Royce Merlin's twelve cylinders with just the right amount of raw fuel. When you pressed the starter the shotgun shell fired into a cylinder that had a piston that whammed downwards and turned over the big crankshaft just enough to send a couple of the twelve pistons up to the compression and firing position — enough to lurch the Merlin into that coughing, hesitant start we've seen in the movies and the newsreels. You had two chances, a second shell being available if you overprimed or underprimed on the first shot. Pilots got the hang of it. The superb engines were beautifully tuned and seldom failed. But it was all pretty daunting at first. There were no training Spitfires equipped with a second seat for the instructor; you just got in and did it. Marion said in a television interview once that her first circuit in a Spitfire nearly overwhelmed her.

The first one I ever had was a real shock. Because I got in it, opened up the power, and everything went numb. That thing just shot right off the ground and up in the air. I was five thousand feet before I even sort of shook my head and thought, good heavens, what was that?

But after they came to terms with a couple of thousand horsepower instead of the forty or fifty they were used to, and learned to decipher the language of the operating manuals, the women began to feel pretty cocky about these warplanes.

"We'd just take it in our lap like this," Marion said in a 1991 television interview, showing an old copy of a Spitfire *Blue Book.* "After we got on the airplane, we checked on here and we looked for everything that was going on down here until we got it started. And then just did what the book said."

"And then you'd taxi out," Violet Milstead said, in the documentary about Marion,

and it's an airplane, you know. Like it's got an engine and a frame and it's got a little more power and you know it's going to do this because you've talked to people who've flown them. So you get into it and you go down to the end of the runway and you turn around. And you'd get a green light, because no radio control, of course, and off you went.

And when they got to their destination, they'd say, "Okay now, what's my letdown speed, what's my landing speed? Well, I'll look in my *Blue Book.*" Once when Violet Milstead delivered a Spitfire, she was told when she landed that there was a Beaufighter that had to be ferried to another base.

So this chap came up to me, a flight lieutenant or some-thing, and said: Did you just bring in the Spitfire? And I said yes. He said, "You're getting in the Beaufighter? Have you ever flown one before?" And I said no. And he said, "Well, what gives you the idea that you can fly one of those?" And I said, "Well, I carry my little book around with me." And he said, "How can you fly an airplane by the book?" And I said, "Oh, it's easy. You know, you just get all your information and know where your knobs and taps are on the airplane before you start it up, and away you go."

. . . When I talk easily about taking off and landing a Spitfire and then people will say to me, well how long does it take to train a Spitfire pilot just on Spitfires. And I'll say to them that the only expertise I needed was to get up and get down. And all the expertise that they need is beyond measure. They're fighting for their lives most of the time.

Historian Shirley Render retailed a story she had from Marion, the story that in fact served as the plot for the *Heritage Minute.*

She was ferrying, I think it was a Spitfire, from Scotland to England and she was flying along the coast. And again, the weather came down. It was a priority one aircraft and when ferry pilots were given the task of taking a priority one aircraft they felt a real pressure on them in taking off and getting that aircraft to the squadron that needed it. And she said she took off in crummy weather and the weather just proceeded to get worse and worse. She said she was just about ready to ditch that aircraft when all of a sudden she saw runway lights and she was able to slip through to safety.

And that was the way it went. Pretty heady times for people in their mid-twenties, especially so for women. "I can remember one morning that we got up," Violet Milstead tells,

I was getting dressed and she was over at the window saying, "They can't make me fly this morning." And I thought to myself, "Oh my." And I said, "Marion, you can't see as far as the backyard." That's not 800 feet and it's not so many yards, no one could — they're not going to make anyone even — they're not going to put chits out this morning, let alone make you fly. But then I said, "We're supposed to drive to the airport. Now get busy and get dressed."

We lost a number of pilots and one in particular, a girl, Jane Winston. Jane was from New Zealand. And we had a Spitfire assembly plant right on Cosford and so this day I guess most of the pool of pilots were taking their first delivery of the day out of the factory and Jane got one that had a problem. Jane took off in hers and had engine trouble. And it would stop and start, you know, it was intermittent. And she tried to turn back to the airport and didn't make it and went straight in and she was killed. Well, that upset of course all of us at the airport, and it was really a shock. That was the only one that we had right in our own pool while I was there.

Now Marion began to hear from Deke again, long tender letters full of regret for their break-up and contrition for his behaviour. It seems that he had been playing around even while they were still together, but now he promised to be faithful, and careful, an attentive husband, respectful of her career and her needs. The old feelings that had been so powerful when the two of them had pounded the circuit together doing her commercial pilot's licence apparently flared up again. She went home on leave, and listened to his proposal that they patch it up again, and then came back to England and her Spitfires, to think it over.

A few weeks after the Normandy invasion, in the summer of 1944, she gave that all up and came home for good. It did not work out. Deke did not stay faithful. Once again they separated, and Marion went back to Barker Field with her eight hundred hours of wartime flying and her radiant confidence and good looks, and started instructing for the Henderson Brothers at an outfit called Aero Activities. When Vi Milstead came home she signed on with a competing flight school at Barker, Leavens Brothers, and the two veteran ferry pilots would meet for coffee at Mrs. Ward's Diner right on the field.

When Marion was offered the chance to buy Aero Activities, she knew that she would have to be able to do virtually everything herself if the place was going to ever get in the black, and so she took an Aero Mechanics' course, and soon she had yet another licence to post up on the wall. Not that Aero Activities actually had a wall. She was operating out of a tent at first. Students came in gratifying numbers though. They found her a warm and personable instructor — inclined to suddenly take the controls from time to time and show off a bit, perhaps throw a bit of a scare into the poor student with a sudden wingover or a surprise cutting of power. But they kept coming. She gave parties in that tent, and scrimped and saved. When Leavens Brothers decided to sell Barker Field as Toronto pushed northward, Marion had saved enough to buy land farther north at Maple, where she set out to develop her own airfield and flying school.

In conventional financial terms it was a totally marginal enterprise. Her pals and colleagues from Barker Field, and many of her students, pitched in to help cut trees and dynamite the roots, dig ditches, lay drainage tiles, seed out the grass runway, set tie-downs, and build a rudimentary clubhouse and office. The Department of Transport regulations required a minimum of 1800 feet for the runway, but there was only 1600 feet available. So when the officials came to check it out, a helpful club member discreetly pulled the hundred-foot tape backwards, step by step, until the measure was correct.

As soon as the runway was approved, there was another setback. A petition by concerned Maple citizens resulted in a new bylaw to stop the airport from opening. Marion decided she needed some high-level support at this point, borrowed a car, drove to Ottawa, found her way to the Prime Minister's office and talked her way in to see him. As anyone who ever met Louis St. Laurent will testify, once you got by the protective wall, this Prime Minister was courteous and direct in his quiet, patrician way. He listened carefully to her account of her wartime career, her commitment to teach flying, and her having put her life savings into Maple. We do not know how the strings were subsequently pulled, but the bylaw was withdrawn. The pals put on an air show for the opening, De Havilland sent over their new Otter, the Air Force flew a formation of jet fighters overhead (CF 100s), and Maple was — however precariously — in business. You can still see it today as you drive north on Highway 400, about fifteen minutes north of Toronto; it's much more elaborate now, with a small control tower and an imposing brick building — which largely masks that original grass runway, still in service.

What happened next indicates an aspect of Marion Orr's character that had not yet revealed itself, even to her. Her ambition from childhood had been to fly. She had achieved that. The thing had taken on the specific form of running her own flying school, and the effort to achieve that had been prodigious. But now that she had it, there came a sense of letdown, of no more horizons. So after a few years, she decided to pull back for a while and consider whether there was anything left to achieve. She put the Maple operation up for sale and went off to Florida to stay with her sister Marge. She dyed her hair blond, spent a lot of time at the beach, and occasionally went over to the local airport, Opalaka, to see what was going on.

Early in 1961 she found herself in conversation with a helicopter pilot, and realized suddenly that here was a very challenging kind of flying about which she knew almost nothing. The difference between flying a fixed-wing airplane and flying a helicopter is largely mechanical and physical. A regular airplane's controls constantly feed back to the pilot a muscular indication of what you are trying to do — climb, descend, bank, turn, hold steady. In normal straight-ahead flight, with everything properly trimmed, you can take your hands and feet off the stick and rudder and the airplane will just keep going the way it has been set to go. But when you move the controls to change course by turning or climbing or descending, the controls resist you, letting you know very precisely that you are asking the machine to do something it is not trimmed to do. The greater the change, the more muscle required to control it.

Not so with a helicopter. The control column is limp, "the wet noodle," they used to call it. There is no muscular information. You are almost totally dependent on your eyes to tell you what's going on. Some fixed-wing pilots find the transition so difficult that they give it up. Marion Orr never gave up on anything, except perhaps her marriage. She hurled her formidable energy into the helicopter challenge, and in a matter of weeks had mastered the new craft sufficiently well to earn an instructor's licence.

But they say that you are not really safe in a helicopter until you have flown a thousand hours. Marion had a hundred hours, if that. One day, with a student at the controls, the engine failed. The Canadian poet Karen Solie wrote of the sensation

> . . . *that first engine stutter lifts a hand*
> *to collarbone. In concussive measures*
> *of the blade the chance*
> *of a guttering pause . . .*
> *. . . Movements*
> *of each pilot's arm look much like*
> *our own, panic the soft spot*
> *we are all born to.**

*Excerpt from "Why I Dream of Helicopter Crashes" from *Short Haul Engine*, by Karen Solie, published by Brick Books, 2001.

There is an altitude below which — unless your forward speed is considerable — you cannot recover. Hovering at less than about four hundred feet you are in deep trouble. Marion was in deep trouble. It is doubtful that she felt the panicky soft spot we are all born to — Marion Orr was not a panic person — but she was not able to stop the machine from falling out of the sky.

Marge's daughter Eileen Hobbs told us that she and her mother, Marion's sister, were in the car on the way to California

> when I was seven or eight. And as we were driving along, my mother became violently ill and we stopped the car. And when she got back into the car, she said, "We have to get to a phone." She goes, "There's something wrong with Marion." And that's when we found out that Marion had had the helicopter accident. So the same time she got very sick was when she had had the accident. My mother just knew instantaneously it had happened.

The impact had broken her back. She came out of the hospital in a brace and with a lot of pain. She stayed on with Marge and got a job as a bookkeeper at the Opalaka Airport. At least she was still around planes and aviators. Marge tried to set her up with eligible men. That did not work, but the sisters remained very close, and Marion became very fond of Marge's daughter Eileen, from whom we had much of this story. Sitting there at Opalaka with her ledgers and invoices, and watching the planes rise and descend, and the young aviators eagerly telling each other war stories and moving their hands about like flying objects as they came and went from the office, Marion began to feel that her time as an instructor in real airplanes had been pretty rewarding after all. She decided to come home and get back to what she was really good at.

The little airport at Buttonville, Ontario, a few miles east of Maple, was expanding in the early 1970s. Its new owners, Michael and Heather Sifton, had decided to turn it into a serious player in the Greater Toronto aviation scene. The northwest-southeast runway, a grass strip when this writer started flying there a decade earlier, was now paved, and the airport was the only privately owned facility in Canada to have a D.O.T. control tower, integrated into the national air traffic control system. The Siftons' flying school was big and growing, and an instructor with Marion Orr's experience, qualifications, and personality was just what they needed. Now in her mid-fifties she was authoritative, distinctive, diligent, energetic . . . and unconventional. Peter Muehlegg, a sixteen-year-old boy who had been hopelessly infected with the flying bug and had saved barely enough to pay for the minimum thirty-five hours of flying time plus ground school, was sent to her to be assessed as a candidate. He asked her if it was really possible to complete his licence with those minimum hours.

Before she answered she said, "Are you really dedicated and is this something you really want to do?" And obviously the answer was yes. "Are you willing to work hard and put your mind into this?" I said, "Oh, absolutely," again without hesitation. And, "Well you may not enjoy it. I'm going to work you real hard and it's a little bit tough sometimes getting [through the course] on minimum hours, but as long as you're willing to work, I'll do it."

On a few occasions if there was a couple of parts of lessons that required a little extra work, there was numerous occasions where we were flying and she would look at her watch and say our hour is up. We'd probably best head back towards the airport. She would look at her watch and realize it was still an hour before her next student and she would pretty much shut off her clock and we would train for another fifteen or twenty minutes and stay in the air that much longer. And we did that on maybe a dozen or more occasions just to get in that little extra flight time and training. And then when we landed and went back in the office, she walked up to the dispatch office and handed him a time sheet that only had one hour written on it.

She was a meticulous person with a sensitive nose. If students were careless about bathing, she let them know it. She carried a packet of breath mints and often pressed one on a student when they got into the cockpit and she got a whiff of the slightest unpleasantness. One of the students who turned out to be problematic — for quite different reasons — was Marion's favourite niece Eileen Hobbs.

I called Marion. I said, "Do you think I could come stay with you and learn to fly with you?" And she said, sure, no problem. So we went up in the end of September or October and on my first flight we did attitudes and movements. So when we got up in the air, she was showing me how by pulling the control column back you go up in the air, and push it down and you go down. Then she looked at me and she said, and this is what happens when you students overcontrol the aircraft. And she reached back the control column and we were just standing straight up.

And then she pushed it forward and you could feel your body just came up out of the seat and we were just diving down. And then she pulled the aircraft level. And then she looked at me and she said, "Aren't the trees beautiful down there this time of the year, so much gorgeous colour." I was petrified in my seat because I thought we were going to die. (laughter) That's pretty well how we ended up the first flight lesson and then we landed and she got out of the plane as if nothing happened and that was that.

After a few more lessons, Buttonville's chief instructor Gordon Craig had become concerned that Marion was being unusually tough on her niece. He proposed that someone else take over Eileen's training. Marion became uncharacteristically angry, and said that if she couldn't teach her niece to fly then nobody would. Eileen decided on a discretionary retreat, and went over to Maple to continue her training. Marion didn't speak to Eileen for the next fifteen years. Then, just after Eileen's father died, and without a word of explanation, Marion called her. They were to remain close for the rest of Marion's life.

The next few years were rich in satisfaction, and teaching people to fly, as it turned out, was in many ways the most rewarding part of this pioneer's long and productive life. Of the nearly 21,000 hours she logged in the air, almost 17,000 of them were while instructing. In 1982 she was inducted into the Canadian Aviation Hall of Fame. "I'll fly till I'm ninety," she said, "as long as I don't lose my licence."

But she did lose it. Friends had begun to notice what

at first seemed a slightly distracted air from time to time, and then a more alarming level of forgetfulness. Memory is a pilot's single most essential protective device. There is a constant list of conditions that must be reviewed as you fly, ranging from the simple and obvious such as altitude and speed, fuel quantity, engine temperature and oil pressure (which are constantly displayed on the panel) as well as the condition of switches for the electric supply and the landing gear and other crucial matters that are not displayed and the pilot must remember to check.

There are, of course, checklists. In a light aircraft of the kind in which Marion did much of her instructing the list would have a dozen or twenty items on it. In an airliner there may be hundreds. The more sophisticated aircraft have mechanical devices to record the pilot's review of those checklists, but the pilot does have to remember to *use* the checklist in the first place; must remember to check fuel levels and the exterior mechanical condition before even climbing into the cockpit; must remember to flick the tabs on the checklist's mechanical reminders if the airplane has such a thing; must constantly remember to check, check, check.

Pilots who do so live a long time; pilots who do not, die. Marion was beginning to show signs of forgetting things.

A friend called her doctor, suggesting that he check it out. And the next time her licence renewal was supposed to arrive in the mail, it never came. Marion was stricken. In 1993 when she was inducted into the Order of Canada, she forgot where she was sitting, and had to be helped back to her seat after the Governor General had placed the medal's ribbon around her neck.

When we spoke to her a couple of years later, about developing the script for our *Heritage Minute*, she sounded alert and pleased at the prospect of the dramatization of her ferry pilot days. She would call as soon as she got back from Florida, she said cheerfully. A few days after she returned she drove to Peterborough to see a friend who had been helping her with her taxes. Ironically she had said in an interview once, when asked about the dangers of flying,

I feel a lot more secure in an aircraft than I do in my car. I feel that in an aircraft that if anything was to happen I could, you know, get out. But in a car, I don't know, you've got so many other people around you that you're driving everybody's car, plus your own, eh?

Coming back from Peterborough she seems to have become confused. One of her friends said that perhaps in her mind she was airborne in the circuit at the Peterborough Airport, and just didn't see the stop sign. It was April 4, 1995. She was seventy-nine years old. Or perhaps seventy-five. Who's counting?

◆ ◆ ◆

The History Television documentary was written and directed by Martin Harbury.

◆ Part Sixteen ◆

NORTHERN DANCER
LITTLE HORSE, BIG HEART

When we approached History Television with the proposal to step out of the frame, so to speak, and produce one episode about an animal instead of a person, in this television series *The Canadians, Biographies of a Nation*, the initial response was a kind of tolerant "Wha-a-at?" until we named the animal. We then discovered an interesting phenomenon, as writer/producer/director Martin Harbury began to develop the documentary. Virtually everyone to whom we mentioned that we had initiated this slightly unorthodox venture in Canadian biography immediately responded with enthusiasm: "Northern Dancer! Of course! What a brilliant idea!" And yet, when asked, few of these respondents could say anything more about The Dancer than that it was a famous Canadian racehorse.

"Well, was this horse a Stallion?" we would ask. "A Mare? A Gelding?" Few knew. Yet this little guy had set himself, icon-like, in their minds as a feature of the Canadian celebrity landscape. So radiant was his fame, at the height of his career, that you would have to be fairly young today not to recognize the name, and even very young people we've talked to, if they are horse people, will say, "Oh yeah, Northern Dancer, great horse."

The little stallion's name is a large part of the legend of E.P. Taylor, himself one of those iconic names for the generations growing up in the 1930s, '40s, and '50s. Born in

Ottawa in 1901, Edward Plunkett Taylor would become the biggest brewing magnate in the country, O'Keefe's being the prime brand, and in the popular mind thought of as the richest man in Canada. But important as his managerial, financial, and technical contributions to Canadian beer certainly were, his most enduring legacy was his dramatic rescue of the track from its messy decline and potential collapse. The fears, preoccupations, and economic focus of World War II had deeply hurt racing throughout North America. But Taylor and others recognized that the postwar euphoria and prosperity were a whole new scene.

And to this scene Taylor and his colleagues and counterparts brought a new tone of adroit marketing, insistence on high standards of safety, cleanliness, honesty, and comfort, and a revival of the old glory around horses who ran clean and brave, and the shared delights among the men and women who shared that passion and worked with the great animals and their housing and facilities to give racing that quality of the regal that it historically has always had.

Taylor was not at first driven by those mythic appetites: he had started in racing as a way to make O'Keefe's famous and sell more beer. Then in 1946, his horse Epic (out of Fairy Imp by Bunty Lawless) won the Queen's Plate, an annual 1 1/4-mile race for four-year-olds foaled in Canada. That win is said to have instantly inoculated him with a life-long passion if not an obsession.

E.P. Taylor had shown from his youth a quick, inventive streak. As a toolmaker's apprentice in 1918 (he was seventeen), he invented an electric toaster, built a prototype, and sold the rights to a Montreal company for one dollar. If this does not sound like an impressively entrepreneurial transaction, note that he also secured royalties of forty cents per toaster sold, and these royalties put him through university. He studied mechanical engineering at McGill. He also was away ahead of the crowd with a primitive propeller-driven snowmobile. He and a friend mounted a motorbike engine on skis, the propeller behind and a seat on top. The noise complaints slowed that one down, and then we don't hear more of E.P. the innovator until he reappears in the brewing industry.

Our documentary begins, appropriately, at the track, the jockeys settling tensely into the stirrups behind the closed white bars of the starting gate, the starter raising his hand, the jangling of the bells, the white bars swinging open and the horses bursting out, straight towards the camera. And as they do, in this film we begin to hear voices talking with affection and in some cases with wonder, about Northern Dancer:

"Northern Dancer had more heart than most." "He epitomized this little guy who no one thought was going to do anything, doing it all . . ." "His running style made you want to admire him . . ." "He was almost invincible up to a mile and a quarter . . ." "He was Canada's horse, and they were proud of him." "For the first time Canadians had a horse that could win the Kentucky Derby . . ."

Let's pick up the thread from the owners of those voices, for our story of this endearing little stallion, and he was disconcertingly small, even for E.P. Taylor, is embedded in the minds of the men and women who raised him, trained him, rode him, and, in the end, cared for him until the end and then buried him with love and honour.

Here's Bernard McCormack, the general manager of the Taylor family's now famous Windfields Farms:

E.P. Taylor was building Canadian racing. At the time he became more heavily involved in breeding. In the late 1940s he was buying the best-bred fillies at the sales in Kentucky. He had asked the bloodstock agent George Blackwell to buy the best mare he could in the Newmarket December sales in 1952, and that mare turned out to be Lady Angela. And to give credit to E.P. Taylor, he insisted on buying the mare but he had the opportunity to breed back the mare before she was imported to Canada one more time to Nearco, who was the greatest stallion of his time.

And Noreen Taylor, E.P.'s daughter-in-law, who is now vice-president of Windfields:

You don't usually breed a mare back to the same stallion twice in a row, and the first breeding wasn't tremendously successful from our point of view but the second one produced Nearctic.

Nearctic looked like a winner, and Taylor entered him in a dollar-laden race in Chicago, which he won. With those winnings in hand he then went to the annual auction at Saratoga, Florida, and was very much taken with and acquired a handsome filly named Natalma, who had raced for two years and was in prime shape to be bred. And why not to the stallion whose winnings had brought her to Windfields Farms?

But Natalma was still a pretty attractive candidate for the track, and her trainer, Horatio Luro, wanted to run her in the Kentucky Oaks. The Kentucky Oaks is the number one race in the world for three-year-old fillies, just as the Kentucky Derby, always run the day after the Oaks, is *the* race for three-year-old colts. It is said that a filly who wins the Kentucky Oaks is one of the premier females of her age — good stuff for breeding of course, but Luro thought, Couldn't he get one more splendid win out of her? However, a few days before the Oaks was to be run, the beautiful Thoroughbred injured her knee on the training track, and Luro and his vet, Alex Harthill, had to think hard about what to do. Dr. Harthill said,

> She would have been a strong favourite, she would have been six to five or even money had she ran. And Horatio wanted to ice her and juice her up and run her and she would have probably won. Anyhow, this was Horatio's thought, and I thought differently. I thought if we ran her she could very well have broken down and we'd be bringing her home in the meat wagon so to speak, and I prevailed upon him not to do it, and I said, "Gee Horatio, we can send her home and get her bred right away."

It might be appropriate here to say a word about exactly what constitutes a Thoroughbred. *The English Jockey Club's Stud Book* of 1949 said:

> Any animal claiming admission to the General Stud Book *(which registers all Thoroughbreds) from now on must be able to prove satisfactorily some eight or nine crosses of pure blood, to trace back for at least a century, and to show such performances of its immediate family on the turf as to warrant the belief in the purity of its blood.*

Half a century earlier an American definition said a

Thoroughbred must be "of Oriental extraction and an animal developed through centuries of cultivation by enlightened nations (Merry, 15)." In both definitions, the ancestry of a horse and the purity of its family tree are primary. In fact every contemporary registered Thoroughbred's genes can be traced to one of three eighteenth-century stallions.

Most Thoroughbreds have strong, muscular hindquarters, and a high withers, but those don't make a Thoroughbred, and they are found in other breeds. A Thoroughbred can be any colour from black through chestnut to roan. So in the end it is ancestry. And Natalma would, as it turns out, make a memorable contribution in that regard.

The American Race Museum's account of the breed says this:

To complement the speed of native Galloway horses, [English] breeders in the late seventeenth and early eighteenth centuries began importing stallions from both the Near East and from Spain. Andalusian horses, native to Spain, were imported heavily in the seventeenth century. The height, size, and agility of these horses made them ideal for inbreeding with the speed of the small, heavy English mares. Stallions imported from Eastern countries, in particular Arabia, Turkey, and the Barbary Coast, offered still more to the mix. Races in England were held over long distances, and were often run in heats. Heats, usually one to four miles each, were repeated until one horse had won twice and proven himself the best of the field. In this system of racing, a horse could be expected to run up to twenty miles in one day. Imported stallions from the East were known for their incredible stamina and strength, two traits essential in the heat style of racing. Eastern stallions, too, were purebred horses. Unlike English breeds, which were indiscriminately mixed by constant cross breeding, Eastern horses were carefully bred to maintain the same characteristics in each new generation. This purity of breeding would add genetic stability to the new breed being developed.

In this century the names of some racing Thoroughbreds became household words, known to millions who weren't even interested in racing: Man O'War, Secretariat, Nashua. Before long, Natalma's first foal would become one of those household words.

Peter Poole, then general manager at Windfields Farms:

Northern Dancer was born fairly early in the evening, everything went well, and he was a good little individual, he was up on his feet fairly quickly, and he wasn't big, but then a mare's first foals usually are a little smaller, but he was very robust, and he was a cocky little guy.

Always careful not to be seen keeping the best of his new colts for himself, E.P. Taylor almost always offered all of his yearlings for a set price — Dancer's was $25,000 — at an annual sale. Everyone who saw him liked him, but, as vet Rolph de Gannes told us, "they were mostly looking for big, good-looking horses that in their opinion would become stakes winners and good race horses." And this colt was very good-looking, but he was, well, small.

Bruce Walker, the former publicity director of the Ontario Jockey Club, says,

He wasn't the top horse in the sale, but there was a lot of interest in him and I recall him, especially because Carl Chapman who trained horses for Larkin Maloney was very interested in the colt and he kept taking me over to the stall door and saying, "Look at this horse, what do you think?" And I said, "Well, he's a little on the small side, don't you think?" And he said, "Yeah, but I really like the breeding." Here was . . . this little runtish-looking [colt] . . . and Chappy said, "I really like that horse, I'd like to get him. But," he said, "the boss wants to get the big colt."

And another potential buyer, Jim Boylen:

Well, my brother and I both liked him and so did the trainer but he didn't like his size. He said he was too small, would take too long to come around.

When the intermission bell went off and the crowd headed for the bar, half of the colts and fillies had still not been sold, and when everybody headed for the bar the sale seemed effectively over, so — as usual — the unsold colts went back to Windfields. Northern Dancer was, happily as it turned out for Taylor and the Windfields gang, too small to have made his proposed $25,000, and back he went to the Taylor acres.

Windfields' yearlings manager then was a man who, when he first appears on the screen in our documentary, almost makes the viewer wonder whether we've accidentally wandered into a ventriloquist's studio. His heavily sculptured eyebrows and almost immobile features above a cartoon-like grin and rigid torso are powerfully reminiscent of some of the great ventriloquists' wooden partners — until he speaks, when the animation and excitement of his recollections are instantly engaging, even though the man scarcely moves as he talks. His name is André Blaettler. He told us:

Northern Dancer I got after the yearling sale in sixty-one, so he wasn't a yearling yet of course, he was a weanling. When he was a yearling you never saw him fly around like some of the other ones. He went more like a . . . he galloped but looked more like a hackney pony than a Thoroughbred to be honest about it. But you really couldn't push him around too much or he would start fighting.

Fortunately for us and for the history of the breed, Taylor's people captured the colt on film almost from his earliest days, the tossing head and distinctively marked forelegs, and the unmistakable action of a creature that rejoices in being alive. Even at normal speed, as the colt moves across screen before the camera he seems to be moving in slow motion, the four legs coming off the ground at once as if he were airborne. Peter Poole says,

You can look at a horse, and see what's obvious, see the confirmation he's got, whether he's going to be able to move well, whether he should stay sound which there's no guarantee. But you can't see what's inside, and I think it's the heart that's the unknown thing. . . . After the sale he left and went to our racing stable, which was just across the road at the old Windfields, and they broke him there. He was quite a handful to break. In fact, I think he bucked about everybody off that got on him at the start. Breaking is a very hard time for a horse to go through, he's into something completely different, and it's not a natural instinct for a horse to have somebody on top of him, so they have a difficult time depending on who's riding them, who's looking after them.

In the film you can see the breaking jockey lying across the saddle, crossways, holding on for dear life. They are in the stable and a strong woman trainer has the colt firmly by his bridle, leading him as quietly as possible in small circles about the straw-floored stall, and the jockey is not having an easy time of it. Even André Blaettler, who was fond of the little guy from the start, didn't think he would amount to much. E.P. Taylor kept hoping he'd grow, and asking the staff if he were getting any bigger, and they were tempted to add an inch or two to their reports because they all liked him so well too and didn't want him to be sold. But they knew they couldn't get away with fabricating that increased stature. Yet, somehow when it was time to start serious training, E.P. Taylor decided to put him into the best hands available, so off he went to Horatio Luro, the same man who had wanted to race the colt's dam with an injured knee.

Luro was a star. They called him "The Latin Lover." He would say things like, "Six days I train horses; the seventh is for making love." About the latter activity not much is reported, but as a man who trained horses for almost fifty years, he is talked about throughout the trade. "Hard to ride for," the jockeys would say. Although a big man, far too tall and heavy to race professionally, the handsome Argentinian had spent so much time in the saddle that nobody could pull any excuses on him. His wealthy family in Argentina had owned Thoroughbreds for years. As a young man, he had been a real Argentinian playboy and his life was polo, fast cars, travel, women, and the good life. But when his father died in 1937 and the family called him home to run the stables, he found his real vocation. They called him *El Gran Señor*. He trained professionally for forty-seven years, retiring in 1984. The frivolous playboy had been replaced by a focused professional for whom patience and care were the central instruments of his work. "You mustn't squeeze the lemon dry," he used to say of his charges. In 1980 the Racing Museum inducted him into the hall of fame. For all his experience and insight, Horatio Luro found The Dancer hard to handle, and suggested to E.P. Taylor that he be gelded to make him more manageable, quite possibly one of the most regrettable decisions he had ever made in his long and illustrious career. Taylor detested the very idea of gelding and would not hear of it. He "almost bit his pipe in half when it was suggested they were gonna geld him," Bruce Walker said,

> *because Mr. Taylor not only liked the pedigree and thought the horse had some chance to be something, but he was a personal favourite of Mrs. Taylor because she had often gone into the fields at Bayview and she had picked this little colt out as one of her favourites, and used to feed him peppermints through the fence.*

Billy Reeves, the exercise boy for Pete McCann who broke The Dancer, had been raving about the colt's speed, and everyone was talking about how well the training was going. And so — perhaps because of all those comments about his size — they decided to get him into a race pretty early: August 1963, a 5 1/2-furlong maiden race at Fort Erie. Horatio Luro's vet, Dr. Harthill, said,

Horatio was a fellow who always wanted to prepare his horses for longer races and he didn't want them used up early because it was his thought that they would last so much longer if they were allowed to settle in stride and not be hoop-de-doo and scrambling out of the gate.

But André Blaettler was there, and saw the little guy get out of the gate, his head and ears straight up, his first time ever. "He just ran!" Blaettler said, still enjoying it. "He just kept flying and he won by eight lengths or something."

On his back in that first race was the legendary Canadian jockey, Ron Turcotte:

Mr. Luro never wanted a jockey to hit his horse first time out. When I rode him I was moving up head in head with the second horse which I'd say was Brockston Boy, and he just did not want to leave him, he was just doggin' it with him, and I switched my stick, and just sneaked my whip to the left-hand side, and just brought it down slowly and tapped him. And when I tapped him we were down to past the eight pole and he just took off.

In his fourth race, the Cup and Saucer Stakes at Woodbine, 1 1/8 miles on turf, when you went up to the pari-mutuel wickets to place your bet, Northern Dancer was the clear favourite, but was beaten at the wire by a 40 to 1 outsider. But of his first nine races, he had seven wins, including four stakes races. In the other two he finished second. Taylor and his people decided it was time for New York, and the colt did not let them down. He won the Remsen Stakes, his first time out on a New York track.

He was two years old, and the sun was really shining

on him, they said, but a bit of a cloud moved over that sun, a bit bigger than a man's hand, when they found out that he had a quarter crack. That is a split up the side of the hoof, very painful and potentially very dangerous. Dr. Harthill met with Horatio Luro, and they decided to anesthetize the foot, with a local, and then with a farrier's knife parallel the crack on either side, and draw the diseased portion down to the bottom, and then immobilize the area as much as possible with a bar shoe. A vet named Bane in California had developed what was called a patch technique. Once again they anesthetized the foot against the high heat levels entailed in applying the patch, gave the colt small doses of tranquillizer, and hoped for the best but worried a lot about the worst.

But the patch held. Let's hear about the next phase from those of the principal players who are still here to recall it. First Dr. Harthill:

> [Horatio] wanted to get him ready for the fall races in New York and the winter racing in Florida to prepare him for the Kentucky Derby. He had high hopes from the moment he got him.

Bruce Walker:

> Bill Shoemaker rode him in the early classics in Florida and they thought they had Bill wrapped up for the Kentucky Derby.

Milt Dunnell:

> The fact that Bill Shoemaker was riding him added considerable prestige. If he was good enough for Bill Shoemaker he was good enough for everybody else.

Dr. Harthill:

[Shoemaker] rode Northern Dancer in the Florida Derby and just the day before the race, in the training procedure, Horatio had told the jockey to go 5/16 of a mile, just a little over a quarter, as a blow out. The exercise boy misunderstood him and went 5/8 of a mile, which is twice as far. And he went in 59 seconds for the 5/8 and galloped out 3/4 in 11, which is racehorse time. So when Shoe rode him the next day he won, but it was just because he was such a great horse. And before we could get to him and tell him what had happened, Horatio hadn't told him prior to the race, and after the race [Shoemaker] had taken a plane, somebody had invited him to go to Cuba, and there was no way to communicate with him. He was out of touch, so he announced to the world in a press release that he was gonna ride Hill Rise [in The Derby.]

Bruce Walker:

[Shoemaker] rode a lot for Mesh Teddy who was the trainer of Hill Rise and so politically, and for business reasons, he had to pretty well jump to Hill Rise. So they were scrambling for a rider. But Horatio had always had a love/hate relationship with Billy Hartack, they had a lot of success together, and it was decided that they would go with the experience of Hartack. He had won the Kentucky Derby a couple of times before that and they felt that having that experienced a rider on the colt would be an advantage.

But enough of an advantage to win? Milt Dunnell wondered aloud about it.

He'd beaten the best horses in the east, if he beats the best horses in the west, why shouldn't he win the Triple Crown?

*Two days before the race I talked to Horatio Luro and I told
him that Hill Rise was going to be the favourite, the morning
line favourite, and Northern Dancer would be second. I said,
"What do you think of it?" He said, "Well, if they beat us,"
he said, "it means they beat two minutes."*

You would have to be a race historian to know that no
horse had ever run the Derby in two minutes, the time that
Luro was now sure the Dancer could make. But you don't
even have to be a race fan to know that the Kentucky
Derby is an event of mythic dimensions; the media are all
over it, fortunes and reputations are made and lost.
Owners, trainers, riders, journalists, fans — they all speak
of it as a once-in-a-lifetime matter, and for the majority of
all of the above, it is exactly and only that. The costs of
entry, of preparing the horse for it, and hiring a name jockey, and even for fans — they can pay up to $4500 (for a
clubhouse package ticket) just to watch the race — mean
that it is never to be taken lightly. Not that its almost sacred
resonance would ever allow such negligence.

Some might argue that the great French and British
races have longer pedigrees, but few will try to designate
any other as more important or better known. Horse folk
will tell you that the horses know that they are in the midst
of extraordinary tension, long before they get near the
track itself and the deafening blare of the bands. Ron
Turcotte says, "When we step on the racetrack, and they
play 'My Old Kentucky Home' and your horse is prancing
to it and all that, it's something to behold, I'll tell ya."

Dr. Harthill, the vet, said he was sure despite the
superb training that The Dancer had had "training to the

minute" and improving all the time, the race would be extremely close. After all, the best horses in North America would be lining up behind those white bars, and every single owner and trainer felt that once-in-a-lifetime urgency.

Hill Rise, as predicted, was the favourite, at two-to-one. The bells clanged and the gates swung open, and the first quarter of a mile took the lead horse twenty-two and two-fifths seconds, with Northern Dancer and Hill Rise just apparently coasting along easily around the fourth or fifth position. The reporters and the fans and the owners could see, it was obvious, that Shoemaker on Hill Rise was watching Hartack on The Dancer "to see he didn't make a move on him," as Milt Dunnell put it. Even Ron Turcotte thought that Shoemaker had Hartack boxed in right where he wanted him, and knew it. But Hartack, as it turns out, also knew that he had a horse he could manoeuvre, a horse that could get him out of Shoemaker's box like a puppet on a spring. Harthill says he is convinced that Hartack outrode the more famous Shoemaker, "beat him to the punch up the backside," he says, and "I believe that's where the race was won." The journalist Milt Dunnell says,

I waited until they got to the mile pole and I took a look to see what the time then was and he had run the mile in 1:36 and then that told me that he had to run that last quarter [mile] in twenty-four seconds. He opened up about two lengths on Shoemaker, before Shoemaker made a move.

As they came down the stretch, those who were there remember that the whole place erupted like a volcano, everyone screaming and jumping about. It was that dramatic. Even in the press box, they said, just the way

Northern Dancer came battling through that stretch had all the hard-nosed old reporters up on their feet cheering him on. Bruce Walker says his running style made you want to admire him: "He just, like he grabbed the bit in his teeth and . . . 'You're not going by me, Hill Rise, that's it, I don't care how far we run, you're not going to get by me on this day.'"

Hill Rise seemed to make a terrific run at The Dancer, right at the end, but they could all see that he would never make it, and that even at the end the little three-year-old from Canada was still "digging in."

When they flashed the time, two minutes flat, all the old hands immediately knew: it was a record. You can see in the news film the quiet look of triumph on E.P. Taylor's face as he leads his little champion into the winner's circle and they put on the blanket of fresh red roses.

Three American races — the Derby, the Preakness at Baltimore's Pimlico track, and the Belmont Stakes at Belmont Park, New York — are called the Triple Crown races, and it is a dream seldom even tried for by owners: to have a horse who wins all three. And to the surprise of some observers the shouting and the tumult had scarcely subsided after the Derby when they heard E.P. Taylor's people talking about Baltimore — just two weeks away — and the phrase the Triple Crown. It is not common to run a horse that hard. Many bettors would anticipate the possibility of the horse's not being up to it that soon, maybe even fall apart. And so despite his win in the Derby, he did not come up as the favourite in Baltimore. Preakness bettors and odds-makers made him, once again, the number two. The too-soon argument did not seem to apply to Hill Rise, though, who had a solid record, and Horatio Luro became furious when the majority of the American sports writers seemed to be putting The Dancer down as a one-trick-pony, a fluke, and saying that this time Hill Rise would just run right over him; he'd only won by a neck, albeit a long one, in Kentucky; he'd get nailed at Pimlico. But Horatio said they were wrong, certainly wrong, they didn't know the horse: the distance was less (1 3/16th of a mile) and the little horse's tactical abilities were perfectly suited to anything up to a mile and a quarter.

Horatio was right. The Dancer won by two-and-a-half lengths. This time the blanket was made of black-eyed Susans. "They traditionally send over a case of champagne on ice," Bruce Walker said,

And Mrs. Taylor was in the tack room and she spread her fur coat over the tack trunks and said, "Come on in boys and have some champagne." And then Horatio was standing at the door like a bouncer and said, "No, he can't come in," and "He can't come in," and "He can't come in." Because he remembered all the writers who had put Northern Dancer down and this was personal to him.

Horatio also had reservations about moving on to the Belmont, after two heavy-duty races in a row. But the pressure must have been irresistible: two legs of the Triple Crown down and one to go. The Dancer had earned his shot at it. Luro said, Yes, but maybe the Belmont's mile and a half is too much so soon after the Preakness. Over the next couple of days he scrutinized the horse's gait, his wind, his attitude, his eyes, his smell. Northern Dancer came bouncing back. They decided to go for it. To this day there is bitterness about how the race was run. Not about the decision to go; The Dancer was apparently in great shape, dying to take the lead, an easy win in Peter Poole's view, who was Windfields"s general manager then. But it seems that Bill Hartack inexplicably held him back, right from the start. "Throttled him," Bruce Walker would say later. A questionable ride, others say now. Not so questionable that Horatio would fire him, but a source of grief, when the little horse came third after Quadrangle and Roman Brother, a sore that for The Dancer's "family" has still not healed.

Well, the Queen's Plate was still ahead. And in the meantime, back in Canada Northern Dancer had become a national hero. People wrote letters to him. Not to E.P. Taylor or Ron Turcotte or Horatio Luro, but to the horse himself. Among them was one that was very special. Bruce Walker tells the story. The letter, he said, was

> *from a boy at the Brantford School for the Blind, saying that he had listened to all of the races and that he would like to meet Northern Dancer. And Mrs. Taylor arranged transportation and she met the boy at the track. Just prior to the arrival of Mrs. Taylor and her special guest, Horatio had had the horse cleaned up and he went into the stall to put the halter on Northern Dancer. And just as he reached for the horse, Northern Dancer turned on a dime and was up on his hind legs and he was flailing at Horatio. He didn't want to be bothered, just leave me alone, and Horatio had to dive under the webbing, and the stall door out into the shed row. And Northern Dancer was right behind, and*

he was intent on doing some damage to Horatio.

Just after Horatio escaped, Mrs. Taylor started walk-
ing down the shed row and she said, "Where's my baby,
where's Northern Dancer?" And the horse stopped, and
he pricked his ears and looked, and he started to nicker,
because he knew that he knew the voice, and he knew that
he was going to get some mints from Mrs. Taylor, because
she had been feeding him mints from the time he was a
baby. And the horse was a perfect gentleman. She walked
right up, gave him a mint, patted him, and was almost
nuzzling with him. And then she brought the boy over
from the school for the blind and she guided his hand to the
horse's head. He just stood there, and slowly patted the
horse's head. And Northern Dancer never moved. Never
moved a muscle. It was amazing.

When they got to Woodbine for the Queen's Plate,
Luro and Hartack had arrived at an understanding, and
Hartack said later that there was no way he could not win
that race unless he fell off the horse. He apparently decided it was time to redeem his reputation and that this would
be his show, Billy Hartack's show, not Northern Dancer's.
And when they came out of the gate The Dancer's fans
were appalled to see Hartack holding him back again, rein-
ing him in. Was he going to make the same mistake all over
again, do another Belmont and humiliate not just the horse
and the trainer and the owner now, but the whole darn
country? Peter Poole described it:

Hartack finally let the horse run and the horse cruised
down the backstretch, and coming into the stretch
Langcrest was on the lead and Northern Dancer went by

him like he was standing still. And he won very easily and in hand, but I'm still convinced that that ride in the Plate hurt the horse. And it wasn't announced that the horse had bowed a tendon or injured his tendon until after the horse had gone back to New York, and they said he injured himself training there. But I'm convinced that he left here with a slight knot on his tendon.

Milt Dunnell is convinced that The Dancer could have broken the track record that day, but that Hartack was right to hold him back.

He said, "I wasn't asked for a track record. If I had been, I would have tried to provide it. All I was asked to do was win the race and that's what we did. We won by seven lengths." So of course he won the race, but after the race was over I was talking to Hartack. I said, "Bill, eight horses in the race, you've got seven in front of you, you've got the Kentucky Derby horse underneath you. Weren't you a little bit concerned that you might run into a little traffic here and get the hero beaten on his homecoming?" And he looked at me and said, "Are you out of your goddamn mind? I'm sitting on the Derby winner and I'm going to get beaten by a bunch of damn Canadian breds?" I said, "What did you think you were on Bill, an Egyptian bred?" He said, "Well, I was on Northern Dancer, he's different."

That tendon was bowed, however, and, at three years old, it was time to retire him to stud, where he would leave an even greater mark on the sport than he had from the track. Ron Turcotte was on his back the first time he appeared on a racetrack, and rode him out again when they retired him, to a clamorous demonstration from the fans at Woodbine in June 1964.

Although he had outstanding records in speed (the two minutes at the Derby) and impressive cash returns for both his owners and those who bet on him, his real contribution was as a sire. A "prepotent sire," Dr. Harthill said, a sire of sires and a sire of fine broodmares, whose progeny are still selling at prime prices and still winning races.

From his own loins were sold 174 yearlings, averaging almost a million dollars a yearling. A world's record sale was established when one of his progeny, My Charmer, son of The Dancer's son Nijinsky (whose dam was Flaming Page), sold for thirteen million dollars.

It is getting to the point now where there are so many superb Thoroughbreds with his genes that every time you see a great winner the chances are very good — perhaps as high as 75 percent according to Peter Poole, that he can be traced back to The Dancer. Bernard McCormack, Windfields' general manager, said,

> There's only one horse that has ever run faster than him in the Kentucky Derby and that was Secretariat. [Northern Dancer] was the most dominant stallion of the Thoroughbred breed in the last hundred years. And he will fulfill, going into the fourth and fifth generation of some very, very good race horses, a role where at some point, if we haven't reached it already, that 50, 60, 70 percent of all Thoroughbreds will trace to him. That's a legacy that perhaps no other stallion has left.

He is the only horse ever inducted into Canada's Sports Hall of Fame, and according to Allan Stewart there, nine of the fourteen starters at the 1999 Kentucky Derby had bloodlines that trace back to The Dancer, thirty-five years after his own Kentucky Derby.

He was so small that as a stud he had difficulty mounting the mare. He got very frisky and rough with his first mare, Flaming Page, and she just turned around and kicked him in the ribs. When he finally did get her in foal it was the legendary Nijinsky. To get over the mounting problem, at Windfields they dug a shallow pit for the mare to stand in. Later, when the aging stud was moved to Chesapeake City, Maryland, they built him a "pitcher's mound" instead. At first his stud fee was a modest ten thousand dollars. Before he was finished it was up to a million dollars a time. The mares are usually at least equally important to or more so than the stud in determining the major characteristics and behavioural tendencies of the foals, but Northern Dancer's offspring tended to look and behave much more like their sire than their dam. "Prepotent" was what they called it. He continued to get pretty excited when a mare was presented. One stud manager still has a horseshoe-shaped scar from being pawed. He would get very rambunctious in his stall when a mare was near. "He couldn't quite understand that anybody else could have mares. . . . He wanted [them all]," said Peter Poole.

He was still breeding mares at the age of twenty-six. Noreen Taylor told us,

There's a thrill that comes off a good stallion. . . . Oh, it's like being a girl at the dance and saying "That boy sure is good-looking." And they had that kind of presence and

they would just say, "Look at me," and you did. He had a
warm, sensitive eye and I think people would say "the look
of eagles," but he had it, a wonderful warm eye. But there'd
be glints of fire in it, just fire and magic and charisma. And
he demanded attention, and he usually got it.

Peter Poole recalled going to see him in Maryland, when he was pretty old,

and he came charging at the fence and his eyes quite star-
tling like he was looking right through you. The good
horses have that look of eagles and they look at you and
they don't look at you like they're seeing you, they're see-
ing whatever's going on through you.

They knew they were managing a legend. There was pressure to bring him home to Canada when he retired from stud, but they told people he was an old man for a horse, and not up to travel. And his last trip was only after he came to the end. He was twenty-eight, and very sick and in a lot of pain, and it was only a mercy to put him down. E.P. was gone now, too. His son, the distinguished foreign correspondent Charles Taylor, and Noreen's husband, took charge. He went to the border to meet this almost unheard-of cortege to do the paperwork and deal with the border officials. They dug a grave at Windfields. The cortege arrived at about midnight, and around two in the morning there were more than thirty people there, family and staff, the Windfields community and The Dancer's family, gathering to say a quiet goodbye. Noreen Taylor, fighting tears, said, "You don't stay up until midnight to throw roses in the grave of a horse you haven't . . . seen for, what, twenty years."

But they did that.

"Heart" was the word they all used about him, the men and women who contributed to this film, their voices still saying softly over the final seemingly slow motion filmic reprise of that gracefully running body and the tossing mane, things like,

Northern Dancer had more heart than most horses on the racetrack. . . . A racehorse cannot perform at the highest level, consistently, without a huge heart. "Heart" is what one always says, on a great racehorse, that he had that competitive desire, that instinctive character, that he would not, that he wasn't willing to lose easily.

And they like to tell a story about his statue at Woodbine, that as the horses circle the paddock there, they look over at the statue and they whinny.

◆　◆　◆

The History Television documentary was written and directed by Martin Harbury.